THE PRECIOUS BLOOD

IN

OUR SPIRITUALITY

REFLECTION ON

CONTEMPORARY

REDEMPTIVE THOUGHT

Edwin G. Kaiser, C.PP.S.

IMPRIMI POTEST
> Charles T. Bricher, C.PP.S.
> Provincial Director, Cincinnati Province
> Society of the Precious Blood

NIHIL OBSTAT
> James H. Kelley, C.PP.S.
> Censor Deputatus

IMPRIMATUR
> ✠ Raymond J. Gallagher, D.D.
> Bishop of Lafayette-in-Indiana
> April 18, 1978

Printed by Messenger Press
Carthagena, Ohio

TO

MARIE

MY SISTER

TABLE OF CHAPTERS

unity of salvation under one divine plan. . . Salvation history . . . Christian spirituality relates to God through Christ with his message of salvation . . . brings OT spirituality to fulfillment . . . Baptism: burial and resurrection in Christ. Central thought of Christian spirituality is our indwelling in mystery of Christ . . . Mystery of Christ proclaimed by *Praedicatio Apostolica* . . . Second Coming . . . Didache . . . Gnosis, Gnosticism . . . Clement of Alexandria . . . Origin . . Martyrs . . . Monasticism . . . Great Fathers: Basil the Great . . . Gregory of Nyssa . . . Gregory of Nazianzus . . . Rule of St. Basil . . . Pseudo-Dionysius, author of great mystic works (4th or 5th century) . . . Maximus Confessor (died 662) . . . Von Balthasar: *Kosmische Liturgie* . . . St. Augustine (died 430) . . . John Cassian (died 435?) . . . Walter Kasper: crises in history of Church, fruitful in providential *kairos*. Spirituality and the Jesus-love . . . *Jesu dulcis memoria* . . . *Stabat Mater Dolorosa* . . . Teresa of Avila . . . Catherine of Siena . . . Woman Doctors of the Church. Unique contemplation in *Therese,* according to Hans Urs von Balthasar . . . Devotion to saints: encouraged by *Mediator Dei.* Vatican II norms guiding devotion to Mary . . . Paul VI: We should know the way of Christ: *Ecclesiam Suam* . . . Spirituality in the World Today . . . John XXIII and current spirituality.

text . . . NT uses term *Sanguis Christi* at least 38 times. Eucharistic Blood
. . . Full meaning of Sanguis Christi: whole new economy of redemption.
Children present joyful picture of Last Supper, explained . . . Thomistic
terms: merit, satisfaction, liberation, efficacy . . . Alfaro . . . Schierse . . .
Larkin . . . Biblical Jesus studies today . . . Leo J. Donovan, art. in T.S.,
Dec. '71: *Evolution Under the Sign of the Cross* . . . Motive of Incarnation
. . . Precious Blood Spirituality: total outpouring, total giving . . . Paschal:
Last Drop of Blood . . . Desolation of Jesus on Cross, explained . . . Meditation on Desolation of Jesus by Jakob Brummet . . . Nanda Herbermann:
experience in concentration camp . . . Wolfgang Borchert: The Man Outside. Lippert: God is great riddle of universe? . . . Title: Precious Blood
in St. Peter 1:9 . . . objective redemption . . . subjective redemption . . .
reconciliation . . . expiation . . . infinite propiatory . . redemptive liberation . . . price paid to devil? . . . justification . . . Luther's *Tower Experience*
. . . Trent: justification . . . discussion on satisfactory merit . . . Piet Schoo-
nenberg, S.J., kenotic passage . . . treasury of merits in *TD* . . . Sanguis
Christi: Redemption Through Sacrifice . . . sacrifice explained, p. 68-75
. . . Liberation: a final note . . . redemption after manner of efficacy . . .
Pauline texts linking death of Jesus and resurrection . . . Lyonnet, S.J. on
Pauline soteriology (p. 76) . . . Gerhard Delling: death of Jesus in early
Christian kerygma . . . resurrection, p. 77-78 . . . critique: Walter Kasper:
Jesus the Christ, p. 78-85 . . . Joy in our spirituality . . . Bonaventure:
horror of suffering in Jesus conceals/reveals hidden splendor . . . Eucharist:
supreme joy.

SANGUIS CHRISTI . . . CHURCH . . . SACRAMENTS . . . Faber
quoted . . . Church flowed from pierced side of Savior . . . baptism by immersion is dying with Christ, rising with Christ . . . Eucharist center of all
sacraments from baptism to sacred anointing and viaticum . . . Mystery of
our death . . . death in art, literature . . . Kuebler-Ross view of afterlife as
scientifically proved . . . Rahner's view . . . Moment of death and final
decision . . . in light of teaching of St. Thomas . . . Rahner and moment
of death.

HUMAN FIGURE . . . SYMBOLS . . . LAMB . . . CROSS . . . Actual
appearance of Christ . . . Legends . . . Christ in all the world: Joseph Jobé
. . . Lamb . . . Blood of Lamb in Revelation . . . Lamb of God: Suffering
Servant: Spilly Study of Joachim Jeremias: early Christian community and

Lamb . . . Siebeneck: PBP I: Lamb in John's gospel. Paschal Lamb . . .
Franz Nagel: Apocalyptical vision: St. Joseph in Schweinfurt . . . Comment
from Schreyer . . . Mystical Lamb in Ghent by H. J. Van Eyck . . . M. de
la Taille, S.J., Icons: unique image . . . Christology . . . mystery of Church
. . . as Corpus Christi in West . . . Cross . . . Biblical meaning . . . *theologia
crucis* . . . devotion to cross . . . cult . . . crucifix . . . shrines . . . relics
. . . descent into hell . . . Cross of horror, beatifying cross.

Gaspar del Bufalo . . . Giorgio Papasogli cited 182-186 . . . Francis Xavier . . . Gaspar letters . . . Merlini . . . Maria De Mattias . . . Francis de Sales Brunner . . . Singular Eucharistic love . . . Perpetual adoration in ten chapels . . . Mother Catherine Aurelia: unique model, p. 197-200 . . . The eschatology . . . Depth Psychology.

THE SPLENDOR . . . Gerard Manley Hopkins . . . Hans Urs von Balthazar . . . A negative note on Hopkins . . . Wreck of the Deutschland . . . Inscape: James Finn Cotter . . . Mystical Heights: Francis of Assisi: the stigmata . . . Juan of the Cross: drawing of Christ on the Cross.

THE EPILOGUE . . . St. Andrae in Salzburg . . . Liturgical Conclusion . . . Explanation by Schreyer.

ULTIMATE FRUIT OF THE PRECIOUS BLOOD . . . Maria Regina . . . Martyrum . . . Berlin Memorial Church.

ACKNOWLEDGEMENTS

The writer is grateful:

For the ecclestiastical approval

For the generous funding:

In addition to the author's contribution there was gracious sharing by Fathers Homco, Fortman, Clayton, Schaefer, Robbins and Brother Wendeln

For the text:

We are most indebted to the Indian priest, A. J. Caetano da Cruz Fernandes for *Sanguis Christi,* in its Italian translation (Precious Blood Fathers, Rome, Italy). We use freely *The Everlasting Covenant,* the writer's own work and the work of Precious Blood Fathers Siebeneck, Spilly, Schreiter, Sullivan. We use the New Catholic Encyclopedia (NCE) (permission: The Publishers Guild, Inc.) the New American Bible (permission: Confraternity of Christian Doctrine), the Jerome Biblical Commentary (permission: Prentice-Hall, Inc.), Jerusalem Bible (permission: Darton, Longman & Todd, Ltd., and Doubleday & Co., Inc.), the Encylopedia of Theology, Concise Sacramentum Mundi; the Theological Dictionary; Ratzinger: Introduction to Christianity (permission: Seabury Press), DOV (permission: America Press), James Finn Cotter — *Inscape* (permission: Pittsburgh University Press). We cite official teaching of The Council of Trent from *The Church Teaches* (TCT) (permission: Tan Books & Publishers). Most significant is the work of the Japanese Evangelical theologian, Kazoh Kitamori, *Theology of the Pain of God* (permission: John Knox Press, Atlanta, Georgia). Two noted theologians of our time, Heribert Muehlen and Hans Urs von Balthasar add much to the enrichment of the text. The former is cited for his profound insight into the doctrine of the Trinity in relation to the Cross and divine life in us. Stressed is the relation of Father and Son in the desolation of Jesus on the Cross (permission: Aschendorff Verlag, publishers also of the T. R. which we cite a number of times, beyond the references of Muehlen). The great theologian Hans Urs von Balthasar we cite particularly because of his profound reflection on the *splendor of theology,* and of his deep insight into the thought of St. Bonaventure and of Gerard Manley Hopkins (permission: Johannes Verlag Einsiedlen). The text embodies much of the complex thought of Lothar Schreyer in *Das Christusbild und die Kunst des* 20 *Jahrhunderts* (permission: Otto Mueller Verlag, Salzburg, and the daughter of Lothar Schreyer). A few pages on *Icons* (pp. 105-107) are based on *Heilige Theophanie,* by Julius Tyciak (permission: Paulinus Verlag, Trier). We are grateful for the meditation by Jakob Brummet in *Das Ueber Alles Ragende Zeichen* (permission: Tyrolia Verlag Wien).

For the study of the Litany of the Most Precious Blood, use was made of our article on this subject, published Sept. 1960 (Permission: *The Priest,* Huntington, Indiana). We also appreciate the personal notes of Cynthia Felch, as indicated in the text.

Studies and critiques were inserted after the text was developed over the years. One such critique of Walter Kasper, *Jesus The Christ,* is inserted on p. 78 (Permission: Search Press, London). For the pages on Gaspar we inserted a few pages from Papasogli in *Vita e Tempi di San Gaspare Del Bufalo* (Permission: the author, through the courtesy of Fr. William Volk). Likewise, we have presumed to make a brief summary of Karl Rahner's critical study of the Vatican declaration on the ordination of women, as it appeared *In Stimmen der Zeit,* May 1977, and inserted on p. 46.

For their efforts:

The present study is based on previous efforts sustained largely by Fr. Joseph Smolar and his good mother, now gone to her reward. Three Fathers of the Precious Blood Society assisted in different ways when the goals never seemed to come within reach: Fr. William Volk, Rome, obtained necessary permissions for use of significant sources; Fr. Charles Robbins furnished the Xeroxing for an endless flow of letters and volumes of material on which the text is based; Fr. Raymond Cera for diligent reading of the proofs. We are deeply grateful, also: to John Groppe who was constantly faithful in what we like to call his *diaconia;* to Marge, in the College library, for providing the many pictures from which were selected the best copies for the lists found on pp. 31-220; to Fr. James Froelich, Sr. Donna and Sr. Paula.

A PREFACE

This enterprise is not a devotional reflection in the restricted traditional sense. It is rather a theological presentation of the essential elements of spiritual union with God in a basic area of Christian thought and life — an area involving all who in some manner relate to the grace of Christ: *directly,* the entire race of man in this visible universe and, in a manner more difficult to explain (though we hesitate to call it *indirect*), the created spirits of good, and of evil. All intellectual creation forms the theological place (*locus theologicus*) of our investigation. Consequently our design is both Christological and in a very comprehensive sense anthropological.

That the Precious Blood of Christ in our redemptive thought involves both Christology and anthropology is evident from our sources. We focus attention directly on what is often called, somewhat clumsily perhaps, *official salvation history,* which is God's proclamation of salvation through his prophets and special messengers, all of whom point to Christ and lead to him — and in a much broader sense and indirectly on that *salvation history* which is the totality of world history. For this too must ultimately lead to Christ as the center of all being and all meaning. In our story of the union with God we underscore *covenant with God* throughout the Old Testament whose end and goal is the *new and everlasting covenant* in Christ's Blood.

A preliminary, selective focus on historical types of Christian spirituality must shed light on significant historic developments relating to Jesus. This cannot fail to furnish some traditional preparation for the *Precious Blood spirituality* in its recent development and enrichment of the whole redemptive reflection in our own time. As far as space permits, we include, quite imperatively, the biblical foundations and the development of a systematic theology which alone can justify our claim to depth and significance in the spiritual life. We do not refer to incidental development or to historic research, but to the very basic and essential development as we find particularly in such writers as Rahner, Urs von Balthasar, Muehlen, and Schillebeeckx, whose in-depth thought has raised our systematic theology to heights of true greatness. Deprived of such biblical and systematic theology, any form of spirituality becomes merely another particular devotion swayed by emotion, attracting many good people by sentiment, and too obviously subject to misguidance and error, producing little fruit.

If the writer draws freely from many sources, but especially from the study and research in the societies of the Precious Blood, he does so in full awareness that we have not adequately expressed in our *kerygma*, our formation programs, our personal motivation as members of these societies what might be called the terrifying paradox of the Precious Blood spirituality. It is the *Infinite Paradox* underlying its true revealed nature: the *infinite condescension* of the *all-powerful One* to *utter weakness* in which the *All Other* becomes the *powerless victim* of his own creatures who have rejected his love. The *highest power* is this renunciation of power, and the greatest force is the *love* freely bestowed which only in its rejection can overcome the greatest violence, even of hatred and sin. Such is the *Paradox of the Sanguis Christi*, the God-made-man whose death is our life. In the infinite bond of God — whom the transcendent world cannot contain — with man who is wrapped in our petty nature, yes, in our sin, we embrace our whole salvation-redemption. Only thus can we formulate the greatness of God in its Christian concept: The greatness which the infinite cannot contain, which yet is contained with all its love and power in a helpless child, who grew up, worked, was guided and instructed, walked the earth, preached, died, and rose to glory.

Many have helped to make this work a study, as engaging as it was arduous, to the point that it is not an object of sale or profit, but a gift. We mention them elsewhere with our deep thanks. May the book they have helped to construct prove a step forward in the study of that devotion which the Pope of the Precious Blood, John XXIII, called objective.

Finally we crave the pardon of our readers for the repetitions unavoidably found in this work. The lack of homogeneity is largely due to insertions made after the type had been set up. Our liturgical references relate to our great theme though they may not all reflect the most recent documentary.

Edwin G. Kaiser, C.PP.S.

CHAPTER ONE

THE PROLOGUE

The Three Mysteries

One God: In Three Divine Persons: The Trinity

One Divine Person In Two Natures: The Incarnation

One Mystical Person In Many Persons: Church-Grace-Vision

Quite freely we interchange the terms *Precious Blood in our spirituality* and *Precious Blood spirituality,* the slight shade of difference in meaning being apparent. If we seem possessive in holding to the term *our* spirituality, it is not merely that we belong to one of the societies of the Precious Blood, but that Pope John himself bade our societies: "It is your duty to promote this spirituality." To the writer it calls to mind a response of Karl Rahner when he suggested to the great theologian of the Sacred Heart and of the Ignatian spirituality, that he also take up this subject: "That is your task" (*Das muessen Sie tun!*). The writer has taken seriously the obligation that members of the societies of the Precious Blood study, practice and promote their own spirituality.

Precious Blood spirituality reflects the infinite life of the Godhead in the three central mysteries: the *Trinity* and the intimate inner self-communication or God-life of the one God in three divine persons; the *incarnation*: the divine life communicated to created nature through the Logos, the divine Word; and *grace*: the communication of the divine life through the Word in his Holy Spirit in the Church which is the continuation of the work of the *incarnate-anointed* through time into the eternity of glory. We express these mysteries in the traditional terms of person and nature (the reader must seek to understand them analogously): three persons in one divine nature: the infinite bliss of Trinity: one person in two natures: Jesus the Christ who is God-man; one mystical person: the Christ, his Spirit, we — all men — in their bond.[1]

The Trinity is the infinite, intimate divine life of the Godhead. The Father, eternal and unbegotten, begets the Son eternally. The Son is begotten, distinct from the Father, from all eternity, yet the same God as the Father. Bond of infinite love of Father and Son is the Holy Spirit, distinct from Father and Son, and yet the same God. The mystery is not lessened by the stark, clear teaching that no unity or oneness is so great as the oneness of the divine nature, no distinctness is so great as the distinctness of persons. *Such Is the First Mystery.*

Only this inner, infinite intimate life, eternally blessed, bereft of nothing (*O beata Trinitas*) can communicate being and life beyond itself. Only Infinity itself which is infinite love can fill the infinite void with being, life and love which is truly not God and is outside God. By creating a universe with its center in his own Son, God linked himself with man and all intellectual creation. Born of a human mother, the fairest of the daughters of men, the *Logos,* Son of God, united God with creature, man, forever. The Christ as man is the supreme acceptance of creature by God and acceptance of God by creature.

The supreme Trinity — we dismiss all mere possibilities of what might have been as beyond any human knowledge — eternally willed and decreed to communicate its inner life after the manner of its own inner self. The Logos-Son who comes forth from the Father in the Holy Spirit communicates the triune life to creation through and in the same Holy Spirit. Creation itself bears the seal of incarnation in the Spirit of love of Father for his Son. He who was born of the Father eternally, given the divine life as Son, communicates this life to all mankind (all intellectual creatures) in the incarnation. He who is linked in eternal love — the Holy Spirit — with the Father, unites himself in his very created existence with all men through the Spirit of his love, the Holy Spirit. We use the term sacred in tradition, the *hypostatic union,* the union of God and man in Jesus Christ the God-made-man, to express the source of the God-life communicated to all intellectual creatures. Herein is the pattern of the fellowship of God and all his intellectual creatures: *The Second Mystery: The Incarnation.* We are again reminded that only infinite *love-causality* can pour forth such likeness-to-self without any diminution of its infinite-self, yet bestowing its own causality, dynamic power to love to all creatures. Such transcendent love is the very basis and essence of Christianity (cf. Hubertus Mynarek: *Der Mensch das Wesen der Zukunft,* p. 20). And it is Hans Urs von Balthasar who calls our attention to the essentialistic reality that the Logos assumed created nature in its entire destiny within himself, and made it truly a manifestation of his relation to the Father in the Holy Spirit (cf. *Wer ist die Kirche,* p. 162).

In Christ, God turns in love to his creatures. In Christ-the-man all creatures are embraced by the divine love. With him and in him they love the Father through the Holy Spirit. In his love, embracing all created being, Jesus hallows his Father's name, submits himself totally to the divine will, and brings redemptive grace to fallen man, grace to all intellectual creatures. So close has God come to man in Christ that incarnation means an anthropology for God without which there is no theology of man. In Jesus is mirrored God the Father in the light of the Holy Spirit. The Father speaks to us through him for he is the divine Word. Enlightened by their Spirit, we hearken and make the divine Word-in-truth our own — and respond with their love as our own.

Only recent theology has brought us to a grasp of the relation of the angels to us in our Christology. In this matter we follow the penetrating analysis of Karl Rahner who is never known to shy away from difficult problems. His is not the casual blitheness of some current writers who ignore the profound sense of both scripture and tradition for a demythologizing semantic. Rightly Rahner relates the angels to Christ and redemptive history:

> Consequently the angelology of revelation has the same function as revelation has for the rest of the created world of man's environment . . . At the point where, and because, the world is spiritual and personal, revelation divides it (progressively) into two radically opposed realms and incorporates them into the one event with which everything in human existence is concerned, the coming of God in Christ into his creation. In this way, angelology appears for the theology of man as a doctrine about the non-human world-setting, whether personal or material, of redemptive history which is a factor in theological anthropology . . . It makes man recognize a section of the world of persons of which he is a member for the decision of faith and prevents him from diminishing its dimensions — he realizes that he stands in a more comprehensive community of salvation and perdition than that of mankind alone . . .

Rahner suggests that the angels

> belong to the world by the very ground of their being, that they stand in a natural unity of reality and history with man, have a supernatural history of salvation with him which has its first design and ultimate goal . . . in Christ. As, however, theological anthropology and Christology are intrinsically connected, the nature of angelology is also determined by this more comprehensive context. If the possibility of the creation (although it could have been realized alone) and the actual creation as it in fact is, are grounded in the possible or actual free decision of God to express himself absolutely in the self-emptying of his

Word, who by his self utterance becomes man, then angelology too can only ultimately be understood as an inner element of Christology. The angels by nature form the society of persons surrounding the Word of the Father uttered and self-emptied, a Word uttered and heard in person. Their difference from man would have to be conceived as a variant (even if a "specific" one) of the one (generic) nature common to angels and man, and which attains its highest grace-given fulfillment in the Word of God. This would provide the basis for the treatment of such traditional themes as "the grace of angels as grace from Christ," "Christ as the head of the angels," the radical unity of the world and of redemptive history with angels and men in their reciprocal relations of subordination and superiority," "the change which occurred in the role of the angels in sacred history." Angelology draws its ultimate measure and basis from Christology (*Encyclopedia of Theology,* art, "Angels" p. 6, Seabury Press, 1975).

In this light we speak of a world which was to be given a redeemer. Essential here is the note of sin, of redemption, but also of struggle between forces of good and evil. We boldly assert that God created the world and man, permitting the sin, permitting the struggle, for the triumph of pardon and the communication of divine life. Greater is the splendor of pardon with the communication of grace than grace without sin. To pardon a sinful world is a more transcendent good than the creation of a world without sin or without struggle (*cf. The Everlasting Covenant,* p. 16ff).

He who had come forth from God sent his Spirit into the world. As the Father had sent him, he sent his Spirit to all mankind: *The Third Mystery.* This we compress into one word *grace.* It comprises the Christ, anointed by the Spirit, and us the redeemed, the anointed; *Christ, the Spirit,* creature: One mystical person embracing many persons: the Church — the identity of the Holy Spirit in Christ and Christians: *Una Mystica Persona* (cf. Heribert Muehlen, *Una Mystica Persona,* Paderborn, 1967).

All spirituality is in the context of these three great mysteries. Our presentation of them is the *Revealed Prologue of the Precious Blood Spirituality.* It is the prologue for the basic study for all Christian spirituality, but most of all for the spirituality of the Precious Blood.

CHAPTER TWO

THE THREE DIVINE MYSTERIES

and

OUR SPIRITUALITY

*The Church Is Aware Of Her Life, Which Began
In The FATHER'S HEART, Germinated In The Blood
Of The CRUCIFIED CHRIST, And Was Guided By
His SANCTIFYING SPIRIT.*
Pope Paul VI, Dec. 22, 1975,
Cited in *Origens*, p. 516, Jan. 20, 1976.

The more splendidly our theology explicates the meaning of Christ in true Christocentrism, the more boldly are we challenged by two great pressing realities: first, the Christ, the Logos in the divine Trinity; second, the Word-made-man, as the center of the universe.

Viewing the two, we must clearly shun a theology which places the Trinity in "splendid isolation" and hazards the cynical charge of making the divine Trinity meaningless for men through a *species of deism*. The total *theologia* (the Trinity, the doctrine of the Trinity) must be profoundly involved in the *economia* of our salvation, with the incarnation of the Word. The God-head must be centered in our very midst through the God-made-man. This vast universe must be embraced, truly bonded with Jesus as its center of action, thought, meaning, in the splendid sense of the first chapter of Colossians, verses 15-29.

The influence of Arianism in the early centuries necessarily meant the stress of the divinity of the Son to counteract the Great Denial. Thus we find the Arian misuse of the *glory be to the Father, through the Son and in the Holy Spirit* (interpreting the *through the Son* as instrumentality) led to the doxology: glory be to the Father *and the Son and the Holy Spirit*. In consequence the West took up an expressly new attitude of prayer in the Church's worship — *kneeling* before God to beg for pardon for sin (Synod of Tours in 813). And secondary forms of mediation were brought into sharp focus: Mary, the angels, the saints, relics, etc. (cf. Josef Andreas Jungmann, *Christliches Beten in Wandel und Bestand,* Ars Sacra, Munich, 1969, p. 74).

In the Eastern Churches the majesty and splendor of Christ was emphasized: the *Rex tremendae majestatis* faced the worshiper in the great churches. Though in the West many centuries later the "human Jesus" and the "Jesus-love" enriched the worship of the Middle Ages down to our own time, still for centuries we placed the Trinity in isolation. Now at long last there is reason to hope that we can present the incarnation and redemption, in a truly trinitarian light, and bring to men the *theologia.* Since the current evolutionary dynamic thinks of man in terms of freedom and maturity in a socialized TURN in the ages of world history and salvation history, the Vatican Council calls for a presentation of the truths of faith appealing to the new man and the new age (cf. *DOV,* the *Pastoral Constitution on the Church in the Modern World,* nos. 4ff and 54ff).

In every way the Precious Blood theology and spirituality eminently serves this purpose, once we avail ourselves of all its resources. Our conviction is confirmed by a brilliant study of the *Church and the Civilization of Work* by M.D. Chenu in *DOC,* no. 124, particularly by the theologian's insight into the civilization of work and recapitulation in Christ. This inspiring concept recalls the profound insight of Irenaeus and extends the scope of his thought to our own magnificent space age.

Heribert Muehlen, already referred to above, has sought the same end by furnishing guidelines for a *Future Christology* and a *Theology of the Cross in Confrontation with the Christology of the Early Church* (Heribert Muehlen, *Die Veraenderlichkeit Gottes als Horizont einer zukuenftigen Christologie,* Aschendorff, Muenster, 1969).

Contemporary scientific and technological reliance on man himself challenges the theologian with the imperative of updating our Christocentrism and developing a God-presentation suited to current attitudes and mindsets. The bizarre "God is dead" movement is not a challenge to prove God's existence in any traditional sense. Rather it calls for a deeper insight into men's minds today and into God's union and contact with his creation through Christ. Muehlen's little book suggests a transformation of the *concept of being* long dominant in Western thought and its philosophical-theological reflection.

> If therefore the Nicene utterance is to be integrated into the horizon of our current understanding, then at the same time the *countenance* of God himself must turn to the gaze of the faithful in a new light. But

this is scarcely possible any longer today in the traditional horizon of the all-cosmic understanding of *being,* within which only the Almighty, but non-suffering countenance of the Platonic God constantly gazes on us. The nature of God's essence will have to be proclaimed *diversely today.* Differently indeed must we speak than under the dominant aspect of God as the *Unmoved Mover,* who in pre-personally presented fixed immutability, and therewith also in a non-suffering reality, is blissful in himself. The non-suffering God, far from us, dominating in "deistic" isolation means little to man who must endure existence in pain. It may be true that the man of the technical age — at least in the highly technological industrialized states — suffers less through diseases and catastrophies. But he nevertheless is exposed to a greater in-depth exquisiteness of pain than the man who could still look upon himself as part and parcel of the earthy world. The experience of existence in all ages was truly experience of human finiteness (we need only recall Greek tragedy) and it always sprang from the frustration of expectation. Nevertheless, perhaps the experience of such frustration of existence is more evident today than in previous times. Our point is that today it stands in a sinister antithesis to the progressive threat of power of the human environment, indeed of man himself. (Muehlen then speaks of the planned evolution of man genetically. Even though man could be developed in a test tube, the individual still could not be the cause of his own existence. Nor could he explain it. Much less could he liberate or redeem himself from death).

The Christian redemptive teaching in our incipient technological phase of the history of mankind would therefore have to reflect more intensely than has been done up to now on its actual center, namely on the message of the redemption from spiritual and physical death through the *death of Jesus.* The future of theology will have to be determined therefore by a sober *theology of the cross* personalized in faith. Still it can hardly find a foothold today in a statically presented immutability of a God *in himself* impassible. Wherefore perhaps the death of his Son must be pondered in a new light and manifestation — though indeed we must avoid the mere anti-theopaschitic confrontation of the primitive Church.

Perhaps through a *theology of the cross* — scarcely adequately elaborated in the Catholic tradition — the way to the *Father* who today is so widely viewed as *dead* could be newly opened: the *way to the Father* as to the end and goal of the self-submission of Jesus, the Father who exists in inaccessible light (pp. 8ff).

How obviously is our approach to a spirituality of the Precious Blood pointed out in this *way to the Father in the cross and the death of Jesus!*

A PARADOXICAL NOTE: MAY WE SPEAK OF THE PAIN OF GOD?

If, as we have just noted, the concept of God as *Unmoved Mover* and *Immutable, Impassible First Being* does not address itself readily to our mod-

ern minds — if this concept places God in isolation, and we must view him
in a less Hellenic light — then the work of Kazoh Kitamori, Japanese Evangelical theologian, should prove of special value. Professor of systematic
theology in the Union Theological Seminary in Tokyo, Kitamori is considered the leading theologian in Japan. His work *Theology of the Pain of
God* (John Knox Press, Richmond, Va.) has been translated into German
and English, and is thoroughly reviewed by Ludwig Wenzler in the *TR*,
1974, no. 2, col. 129ff.

The texts of Isaiah, 63:15 and Jeremiah 31:20 suggest the approach
of Kitamori. But only the Jeremian text points to the reality revealing the
concept of the pain of God. After the verses telling of Ephraim's sin and
repentance, Yahweh exclaims:

> Is Ephraim not my favored son,
>   the child in whom I delight?
> Often as I threaten him,
>   I still remember him with favor;
> My heart stirs for him,
>   I must show him mercy, says the Lord.

The thought is designed to shed light on the divine love in its effectiveness
— after God returns love to the ungrateful sinner who has wounded that
love. This concept is called the *pain of God*. Ephraim yearns to turn back
to God, repenting after the shame and disgrace of his youth. The *pain of
God* is not mere rhetoric, the cry of wounded love calling out again to the
sinner. But it is the divine appeal to the one who has sinned and turned
against the *love of God*. Man so often flaunts the direct love of God. But,
such is Kitamori's point, he is unable to resist the love, once bestowed and
rejected, which again reaches out to him. We cannot know what the *pain
of God* actually is, but we know what pain is in our hearts and God wills
to show that this reality is in his heart. This we cannot know through the
analogia entis of Thomas but through the mercy of God. The sinner turns
God's love to wrath, forces God to anger. God cannot forgive him, such
is his anger. But the will of God to love even the object of his wrath, this
is the *pain of God*. This pain of God is the background of the historic Jesus.
The *pain of God* means God's love in this historic world, which must bear
his wrath, the pain of God which has overcome the wrath. In consequence
the *pain of God* must enter the world in person, and God's coming into the
world already means his death. The God of the Gospel is the God who as
Father permits his Son to die and in such action he is said to suffer pain.
The act of the cross reflects the axiom of theological thought: the nature
of God can be understood only from the word of the cross. *The pain of
God is the nature of God.*

Kitamori rejects all other analogies, accepting only the *analogia doloris,* rejecting the *analogia entis.* The pain of God is the power of God which can fully overcome the disobedience which penetrates all activity of man. If Christians can follow God as pattern of their relation to others, then pain is also characteristic of Christian ethic. If the pain of God belongs to the inmost nature of God, then we reject the *ousia* or *substantia* concept of God. Not the Greeks, Kitamori avers, but the Japanese made the discovery of the true nature of God and rightly understand the gospel. Obviously what is decisive for Kitamori is not God in himself, but God for us. His is an intuition rather than a system, seeking to express the relation of God to man the sinner and the meaning of redemption in Jesus.

ECONOMIA INVOLVES THEOLOGIA

As indicated above our Precious Blood spirituality strikes its most profound roots in the concept of the involvement of the *theologia* (Trinity, doctrine of Trinity) in the *economia* (creation-incarnation-redemption). This means: the very nature of God, the God-ness must be the pattern and measure of the entire *economia,* the work of God in his creation. The very inner life of the Trinity is the pattern of God's action in creation-incarnation-redemption (cf. Herbert Vorgrimler, *Karl Rahner, His Life, Thought and Work,* Palm Publishers, 1965, p. 56f). It may be suggested that *perhaps* it could not have been otherwise intrinsically and absolutely. Then only the Son could have become man, sent by the Father in the Holy Spirit.

Throughout we have in mind the current pneumatological theology with its deeper, richer insight into the Trinity beyond that of past ages. When Jesus in his prayer of agony says, "I and the Father are one," we think of this eternal unity of Father and Son continuing into the *economia.* It is not, as the manuals have been wont to say, the unity of a common substance, simple, indivisible, with the *De Deo Uno, De Deo Trino, etc.* Rather it is the *we* of personal unity (call to mind the current phenomenological concept of person as *directed to other*). The *we-ness* is also salvation history *we-ness.* The divine nature, the God-ness, which manifests the mutual one-ness in love of the three distinct persons is the Holy Spirit in person. God the Father, the *I* confronts the *Thou,* his Son. The Holy Spirit is the *we* as love bond between the *I* and the *Thou.* The Son coming forth from the Father in the love of their Holy Spirit has come to men, sent by the Father in the same Holy Spirit. In this Spirit he forms with us the one mystical person: many persons in the one Holy Spirit.

Pertinent to this involvement is Paul's splendid theology found in numerous texts. We can refer only to a few of the better known, and direct the reader's attention to more extensive commentaries. The eighth chapter of Romans is magnificent. It is the very heart of the letter which is rather a theological treatise than an epistle. Though the first seven verses of chapter one state the full theme of the entire letter, it is chapter eight which sets forth the divine plan of predestination by which men share the *image of God's Son*. The Son, the Father's only begotten, embraces us as firstborn brothers and sisters. Thus we are *called* by the Father, we are *justified*, we share the divine external glory. The following verses (in the Jerusalem Bible) are a *hymn to God's love*:

> After saying this, what can we add? With God on our side who can be against us? Since God did not spare his own Son, but gave him up to benefit us all, we may be certain, after such a gift, that he will not refuse anything he can give. Could anyone accuse those that God has chosen? When God acquits, could anyone condemn? Could Christ Jesus? No! He not only died for us — he rose from the dead, and there at God's right hand he stands and pleads for us (Rom 8:31-34).

We conclude: In the innermost Trinitarian life, the Father eternally begets, gives, sends forth his Son. Precisely in this is he *Father*: such is his *being-ness*. What God sends therefore is most *his own*. Herein too lies the permanence of his covenant which like the Father is totally unalterable, the result of his eternal decree. We may well speak of covenant-loyalty. He did not spare his only begotten Son, but in *not-sparing* his Son, he gave himself as well.

But this Son also delivered himself (Eph 5: 2.25). God who is love manifested his love by sending his Son to save mankind (the total universe), to communicate to creatures the divine life (1 Jn 4:9; Jn 3:16). Such was his love, for *God is love*: *ho theos agape estin*. He gave us his love for he gave us himself. May we not say with Muehlen: "The Einai of God, the essence of his being is the giving up of that which is most his own?" (*op. cit.,* p. 31).

GOD'S MERCY IS OVER ALL

What we have said thus far is to proclaim the infinite mercy of God. Our dogmatic reflection on God's nature and attributes offers the most fruitful meditation on that *proper and formal attribute* which is the mercy of God, so essential for our entire social-religious order today. In his mercy the Infinite Goodness relieves his creatures in their sin and distress, in their lowliness and misery. The Old Testament uses terms mindful of "motherliness" and kindly condescension. Mercy outweighs all thought of wrath and punishment. But in the New Testament the mercy of God is the dominant concept. Mercy is the root concept of all the action of God toward men, the very end and term of salvation history in Christ, the God-man.

It is a most beautiful and consoling thought that God himself — such is his supreme spirituality — can have no "affective" (emotional) mercy, but its very substance and effectiveness in the transcendent plan of redemption as we have explained. It is all the more resplendent because fallen man can claim nothing on his own, and because the prodigality of grace makes this fallen man rich with the very justice of God-love. But the very depth and height of human mercy, the deep pity and tender kindness, the anxious readiness to help those in need, the deep acceptance of all human suffering, all this we find in the God-man. How deeply must we ponder that what God could not possess in his divinity, he took upon himself through the humanity of Jesus, in whom all human mercy becomes divine. The supreme act of divine mercy was wrought in man's redemption.

The central theme of all God's action rooted in his divine mercy we proclaim in our spirituality of the Precious Blood: the divine-human mercy manifested in that giving, that outpouring which is this shedding of Jesus' Blood. Especially in the litanies do we appeal to the divine mercy (Jesus in his suffering is depicted in art as the Christ of pity). Precisely because he lowered himself to the depths of sin, though free from all sin, does the Church exalt and proclaim him Lord. Such indeed is the climax of this chapter.

The Climax

The great *kenotic* passage of Philippians, probably a hymn of the early Church taken over by Paul, is the climax or high point in *Our Spirituality and the Divine Trinity*:

> Though he was in the form of God,
>   he did not deem equality with God
>   something to be grasped at.
> Rather, he *emptied* himself
>   and took the form of a slave,
>   being born in the likeness of men.
> He was known to be of human estate,
>   and it was thus that he humbled himself,
>   obediently accepting even death,
>   death on a cross!
> Because of this,
>   God highly exalted him
>   and bestowed on him the name
>   above every other name,
> So that at Jesus' name
>   every knee must bend

in the heavens, on the earth,
and under the earth,
and every tongue proclaim
to the glory of God the Father:
JESUS CHRIST IS LORD! (2:6ff)

This much discussed hymn should become a part of our Precious Blood prayer, recited frequently, pondered profoundly. It is for this reason that it is repeated with such stress in our work. The meaning regarding the *kenosis* is debated. Piet Schoonenberg, S.J., thinks of the choice or decision not as that of the *Logos,* a divine decision, but rather of the *Word-made-flesh.* Nevertheless, it is the act of the Second Person who chooses suffering and death. Indeed, it is the very mystery of the incarnation-redemption, that the divine Logos (in his human nature) suffered and died. The noted author concludes (and this also is the clear doctrine of faith) that the humanity will not vanish but be glorified. He adds, however, that there are two decisions implied in the *kenotic* text, one at the beginning of Jesus' preaching, to become THE SER-VANT, the other at the approach of his passion: here lies the supreme self-humiliation, the obedience even to the death of the cross (cf. *Concilium* 11, "Who is Jesus of Nazareth?" Paulist Press, 1966, p. 57 and 56). The reader is urged also to read the little study of John L. McKenzie, *Light on the Epistles,* Thomas More Press, 1975, p. 123f. In the light of post-biblical Nicene thought, Muehlen views the verse somewhat differently:

> The Son did not cling greedily to his pre-existent same-ness-of-being with the Father, so that this reveals itself in salvation history as "alteration," as self-alienation and obedience unto death on the cross (*ibid.,* p. 32).

The writer adds an *eschatological note:* Paul admonishes his readers to remain innocent amid the moral evil and depravity surrounding them, warning that he "looks to the Day of Christ." His work is a *"libation over the spiritual service"* of their faith. We of the Precious Blood spirituality must also labor, make our lives a similar sacrificial service for all mankind redeemed by the Blood. This as we chant the great hymn. In consequence ours should be the gladness and joy to which Paul refers in the verses of the second chapter of Philippians (cf. Phil 2: 17-18).

THE SCANDAL OF THE CROSS

Penetrating more profoundly into the *kenotic* concept, Muehlen comments on the *scandal of the cross,* the utter lowliness of God-made-man, which lies at the very heart of our Precious Blood spirituality.

In its total depth and breadth the *scandal of the cross* becomes manifest only after we have pondered the reality that the Father made the divine *Thou* — who was co-equal to himself — *sin* and *malediction* (2 Cor 5:21; Gal 3:13; cf. Rom 8:3). Hence the Son has not only become *other* to himself, namely creature, but he was made into the totally *alien* to himself, into *sin*. And hereby is made manifest with all clarity that the Father and the Son, insofar as they are persons, have nothing, indeed totally nothing in common. Hence the cry of desolation of Jesus on the cross reaches to its incomprehensible depth (Mk 15:34; Mt 27:46). This cry of Jesus manifests first of all that the deliverance of the Son unto sin by the Father means that the Son in salvation history is uniquely distinctive, with a distinctiveness so great that none greater can be conceived, namely, utter, God-forsakenness. And yet at the same time — the point is indeed important for an understanding of the divine equality-in-unity — there is manifest in this absolute distinctiveness the absolute closeness between Father and Son. This likewise is so great that it cannot be conceived as possibly greater. If, according to Romans 8:32, the Father did not spare what is most his very own, and the Son does not spare himself in obedient submission to the cross, then this *non-sparing* in the Father and in the Son is strictly one and the same. In every respect it is identical in them. The love with which the Father delivered up his Son for us is none other than that love with which the Son gives up himself *for us*. Indeed, insofar as the Holy Spirit is simply this identical love (as person), he is (as person) the absolute closeness and identity in the distinctiveness between Father and Son themselves. According to Hebrews 9:14, indeed, Jesus offered himself to God *dia pneumatos aioniou,* that is in the power of the eternal or more specifically, the divine Spirit. This *pneuma* present in the offering of Jesus on the cross is, however, none other than the *pneuma ek tou theou* or specifically the *pneuma tou theou.*

If in accordance with the considerations indicated above, we interpret the divine *homoousie* on the basis of an understanding of persons in the perichoresis of divine persons, then the *pneuma* as one and the same in Father and Son is likewise the divine *homoousie* in person insofar as indeed it is the divine love in person which in the death of Jesus manifests itself as the love of the Father. The *pneuma* as one person in two persons is the one *we-center* of divine existence. In this *we-center* manner of the divine existence the *I-center* and the *Thou-center* with total antithesis are indeed the *pneuma*. In this sense the *cross event* is the historical *self-effecting* of the Trinitarian *we-act*. It is not as though the Father and Son offer themselves in common, or as though the Father himself had suffered, but rather that indeed in the most radical antithesis between Father and Son their most radical closeness and unity become manifest.

Our thought may also be expressed in the following manner:

In the context of salvation history the essence of God's being is the *giving-over,* or more specifically the *self-giving*: here the divine *einai* manifests itself as truly the *agape*. The *Trinitarian* structure of this *event* is made evident in this, the Father is the *one who delivers over* his Son, the Son the *one who delivers himself,* and the *pneuma* the *event of the giving over,* the *pneuma* who is strictly identical in Father and Son. One could therefore also say that the *cross event* is in *salvation history context* the procession of the Holy Spirit, the so-called *spiratio activa* as salvation history event, which first of all makes possible and liberates every delivery of word, office and sacrament in the Church. According to the marvellous twofold significance of John 19:30 *paredoken to pneuma,* Jesus not only breathed forth his human spirit, as indicated in Luke 23:46, but indeed he also in his utter God-forsakenness, and on the basis of this forsakenness, delivered over to the Church his divine Spirit, his likeness-of-being with the Father (according to John 7:39 there was no Spirit because Jesus had not as yet been glorified). Accordingly, the *cross event* is the actual occurrence in time of the *procession of the divine love* as the divine being-ness itself. A procession effected by the Father and Son in strict identity. At the same time it is that procession in which the *a priori we-centered* divine being-ness or more specifically divine love concretizes itself unto the third divine manner of existence and therefore emits from itself the Church. Since the incarnation of the Son is the becoming in time of the divine *Thou* insofar as the Man Jesus of Nazareth is taken up into the *Thou-relationship* of the Son to the Father, the cross event is the becoming-in-time of the divine *we.* (H. Muehlen, *op. cit.,* pp. 32-34).

As in other parts of this study, though we always seek to follow approved authors and interpreters and offer divergent points of view, we do attempt to indicate such division of opinions. Here we meet the hazard of ambiguity in the biblical references to the giving up of the spirit, dying, breathing one's last, and sending forth the Spirit to form the Church. (Elsewhere we shall refer to the teaching of Pius XII in *Mystici Corporis* that the birth of the Church was on Calvary, through the riven side). We find a striking corroboration of the concept of the Spirit as forming the Church in the post resurrection apparition to the apostles, recorded in John 20:22f. According to the *NAB, breathing* on the apostles was more than symbolic, for when he gave them the Holy Spirit, he gave them the power of pardoning sins. The Council of Trent made the cautious but definitive decision that on this occasion the Lord *principally* instituted the sacrament of penance (D 894) and condemns those who hold that the words are not to be understood in the sense of conferring the power of forgiving sins in the sacrament (D 913).

Indeed, if through the power of the Spirit Jesus offers himself and rises again from the dead, then cross and resurrection are only two *moments* of one and the same *event,* namely the entry into time of the divine

love in the divine *We-set* of existence. And the Precious Blood theology
and spirituality must be focused on the divine Trinity in the sublime context of cross, resurrection, and the continuous *Christ-presence* and *Christ-
action* in the Church through his Holy Spirit. No one, to our knowledge,
has expressed this thought as splendidly as Muehlen:

> The cross itself as the *event* (*Vorgang*) and the *procession* (*Hervor-
> gang*) of the divine unity in absolute distinctiveness of Father and
> Son would then be the *beginning,* the *center,* and the *end* of all Chris-
> tology, and therewith of all theology. The elaboration of a *non-
> aprioristic* theology-in-history (*Geschichtstheologie*) which takes hold
> of the newness — the not-to-be-anticipated, the staggering or even
> shocking newness of the truly divine (and in no manner manifesting
> itself in an all *cosmic* understanding of *totality*) fidelity of God —
> effectively reacting on man — such a theology would indeed be the
> desired goal of a future Christology of the cross (*op. cit.,* p. 37).

CHAPTER THREE

CHRISTIAN SPIRITUALITY

Unless We See Redeemed Man, We
Cannot Believe In A Redeemer.
(From St. Augustine, quoted in *Origens*,
March 11, 1976, Vol. 5, no. 38, p. 601.)

God is love and man the creation of his love. Hence all spiritual reference to God arises from the "acceptance of the ineffable mystery of God as love" (Rahner). The term clearly suggests that Christian spirituality is fashioned by the bond of love in Christ through his Holy Spirit, a bond which integrates us into the life and mission of Jesus and the Spirit of Jesus. Incarnation-redemption communicates the God-life with all its love to mankind. Only through this divine life, this bond of love, coming to us through the Son-of-God-made-man, does human existence and human fellowship possess true, interior, in-depth meaning. Christ, the Man, Son of God, unites to his divine person all of mankind — its cultures, manifestations, all its ages and stages, its total existence in this universe. But, as we point out elsewhere, we speak of man largely because of the ready incompleteness of our grasp of the universe, of creation in its totality. We positively include all intellectual creatures in our concept — the totality of grace-borne creatures and, in a manner, the material universe itself. Nothing in creation can escape the Christ who is the center and goal of all things.

Only the most PERFECT MAN — perfect by his very closeness to God in the divine Logos — could so unite to God the totality of created-intellectual-grace-borne reality. Herein lies the mystery of Christ revealed by the Spirit to the holy apostles and prophets (Eph 3:4ff).

Christian spirituality with its origins in God's self-communication through the divine revelation of his own inner life, his word of truth, his sacred action in history and in every human life, is disclosed to us in the divine scriptures throughout, most manifestly in the proclamation of the prophets, and finally and definitively in his Son, the God-man. This announced plan of salvation is salvation history. It may be called *official salvation history,* the center and term of all history which, as we noted above, is salvation history in the more comprehensive sense. Always involved is the divine call, eliciting creature response, the impulse of divine grace in the context of creature's needs and aspirations throughout all stages of life and culture.

Though contemporary theological reflection so enriches our Christocentrism by its deep insight into the impressive reality that our Christology has become our anthropology, profound theological study still challenges us to further serious discussion and development. The great world religions have elements of high spirituality. Already before Vatican II Thomas Ohm, O.S.B., found traces of the love of God in all non-Christian religions.[2] Something of the divine truth has always been present in the pagan background, despite a depth of error and perversity. We underscore all this with the Christocentric concept of divine love for all men. The grace of Christ is everywhere. This consoling doctrine has a beautiful and impressive background among the Fathers of the Church, to which we can refer only briefly. In the early *Christian Apology* it is Justin Martyr (died about 165) who maintains that a *seed of truth* rested in every man. The fullness of truth, however, was in the Logos, Christ. Even the ancient philosophers might be considered Christians in a broader sense (*Patrologie,* Altaner, p. 93, Herder, Freiburg). Clement of Alexandria (died before 215), first of learned Christians, attempted to write a summa of truth. He found truth everywhere, in the conviction that all truth was summed up in revelation in Christ. In unity in Christ he sought to garner all truth, all philosophy (*ibid.,* p. 160). From earliest times the Church christianized many pagan rites, festivals and customs, purging their error and directing them to lofty Christian levels. The Second Vatican Council had in mind the direction of all studies to the mystery of Christ in the history of salvation.[3]

The Council's *Declaration on the Relationship of the Church to Non-Christian Religions* recognizes

> a certain perception of that hidden power which hovers over the course of things and over the events of human life; at times, indeed, recognition can be found of a Supreme Divinity and of a Supreme Father too. Such a perception and such a recognition instill the lives of these peoples with a profound religious sense. Religions bound up with cultural advancement have struggled to reply to these same questions with more refined concepts and in more highly developed language.
> Thus in Hinduism men contemplate the divine mystery and express it through an unspent fruitfulness of myths and through searching philosophical inquiry. They seek release from the anguish of our condition

through ascetical practices or deep meditation or a loving, trusting flight toward God.

Buddhism in its multiple forms acknowledges the radical insufficiency of this shifting world. It teaches a path by which men, in a devout and confident spirit, can either reach a state of absolute freedom or attain supreme enlightenment by their own efforts or by higher assistance. . . .

Upon the Moslems, too, the Church looks with esteem. They adore one God, living and enduring, merciful and all-powerful, Maker of heaven and earth and Speaker to men . . . Though they do not acknowledge Jesus as God, they revere him as a prophet. They also honor Mary, his Virgin Mother (nos. 2, 3).[4]

We do not look upon these noble religious elements in the non-Christian religions as justification for indifference toward the mission of bringing the fullness of Christ to them, as to all mankind, but rather as evidence of the grace of Christ beckoning us toward a fuller and richer Christocentrism. Magnificent indeed is the Christocentric concept of the Church as the "Sacrament of the World's Salvation" (*sacramentum salutis totius mundi*), reflecting the sacramental insights of such theologians as Henri de Lubac, Otto Semmelroth, and Karl Rahner. The latter speaks of her as the visible form of what is already binding interiorly (*The Christian of the Future*, p. 88, *QD*, no. 18, Herder). In the divine will to bring all men to salvation God communicates his grace — and with it the revelation of himself — to all men: He meets all in his Son in what we appropriately call the *cosmic covenant*. God "wants all men to be saved and come to know the truth. And the truth is this:

'God is one.
One also is the mediator between God and men,
the man Christ Jesus,
who gave himself as a ransom for all' " (1 Tm 2:4-6).

With cosmic background and Jesus the universal Mediator in mind, his grace imparted to all men, we now readily link our broad theme of Christian spirituality (and the Precious Blood spirituality) in this context to the all-embracing concept of covenant, covenant with God in the Old and the New Testaments. Shall we call it the central dogma of all revelation?

John E. Huesman, S.J., calls the *Exodus* with its "choice, deliverance, and covenant . . . the cardinal dogma of Old Testament religion . . . What the incarnation is to Christianity, the Exodus is to the Old Testament" *JBC*, 3:2, p. 47).

In the same vein is the following authoritative statement from the New Catholic Encyclopedia:

Jewish religion was above all the religion of the covenant. This covenant was the source of unshakable trust in God's divine power and of the nearness of God, who condescended to make himself the companion of his people. The prayers of the Jewish religion were permeated with the sense of God's nearness and at the same time of his elevation (*NCE*, History of Spirituality, Vol. 13, p. 594).

THE PEOPLE OF THE COVENANT

The spirituality of the Jewish people is best understood by the unique relation in the covenant between Yahweh and his covenanted people. He is the *living God*. He possesses life, power and personality.

The election of Israel, the formation of the covenant, and the saving acts by which Yahweh made Israel a people are acts of favor arising from personal benevolence. The law that is imposed upon Israel in the covenant is the externalization of a vital personal will. The response of Yahweh to love or to disobedience is a personal response of love or anger . . . The personal relation of Yahweh to Israel demands a personal response and not merely an official or a cultic posture toward him. It becomes almost a commonplace in the prophetic books that cult without personal commitment is vain and hypocritical. The total demands of Yahweh can be met only by total surrender. Personal communication becomes possible: Yahweh speaks to Israel, and Israel can speak to Yahweh . . . In prayer the speech of the OT attains through anthropomorphism an intimacy and an urgency that is scarcely paralleled elsewhere, and cannot be achieved in any other way (*JBC*, 77, no. 22, p. 740).

The hallmark of the spiritual relation of Yahweh to Israel — the same is true of his relation to the universe — is the positive *free action* which calls for free response on the part of Israel. (This is characteristic of all Western religious culture). We here face a basic Israelitic spirituality unique among the religions of the ancient world.

The relation is not a given necessary component of human existence but a freely instituted community of persons (*JBC*, 77, no. 74, p. 749).

Springing from the covenant relationship on the most basic level is the bond of father and offspring, Israel is *begotten* not by carnal relationship, but lovingly formed as God's people, by divine adoption, involving the free personal attitudes of love, devotion and obedience. Basic love and fidelity also underlie the relationship of marriage. As the bride of Yahweh, Israel owes fidelity in love. Infidelity is personal offense against her Spouse. She is the flock he shepherds, protects, and redeems. He is her Lord whom she obeys and whose law she respects and observes. She becomes a community of law and worship. Covenant, law, and worship imply and involve holiness, consciousness of sin, repentance and an eventual hope of resurrection.

In summation, Israelitic spirituality centers in covenant which embraces the love initiating it, the love and mercy which is a lavish kindness surpassing any mere minimum requirement. God's fidelity to his promises, his willingness to save, make of covenant love the total complex of salvation. Profoundly Jeremiah at Yahweh's bidding cries out to Jerusalem:

> I remember the devotion of your youth,
> how you loved me as a bride, (2:2).

And again Yahweh forgives and restores:

> The people that escaped the sword
>   have found favor in the desert.
> As Israel comes forward to be given his rest,
>   the Lord appears to him from afar:
> With age-old love I have loved you;
>   so I have kept my mercy toward you.
> Again I will restore you, and you shall be rebuilt,
> O virgin Israel; (31:2-4).

The entire history of Israel is "one act of covenant love." This gives purpose and understanding to God's dealing with men, even in his anger and judgment. This love identifies Yahweh. "It is the key to the understanding of his character" (cf. *JBC*, 77, no. 98, p. 753).

Obviously this clearly shows that the Old Testament relates to the New Testament as promise to fulfillment. And the New Testament proclamation of Jesus as Messiah implies the unity of salvation under a single divine plan. Here the acts of Yahweh converge and reach their fulfillment. The Old Testament idea of history and hope of future ages is brought to term. Israel can look to no further destiny. In Jesus the saving and judging acts of God are accomplished. Such is the unified design of *official salvation history*.

In consequence Christian spirituality relates to God through Christ with his message of salvation and brings to fulfillment OT spirituality. It looks to Christ and this message in faith-acceptance of a unique loving revelation and specifically reaches out to all men through the Christ-presence and Christ-action. Through and in the Mystical Body, the Christ anointed by the Holy Spirit is the salvific communion of all men. The letter to Hebrews sheds a splendid light upon this Christ of the new covenant (cf. *Encyclopedia of Theology*, Seabury Press, 1975, art. "Covenant," p. 308ff).

Since its object, origin and goal is God in his personal life, Christian spirituality is interpersonal; it is the life of man with God. Men are given this new relationship with the Trinity gratuitously, and they express it in acts that are at once human and transcendent. The open, free, and in some sense unlimited human spirit can express itself only in dependence on the material, the finite and particular, hence little by little and in time. This particularized condition of existence is reinforced in Christianity by the fact that grace is union with an historical person, Christ (Acts 2:38), and a participation in the sacred events called mysteries in his life. At the same time the new life in Christ is transhistorical and supernatural (Gal 2:20); it is nothing less than the life of the Holy Spirit, the Spirit of the Son, in man (Rom 8:14-16) (NCE, Vol. 13, "Christian Spirituality," p. 598).

Christian spirituality, reflecting the mystery of the God-life in man (with special relation to angels, and the conflict of the forces of evil) is always deep and diverse. The finite grasp of infinite treasure, the diversity of men in time and place, must mirror the highest aspirations of the human spirit. Unfortunately, however, it may also reflect external and partisan zeal and factional piety if it yield too readily to external and party loyalty. The writer cautions especially against the partisan spirit in the promotion of certain devotions and exercises of piety. Obviously this caution should not temper the zeal of the great societies in the Church for their special devotion. Again we call to mind the example of those who further the Ignatian spirituality — and the reference to *our* spirituality as we use it in these pages.

In the same vein we point out that *our spirituality* must relate to the God-man as redeemer and the source of all grace. It begins with the self-giving of Jesus and his bearing of our sins on the cross. To Jesus in his death and resurrection the Christian is united by baptism: there is a profound mystery-sense in which the Christian dies to sin and rises to new life in the resurrection of the Savior through his Holy Spirit.

Are you not aware that we who were baptized into Christ Jesus were baptized into his death? Through baptism into his death we were buried with him, so that, just as Christ was raised from the dead by the glory of the Father, we too might live a new life. If we have been united with him through likeness to his death, so shall we be through a like resurrection (Rom 6: 3-5).

The text focuses on the central thought of the Christian spirituality — our indwelling in the mystery of Christ. This mystery of mysteries embraces the total work of incarnation-redemption, culminating in the paschal mystery of death-resurrection. This present age — between resurrection-ascension and the Second Coming — involves what we somewhat ineptly call the *application* of Christ's work to men. The mystery of Christ — as of now —

is the risen *Kyrios* in glory and in the Church. John sees him lifted up on the cross and drawing all men and all creation to himself (Jn 12:32). For Paul his commission is to preach

> his word in its fullness, that mystery hidden from ages and generations past but now revealed to his holy ones. God has willed to make known to them the glory beyond price which this mystery brings to the Gentiles — the mystery of Christ in you, your hope of glory. This is the Christ *we proclaim* while we admonish all men and teach them in the full measure of wisdom, hoping to make every man complete in Christ (Col 1:25-28).

This mystery of Christ thus proclaimed in the *Praedicatio Apostolica* is communicated to all men — in word, in power, in sacrament. Man's loving response in and through the Word-made-flesh is the basis of the most diverse Christian spirituality. For, indeed, the mystery always transcends any manifestation and acceptance of it in men's lives. But it will always be structured in the Church: it will always be Christ-centered, moved by his Spirit, impelled to worshipful dedication in the liturgy and every form of prayer, and diversity of holy exercise. It will assume the most diverse forms as men diversely apply, interrelate, and stress the doctrines of faith in this one great mystery of Christ. Always striving toward the full measure of Christ, only the most diverse spiritualities can reflect the *full measure of wisdom* and our completeness in Christ through the working of his Holy Spirit (cf. *NCE*, Vol. 13, "Christian Spirituality," p. 600).

THE EARLY CHURCH

Shall we say the early Christians were fond of the risen Lord, tender and intimate with him? They deeply sensed his promise of return. They yearned for the Second Coming. This very yearning — which we all must learn to share — even merited what seems a rebuke from Paul who surely did not think of it in terms of unknown ages away. His rebuke rather censures the *dating* of the event, and a certain slovenliness toward this present world. How often has his warning (and that of such minds as Augustine and Thomas) been unheeded even to our own time!

> On the question of the coming of our Lord Jesus Christ and our being gathered to him, we beg you, brothers, not to be so easily agitated or terrified, whether by an oracular utterance, or rumor, or a letter alleged to be ours, into believing that the day of the Lord is here (2 Thes 2:1f).

Though this eschatological awareness deepened the Eucharistic unity and tender togetherness — for the Lord is always at hand in the Christian fellowship — it did not stifle the sense of social justice and social love, nor the consciousness of the Church's continuous mission. Clearly the *Didache* or *Teaching of the Apostles* offers us a nostalgic insight into this other-worldly spirituality with its reflection of the unique organization of the post-Apostolic age. As the Church expanded, however, and faced the Hellenistic world, the perspective of a Second Coming rather assumed the nature of a distant hope. There followed greater spiritual depth and intellectual breadth with a far more complex outlook on the realities of life. Nowhere did this become more evident than in the response to the challenge of Gnosticism, which was both positive and negative. Even today it is a complex and widespread phenomenon for the student of history.

Striking at the very heart of the doctrine of redemption through Christ the doctrine of a *Gnosis* or unique *knowledge* of the elite and arcane intellectualism offered one of the greatest, if not the greatest of challenges to the Church in all her history up to our own time. The material world, the entire universe in point of fact, was viewed with jaundiced eyes, and the divine revelation distorted in the most bizarre perspective. Ignored was the true *Gnosis* which is "intimate knowledge of and participation in the love that is communicated by God to men through Christ." This "surpasses all natural knowledge to lose itself in the fulness of God" (*NCE, loc. cit.*, 594). The very aberrations of Gnosticism in complex manifestations providentially provided the Church with a massive anti-Gnostic literature and brilliant Christian writers who revealed true insight into the world, its history, and human knowledge. The result was a great enrichment of the faith in the development of the true *Gnosis*. We single out two stalwart figures, true *greats* from the school of Alexandria, a world center of learning — *Clement of Alexandria* and *Origen*. Clement's thought stresses sublime love: The

> supreme state is that in which one knows the God of love by loving as he loves. The attainment of the summit of the Gnostic life, i.e., assimilation to God, was made possible by *apatheia,* a term he introduced into Christian language. By this term, he meant a domination, acquired through grace, over everything that is opposed to charity. The resulting stable condition is, as it were, a foretaste of eternity (*NCE,* "History of Spirituality," Vol. 13, p. 594).

The imitation of Christ and participation in the life of Christ was necessary to uproot the soul from the world in which it was buried in egotistic desires.

> Like Clement, Origen wrote about vocal prayer, saying that as it is interiorized, it goes beyond itself into the prayer of silence, which characterizes the state of union with God and liberation from the body (*NCE, ibid.*, p. 594).

The Martyrs — Monasticism — The Great Fathers

Dying in Christ through baptism did indeed mean baptism into his death. In the baptism this was graphically symbolized as *burial* (we *visualize* the catechumen being submerged into the water) and *rising again* (emerging from the water). This luminous, symbolical concept was realized in its most lofty form in the martyr who actually gave up his life, by physical death, for Christ. The martyr (the Greek term means witness) was witness to Christ, the *Faithful Witness* (Rv 1:5, 3:14). The Church has always looked upon him as witness to her truth, *proof* of her relation to Christ and the Father.

Martyrdom was a part of her very nature, the uttermost commitment in her faith. It was the peak of Christian spirituality for it summed up the totality of the Christian life, as death sums up man's whole life for salvation or perdition. Consequently the early Christian martyrs were honored as united immediately with Christ in glory, the first of the saints to be venerated and commemorated in her public prayer (cf. *TD*, "Martyrdom," p. 275f).

As martyrdom meant the ultimate and total commitment in witness to Christ, so unique forms of renunciation were held to free man from the entanglements and allurements of the world. Consecrated virginity was a most exalted form of spirituality in union with Christ and in imitation of him. Flight from the world into the desert meant not only disengagement from the flesh and the world, but also imitation of the solitude and loneliness of the Savior. Particularly significant was the shunning of the temptations of the world — through penitential practices of special harshness combined with fasting, work, and prayer — by the countless holy men and women who fled to the desert in Egypt and other desolate areas.

Gradually the hermits merged into communities or monasteries under a spiritual father, upholding the early Christian ideal of perseverance in prayer, community of goods, and the breaking of bread. Often noble women dedicated themselves totally to most menial forms of monastic life, as Saint Jerome eloquently testifies. The spirituality which is deeply rooted in the heart of man came to flower under the influence of the example of Christ and the power of his grace.

> In the period when monasticism in general came to be organized, the practice of consecrating one's virginity to Christ was solemnized by profession and public consecration before the Church. By virginity the Christian sought to achieve the reality of which marriage offers an image: the union of Christ and the Church. (*NCE*, "History of Spirituality," Vol. 13, p. 595).

Despite all diversity between East and West (the terms are probably too broad) the history of spirituality in both is very largely the history of monasticism. With the East in mind, we must note such true giants as the Cappadocians, Basil the Great, Gregory of Nyssa, and Gregory of Nazianzus: a great debt in theological theory and practice is owing them in both East and West. *The Rule of St. Basil* entitles him to be called the founder of the monasticism of the Eastern Church.

> Gregory of Nyssa's thought was transmitted in two different ways: one was more learned, and the other was more popular and practical. In Syria what was most personal in this thought came to be the seed of a new development: the Areopagitical writings.
>
> According to Pseudo-Dionysius (4th or 5th century), the soul finds God by going beyond itself, by rejecting all particular knowledge and by being united to him, who is transcendent, in the luminous darkness where he awaits it. Spiritual writers were very numerous in the East during the 5th and 6th centuries, and certain of them were masters whose influence was considerable throughout the later history of spirituality. But only with St. Maximus (580?-662) was a new departure sketched out: that of Byzantine spirituality (*NCE,* "History of Spirituality," Vol. 13, *ibid.,* p. 595).

Dionysius, for centuries mistakenly associated with the Dionysius mentioned in the Acts 17:34 and Paul's discourse in Athens, is an unknown writer of a much later date. Research has failed to discover the real author of his immensely influential writings. There are four works, highly esteemed, and ten letters written in Greek around the year 500. We may list Dionysius as a fountain source of deep mystical thought. In this context we mention also Maximus the Confessor (died 662) — mystical forerunner of scholasticism, interpreter of our Dionysius — to whom belongs the credit of synthesizing Rome and Byzantium, Asian and Western theology, antiquity and the Middle Ages. He is rightly called a co-founder of medieval thought, who brought to light the rich treasures of the ancient Christian tradition. Here we should like to stress his significance for our current spirituality as brought out in the great work of Hans Urs von Balthasar's classic *Kosmische Liturgie.*

Turning to the West, we are restricted by space to two names: *Augustine* (died 430) and *John Cassian* (died 435?). The former dominated the spiritual and intellectual life of the Church for centuries and in a sense is now enjoying something of a revival.

> Augustinian wisdom . . . is distinguished particularly by its psychological reflexive orientation. It does not deal directly with the mystery of God in Christ, but with the mystery of men's selves that Christ helps them to discern (*NCE,* "History of Spirituality," Vol. 13, p. 595).

John Cassian transmitted to the West monastic practice and spiritual thought from the East:

> Throughout the whole work of asceticism, the monk is not to seek anything but the kingdom of God. He will attain this kingdom by purity of heart, which is the condition and counterpart of the full development of charity. The summits of Cassian's mysticism are described by him as a constant prayer, a prayer of fire wholly inspired by the Gospel (*NCE, ibid.,* p. 595).

According to Walter Kasper in his *Einfuehrung in den Glauben* the great crises in the Church from her very origins led to immense historical transformations, created tremendous challenges to her faith. The hazard or ruin, however, was accompanied by a providential summons for a deepening of faith and its spiritual enrichment. These crises, under the influence of the Holy Spirit, prove to be the *Kairos,* the providential call to unique spiritualities. The age-long medieval Christianization of the barbarian hordes could not fail to produce what we must designate as *crude spirituality,* often manifested in the display and stress of *Schaureligion*: devotion to relics, pilgrimages to tombs and shrines of saints, especially to Mary and her mysteries.

But even these ages did manifest a more profound sense of sin, consciousness of the distinction of sins in the administration of penance (Irish monks), deep interior sorrow with sense of expiation, and also in-depth prayer of contemplation. Simple and gentle humanization of the life of Christ and the Holy Family manifested itself in noble forms of art, architecture, and poetry. Some of the medieval hymns rank among the world's great poetry. In this sense a religious atmosphere permeated the entire medieval life style.

The decline of the Middle Ages, the beginnings of the modern age, Renaissance, Reformation, revolution, all swept away much of the religious spirit of the past, but also created various forms of special spirituality. Our polemics have caused us to disregard the piety and spirituality of many dissident groups even in the midst of the Reformation and the religious wars. Luther and Calvin had a deep prayer life, not to speak of William Penn and the Wesleys. Why should we not learn much from Martin Luther's theology of the cross, especially in the current age of ecumenism? Worthy of special note is the cultivation of the sacred pages, the love of religious hymns, and the strong strains of the unique *Jesus-love*. To this we now turn.

SPIRITUALITY AND THE JESUS-LOVE

The medieval spirituality which centers in the *Jesus-love* is of particular significance for our current devotion to the Savior and our Precious Blood spirituality. For all its precision in explaining the human nature of the God-man (like to us in all things, sin alone excepted) Chalcedon and the Greek theologians never quite developed the warmth of the spirituality of this approach to the Jesus-love. The affection, the tenderness, is nourished in fancy and legend about the infancy, deep human sympathy is stirred over the passion and death: a love of pity. Only such spirituality could have produced the *Jesu, dulcis memoria* and the *Stabat Mater Dolorosa*. This tender spirituality identified with all the mysteries of the life of Jesus, his birth, his childhood, his passion and death, we feel, would have amazed (and delighted) Augustine.

The Franciscan spirituality is close to Jesus in its simple discipleship, in imitation of the Savior (utter poverty), recreating the atmosphere of the events of his life, identifying with the common people through the hearing of confessions, preaching in simple folk-like style. The meditation on Jesus' life (*Meditationes vitae Christi*) profoundly influenced Christian art and literature for centuries (*NCE*, Vol. 7, p. 950). In unbelievable simplicity Francis sang to the beauty of God's creation, and brought to his own body the passion of the Savior. His stigmata and his joy in suffering is unique in all the annals of spiritual thought: mankind could never be the same after Francis of Assisi [See: The Mystical Heights].

This humanized Christ, whom we call Jesus and love with affection, is also the font of *mystical experience* in many chosen souls. Union with him is sharing his suffering in atonement for sin, extending the kingdom. Here too is the basis of the mission efficacy of prayer and self-oblation for the Church, for all the needs of mankind, including the suffering souls. There is a unique list of saintly women. Two have been declared Doctors of the Church. In Catherine of Siena (1380) love for the Blood of Jesus and his tortured Mystic Body, the Church, in the troubled times of the so-called Babylonian Captivity of the Church and the Avignon Schism, mark her as the most apostolic figure of the age. In Teresa of Avila (1582) mystic love for Jesus, like an interchange of hearts, was the source of tremendous reform activity in the monasteries of her time.

Closer to our own days is that other Therese whose true spirituality is often blurred by the mushy sentimentality of the *Little Flower literature*. Her all embracing love transcends both contemplation and action in a mission for the Church, for which she has been called the "greatest saint of modern times" by none other than Hans Urs von Balthasar. In Therese he finds not the *contemplata tradere,* but rather the contemplation which is itself dynamic grace-action for the priestly work of the Church (*Theologians Today,* p. 37).

We associate all this with an essential theme or note in the Precious Blood spirituality: all the acts and sufferings of Jesus are efficacious for the salvation of man. It also calls to mind the doctrine of the *Mystery Presence of Christ* in the Church. The intimate affection of the mystical saints we have just referred to, Catherine of Siena, Teresa of Avila, and Therese of Lisieux, sheds a vivid light on our contemporary theology which seeks to answer the question: *Who is this Man, Jesus?*

As living theology, our current Christology combines the fruits of our biblical research with modern psychological concepts in explaining the man Jesus. Thus Jesus makes known to us the Father and the Holy Spirit in living theology. We repeat what we noted above, no longer is the divine Trinity viewed as from afar, in splendid isolation, but as within us, in our experienced love for Jesus, in our worship and daily life and in our whole theological approach through mystery of incarnation-redemption. An understanding and intelligent piety without snobbery lovingly embraces all Christians (and potentially all mankind) as the *una mystica persona* with the Holy Spirit (cf. again Heribert Muehlen). The previous paragraphs clearly reveal how such an atmosphere must be favorable to continual study of the Church's great mysticism. Rightly understood the current Pentecostal Movement, with all its diversity and perplexity, reflects the *Spirit of Jesus.*

> Because of the great strides forward in the study of man, and perhaps from an instinctive awareness of the need to counteract the aberrations of a materialistic culture, contemporary spirituality has assigned the major role to Christ, the God-man. Previously, the saints had great influence upon the lives of the faithful, particularly in their acts of piety: 20th century spirituality tends to view them more realistically, that is, in their relationship to the Redeemer. In *Mediator Dei,* his encyclical letter on the liturgy, Pius XII encouraged devotion to the saints precisely as imitators of Christ, "for in their virtues there shines forth under different aspects the splendor of Jesus Christ" (*Mediator Dei, NCWC* translation, par. 167). Mindful of the excesses in certain parts of the Catholic world that would place Marian devotion before that of Christ, some Fathers at Vatican Council II strongly advocated severe norms to guide devotion to the Blessed Virgin Mary (*NCE,* Vol. 13, "Contemporary Spirituality," p. 603).

The present pope directed the people of God to know the ways of Christ:

> A strong desire to know the ways of Christ is and ought to remain ever present in the Church, and its discussion must always be fruitful and varied . . . We should like to see the unique interest that the life of Christ deserves reawakened, not so much for the sake of elaborating new theories as for generating new energies. They should be used for

acquiring that sanctity which Christ teaches. His example, His word, His grace, and His method, sustained by ecclesiastical tradition, strengthened by divine action and exemplified in the lives of the saints, make it possible for us to know, desire, and follow the path of sanctity (*Ecclesiam Suam, NCWC* translation, par. 43).

SPIRITUALITY IN THE WORLD TODAY

Current Christocentrism in the totality of the universe not only involves a relation to the world, but a totally different approach than could have been thought of in former ages. It cannot be reconciled with a mere flight from the world, nor being in the world and in no way a part of it. We must be guided by a twofold concept: the *incarnational* rightly looks upon a world redeemed with redemption as essential motive of creative-incarnation, as essential to the meaning of the total reality. In consequence, consecration of the world marks a new term in our spiritual conception. But Christian tradition also calls for an *eschatological* emphasis which looks to the end of all and the Second Coming.

From this dual viewpoint we turn to a world (the term universe is probably more apposite) not to be shunned, but rather to be more fully redeemed (cf. Rom 8:18ff). We share a redemptive apostolate of action. Man is responsible for building the world as completion of the work of full redemption: we look to the Second Coming. We have already indicated our conviction that to *share* transcends men and the visible world, and involves also the *superhuman powers,* the cooperation of the angelic, the conflict with the demoniac, in the war of the kingdom of darkness with the kingdom of light. But in this we must tread cautiously and seek guidance of the most carefully constructed systematic theology.

Our immediate point of departure is *community* rather than individual (the avoidance of rugged spiritual individualism does not exclude the fullest maturity of individual responsibility). Liturgy and common prayer are the center to which private prayer (always necessary) is directed. Activity and involvement must conspire with *holiness in the world.* Translated into action, incarnational and eschatological elements of Catholic ideals set up the balance between antinomies of *withdrawal* and *engagement, renunciation* and *use* (cf. *NCE*, Vol. 13, "Christian Spirituality," p. 602). Significant is the thought of Chenu, that the utter vastness of automation and world-oneness must lead to love and justice embracing all our race (in a sense we add: *one race, no races*) with the most comprehensive Christocentrism. Paradoxically the very depersonalization of our modern *civilization of work* which is also our *technology of work* must lead to the personalization of every man: the new swift communications have made every man our *next door neighbor.*[5]

JOHN XXIII AND CURRENT SPIRITUALITY

The vast epochal turn in the life of the Church in the last two decades is associated with the Second Vatican Council and with the great pontiff whose life was so much a part of the world which preceded it. With his personal piety or spirituality we associate no boldness, yet his convocation of the council might well be called *audacious* as was the pontiff's turning to all the world in a spirit of ecumenism and love for all mankind. His was the first encyclical to be addressed to all men, an open letter to all the world. Such is the *Pacem in Terris* addressed to all men of good will.

The personal or private declarations of this pontiff underscoring his official pronouncements embolden the writer to present the *Precious Blood* in the stark terms of these pages. In a most singular way John XXIII is associated with the *Precious Blood spirituality*. In his private devotional life, he himself tells us, he learned of the devotion to the Blood of the Redeemer in his parental home. In official documents (as we shall see) he promoted this spirituality, and took every occasion to encourage its practice and exercise. To the societies of the Precious Blood he gave the *injunction* that their members make known the values and merits of their spirituality. For this reason our special and specific treatise on the Precious Blood spirituality rests on the official position of John XXIII. Since we find the center of all spirituality in Christ, all graces and virtues in his priesthood (notably in the supreme sacrifice on the cross, and the mystic oblation in the Eucharist) we introduce the thought of John XXIII by a few pages on the priesthood of Christ in us.

Lord of the Heavenly Banquet

Fresco by Rudolf Kaufhold in Holy Trinity Church in Freiburg, Breisgau, Germany (cf. jpage 31).

Children Rejoice in the Last Supper

Done with clippings by kindergarten children in Kirchen-Hausen, for the feast of Corpus Christi (cf. page 55).

CHAPTER FOUR

PRECIOUS BLOOD SPIRITUALITY
The Priesthood of Christ In Us

What, then, is the Priesthood of the Incarnate Son? It is the office he assumed for the redemption of the world by the oblation of himself in the vestments of our manhood. He is altar, victim, and priest, by an eternal consecration of himself. This is the priesthood forever after the order of Melchisedech . . . These striking words by Cardinal Manning in "The Eternal Priesthood" (Burns and Oates, p. 3f) *call to mind the Prayer of Christ before his sacrifice of himself on the cross. In John 17:17-19 Jesus prays to his Father, that he "consecrate" his disciples "in the truth". And Jesus "consecrates" himself for the sake of the disciples "so that they too may be consecrated in truth." Here we feel that Jesus the priest is to send his disciples as priests, more intimately bound up with him for "the Word of God," "truth" itself is their "consecration." Linked with them will be all to whom the disciples bring the word of truth* (cf. *JBC,* 63:156-158, p. 457, Bruce Vawter).

THE ARTIST'S VISION

We insert here the lofty vision of the Christ, Lord of the heavenly banquet. It is the creation of Rudolph Kaufhold in the church of the Holy Trinity at Freiburg in Breisgau, Germany. For the reproduction and theological insight we are indebted to Lothar Schreyer, *Das Christusbild und die Kunst des* 20 *Jahrhunderts* (Mueller, Salzburg, 1960), to which we shall have occasion to refer frequently in our study.

The Wedding Banquet of the Lamb of Revelation (19:6-9) looms up before us in all its glory. The white garments symbolize the purity of life and good works of the saints who have been invited to the celestial feast. The pledge in this life is the Eucharistic liturgy. Holy Communion is a foretaste of the eternal participation.

> Obviously such are our inadequacies that this *foretaste* cannot fully be a measure of our participation in the heavenly liturgy. As a rule, we should say, that we share in the obscurity of faith, nurtured on hope and love, and insofar we possess a true though imperfect foretaste of the *lumen gloriae.* Yet it is truly profitable spiritually for one who prays if both the earthly and heavenly banquet of Christ are proclaimed to him in their unity" (*op. cit.,* p. 226f).

The writer underscores the point that the proclamation by men in word and in picture directs attention to the mystery which is enclosed and presented to us in the words of the institution of the Eucharist at the Last Supper, as found in the evangelists and in the Consecration at Mass. Then he quotes at length from Claudel on Holy Communion and the mystery of the Presence with its deep hope of the mystery of the heavenly banquet (*op. cit.,* p. 227ff). "Though Claudel wrote his words of rhythmic beauty in 1917, and Kaufhold created his vision-in-image in 1953, we sense in both the natural-supernatural tension involved in the banquet of Christ in the liturgy on earth and the liturgy in the celestial realm, the tension between the temporal here and now of the union with Christ and the promised gift of the eternal union with him in heaven" (*op. cit.,* p. 231 adapted).

> The content of the proclamation-in-picture manifests symbolically the triune God: in the loftiest heights is the symbol of the *Divine Eye* peering out from the triangle within the triangulated structure shrouded by the cloud of the night of God. Symbolized is the deep hidden vision of the invisible God-the-Father. From this night, the Dove or symbol of the Holy Spirit hovers over the throne of the Son-of-God who manifests himself as the God-man. Radiant in the very obscurity of faith his sphere is turned toward all mankind. Expression and gesture of the God-man seem visibly filled with benign and loving self-giving. Beneath the great Christ-circle appear the smaller spheres of light, the two *thrones of angels* which uphold the Christ-sphere, presenting thereby to heaven and earth the incarnate God. From right and left near the rim of the Christ-circle blessed men approach the Lord of the Heavenly Banquet, who extends to the blessed ones his open welcoming hands. From the world of the Christ the light-in-shadow descends to the altar, with the picture-proclamation erected behind and over it.

Form and figure derive their vital meaning from the Trinitarian structure, from the merging of *cross, cycle,* and *triangle* in structure. The cross structure descends directly from the head of the Holy-Spirit-Dove through the Head of Christ to the center of the altar with its cross and tabernacle. Balanced are the hands of Christ outstretched to right and left, meeting the sainted forms approaching the Christ-cycle. The *cycle structure* separates by a flat and upward moving line the world-of-the-Father from the world-of-the-Son. Similarly, a cycle turned upward separates the world of the Son of the Celestial Banquet from the space in which the earthly liturgy is carried out. We may say that cycle structure is focused on the great cycle which surrounds the throning Christ and concentrates luminously in the nimbus of Christ and in the spheres of the two *thrones*. The triangular structure is formed by two equal lines whose tip rests on the center of the altar. The sides of the triangle descend from the world of the Father, enclosing the symbols of Father and Holy Spirit, through the world of the Son enclosing the darkly-glowing cycle-of-Christ, overshadowing the place of the altar and pointing to the God-Man-Oblation of the Eucharist. The triangular structure is emphatic in the downward turn of the tip of the triangle in the area of the mystery-celebration. Note also the upward pointing of the tip of the God-the-Father symbol, with the bond of unity in the center in the upward surge of the triangle from the hands of Christ extended and the lines to the Sacred Head. Finally, the triangle pointed downward to earth between the same sacred hands extended and the hand of the angel who prayerfully touches the lower rim of the Christ-circle as he presents it to us. Very clear is the threefold rhythm of the whole structure: the division of the whole wall into three realms by the two cycles, the clear imaging of the three divine persons. The Christ-world is structured into six members, hence in dual threefold rhythm: Christ, with the two holy groups to right and left, the Christ-cycle and the dual Angel-cycle. The rows of the blessed figures are three times three. Hence there are nine Blessed in all who approach the Love-Banquet. The ninth is a child: we are reminded of the Lord's word: Unless you become as little children.

The picture is rightly complete and meaningful if the priest is standing at the altar, says Rudolph Kaufhold. If the prayer of the priest and the faithful mingles with the clouds of incense, then there is manifested to interior and exterior view the vivid picture-proclamation. Profitable indeed is this proclamation of the celestial banquet emerging from the clouds. The bright colors in full light prepare us for spiritual uplifting in our celebration of the mysteries. Such is the significance of the proclamation through picture and allegory (*op. cit.,* adapted p. 231f).

Our reflection on the Precious Blood spirituality is focused on the redemptive work wrought in the priestly mediation and ministry of Christ for all mankind, a ministry shared by the diversity of ministries in the Church. In her, Christ is present and active with the total ministry of his life, death, and resurrection; men and women share diversely in this supreme ministry, unto the fullness of Christ. They proclaim the faith of the Apostolic preaching, exploring, expanding, pastoralizing the divine revelation. In every diverse age and diverse culture they direct *one great mission* to its end and goal, enacting salvation history to its final and eternal goal. They preside at the sacral communal celebration of the community of Christ. They share in it and participate in its fruits.

By grace-cooperation they manifest to all the world the visible unity of a visible Church guided by the Spirit of Christ. This ministry of many in unity is the living Church. Though we speak of many ministries, yet there is but one ministry, the priesthood of Christ which we all share in some measure. Though we stand in awe of its dignity, it is only in the light of *service* that we love and embrace it as essential and fruitful for our spirituality of the Precious Blood.

We would be in error if we were to state that the early Church had clearly defined and established norms or orders with ministers, all of which must be reflected clearly in the Church today. No less would be the error of expecting an exact and clear terminology for the multiple offices that existed in the Church. This would imply a misconception of a living Church meeting the needs of the changing world in time. The entire Apostolic period was fluid and developmental. Development and clarification, as essential elements of the Church's founding, could be complete only when the Apostolic preaching merged and crystallized in the founded Church. Even here exact dates and terminology are not possible. We feel that no past isolated instance of Eucharistic celebration, no single designation of office, or function (which is unique as differing from the present practice) can be cited for the Church today as definitively acceptable and binding pattern. Nevertheless, we do hold that there was present in the Church the full priestly ministry and service of Christ from the beginning. (In *Light on the Epistles,* John L. McKenzie maintains that the Greek word *hiereus* (priest) is never used for any Church office in the New Testament. cf. p. 115).

This writer clearly recalls that only a few decades ago in our instruction the concept of priesthood itself was almost exclusively bound up with the *cultal*: the essential duty and function of the priest was to offer sacrifice. Obviously this included the exclusive power to administer other sacraments besides the Eucharist, e.g., confirmation, penance, anointing the sick (somewhat crudely called extreme unction), holy order (with certain differentiations between the power of bishop who possessed the priesthood in its fullness and the simple priest). Today we are cautioned against exclusive emphasis of the priestly function as cultal or cultal-sacrificial.

> Rightly (Heinrich) Schlier rejects the exclusive grounding of the priestly character of the Church office in the right to preside at the Eucharistic celebration. Such a view is often found among representa-

tives as well as opponents of the desacralization. "There is no express mention in the New Testament of a connection between the presbyterial and episcopal office and presiding over the Eucharist. . . . Only gradually did it become clear that the Eucharist is the most objective and the inmost *making-present* of the sacrifice of Christ and the central *constitutive reality* in building up the Church. In consequence, the priestly ministry is found to be directed ultimately, though not by any means exclusively, to this manner of *making present* the priestly action of Jesus Christ" (cf. *TR,* 1973, no. 3, col. 181. Cf. also *Decree on the Ministry and Life of Priests* from Vatican II).

Biblical sources indicate that the Old Testament priesthood was not restricted to the divinely prescribed sacrificial ritual. The Old Testament priest bore the mark of Yahweh's covenant, was his messenger, custodian of his wisdom, and made known God's will to the cultal community. Old Testament religion bore the stamp and character of its priesthood, but it is clear that this Old Testament priesthood as the Old Testament covenant pointed to Christ and the New Testament priesthood and had its term in Christ.

The New Testament priesthood, however, is unique, transcendent, once-and-for-all. It centers in and derives totally from Christ whose work is consummated in the Last Supper-Passion-Death-Resurrection. This absolute uniqueness demands that its purpose be fulfilled by communication to all men, who through it are to become the redeemed people of God, priestly, sanctified, offered to God. Basic to New Testament priesthood, therefore, is a ministry which brings all men into union with Christ, crucified, risen. Hence: *Priesthood in Christ and in us.* We may not overlook in this priesthood that Christ is both *priest* who *offers* and *victim* who is *offered.* Similarly we share in both the priesthood offering and in the victimhood. This is especially important for us of the Precious Blood spirituality. We are offered with Christ, with his Blood. (The writer suggests the careful study of the leading article in *TR,* 1973, no. 3: "Der priesterliche Dienst." The article which is concerned with a series of *QD,* nos. 46, 47, 48, 49, has proved very helpful for our study).

Paul in Romans 15:16 speaks of himself as a "minister of Christ Jesus among the Gentiles." His proclamation of the gospel is a *"priestly* duty" whose purpose is that the "Gentiles may be offered as a pleasing sacrifice, consecrated by the Holy Spirit." According to Schlier, Paul considers his priesthood a "public official sacrificial-leiturgia for the total fellowship of the world" (*ibid.,* col. 180). McKenzie views the matter somewhat differently in *Light on the Epistles* (p. 115). He rejects the translation *priest* (priestly) as inaccurate, though it is used in our best English versions. (The words quoted in the first several lines above are from the *NAB*).

Thus far we noted three points: a) the *source* of priesthood or ministry: the Christ who suffered and died in total submission to God his Father and was raised to the glory of *Kyrios*. b) the direction of this ministry is to the Gentiles and all men to whom Christ was communicated and who with him were offered to God. As a priestly people, redeemed, sanctified, they dedicate themselves to God their Father. c) the priestly ministry or function in Paul which communicated to men Christ crucified and risen from the dead. This ministry of Paul is stressed as preaching Christ, but includes the total redemptive work of Christ, his presence, his grace-action, his whole priestly commitment.

This concept of priesthood seems basic and correct, though we may not expand the cultal power and function into a generic bracket including all that belongs to priesthood. That is, we should not subordinate all priestly functions to the cultal, much less all ministerial functions. But it is totally unsound theologically to slight the whole Christological ministry in favor of a sociological one. Paul's entire ministerial duty implies mission, proclamation, formation of the people of God by word, example, precept. Forming the people of God in Christ, making Christ present in them, making them holy and dear to God, of course, includes the cultal-sacrificial. In a most exalted sense the sociological is included. The exalted *Kyrios* of Hebrews is indeed the High Priest, fulfillment of Old Testament priesthood, who offered the sacrifice of his Blood for his people, and raised to highest heavens, even now intercedes for us before God his Father. As we look forward to this heavenly liturgy we assemble in our earthly liturgy, in the Eucharistic sacrifice. Most splendid is the *synodal concelebration* with all the gradations of order and the devout laity of every type. Ideally, this occurs at every Eucharistic celebration.

Here we call to mind again the splendid insight of *Muehlen*: the Church, as *one mystic person* — the Holy Spirit — unites us with Christ as *many persons*. How lofty our liturgical action!

In the light of what we have already said the most exalted *function of priesthood* and all the ministeries in the Church center in the Eucharist which builds up the whole Church and forms individual and group in Christ. The Eucharist is the heart of the society of worship which adores the Father in spirit and truth. The name of the Father is hallowed and thereby men are made just and holy. All the sacred signs, symbols, prayers, chants, converge in this central sacrament-sacrifice, the covenanted "Opfermahl" and "Mahlopfer" (*sacrificial banquet* and *banquet-sacrifice*). Sanctified also are the proclamation and prophecy, for which we must seek ever newer avenues in the world of our time, by no means restricting it to any order or group in the people of God. The very riches of the Eucharist make it impossible to uniformly stress all: the sacrifice, the Communion, the Presence, the blessing, the procession with solemn chant, the bearing of the Viaticum to the sick, the Communion to prisoners or those hiding from the enemies of Christ. All center in the Eucharistic liturgy or radiate from it.

Warm and affectionate is the Eucharistic offering of the Breaking of the Bread and the Cup in fellowship with the hungry in our society (cf. the beautifully written article "Eucharist and Society" in *America,* August 7, 1976, by William J. Byron, with its "accent . . . on the Eucharist as meal"). But we must caution against a current tendency to ignore the Eucharistic *sacrifice* by some, whose flippancy occasionally approaches blasphemy and destroys the loving reverence which must encompass the entire Eucharistic gift. At all times a well-rounded understanding of the Eucharist in all its "accents" is essential to our Eucharistic faith and worship. (It is well to recall that a narrow and badly-presented concept of Eucharistic sacrifice shared the blame psychologically in Luther's repudiation of the sacrifice and with the appalling commercialism made its own melancholy contribution to a basic heresy).

In vital Christian life and thought, in vital expanding theology we are in duty-bound to study and be ready to accept far-reaching conclusions regarding the *priesthood in Christ and in us.* Yet, as we cautioned above, we may not proceed uncritically, and with intemperate haste. Our technological age does not offer safe guidelines for theological development. If the innovative theologian follows the law of progress which governs vital theology he must still build on the past, grasp it thoroughly, though rejecting the role of mere theological reporter of the past, a *laudator temporis acti,* clasping fast the shopworn manuals of his school days. But the advanced must ponder 1 Cor 13:4-7 on love.

We suggest the application: Theology is patient, theology is kind, it is not snobbish nor arrogant. Without limit is its forbearance. Above all, it must shun the flippancy of the superficial claim to be up-to-date. Something of this was in the mind of the writer who coined the phrase *considerate theology,* which we have from his German text, *Barmherzigkeitstheologie.*

Suggested in conclusion, as we ponder the priesthood of Christ in all of us: Let us abandon the chasmal cleavage between laity and clergy, the harsh confrontation between any rank or order, the quarrel with women in the Church, without abandonment of essential structures. Jean-Paul Audet suggests that basic to this divisive reality is the gradual merging of the tiny family community in the Church, called the *Communauté de base* or *Stammgemeinde* into the vast mass expansion often patterned on secular lines. We have lost the intimate familial contact, the person-to-person relation and the familiar name, sharing the vocation, with all essential structures preserved lovingly. In the massive organizational and hierarchical Church the *Stammgemeinde* or *Communauté de base* became passive with diminished power to mediate brotherly love. Passive acceptance rather than loving response often marked the entire mass of the *ecclesia discens* confronting the *ecclesia docens*. Can we revivify the vital *Stammgemeinde*? How? (cf. *TR,* no. 3, 1973, col. 181f).

The problems involved seem endless. We shall not even attempt to list or suggest them. But we do suggest to those who lovingly study their Precious Blood spirituality and the Precious Blood vocation that they alert themselves to this basic need of the Church. The beginnings of revitalization must stir in all community groups. Here, too, *life is in the Blood.* Conciliation is from the Blood. Hence the grace of Christ's priesthood in us must be the source of *our* inspiration, our pulsing to life. All men must be our *Stammgemeinde* — every man our neighbor, every man our brother. The priesthood of Christ must embrace all men, even the least lovely — perhaps these most of all — making precious, holy, pleasing to God all the redeemed who have been washed in the Blood of Christ's priesthood — and ours. Our duty in our Precious Blood spirituality is to bring Christ to them in the spirit of the priesthood of St. Paul (we again refer to Rom 15: 16ff).

We cannot, however, speak of *all* without responding to a current challenge: In what measure does the *ministry to all* include sharing with that vast half of the Church — the women (a great variation in the percentage of men and women exists in many parts of the world)? In response we take up, first, that which is most controversial, which sheds light on the total ministry of women, and which the theologians may not disregard or evade — priestly ministry. Are women merely ministered to, objects of sincere ministerial action? Or, perchance, can they share the ministry, participate in it, minister to others, to all?

THE PRIESTLY MINISTRY OF WOMEN

By way of preliminary statement to this problem the writer directs attention to the serious discussion on the diaconate — and not as step to priesthood but as permanent status and function, especially the establishment of *married deacons.* Before the Second Vatican Council immense studies had been under way by the most noted theologians pondering all phases of the problem. We instance particularly one such work. More than a decade ago Karl Rahner and Herbert Vorgrimler published the most massive volume in the series of *Questiones Disputatae:* the *Diaconia in Christo: Ueber die Erneuerung des Diaconates* (Herder, 1962). The title indicates the concern for the *Renewal of the Diaconate.* With its fourteen pages of bibliography, it takes up the problem in all its breadth and depth — the diaconate in the early Church, in East and West, the efforts toward renewal, even the deacon in the Evangelical churches. Many distinguished writers contributed. It is obviously the desire of the writers to produce a thorough study in every area, without which the problems can find no practical solution.

We cite all this for the serious consideration of many who today advocate the immediate ordination of women to the priesthood, and who, in fact, seem to find no difficulty involved. The writer recalls a meeting for Contemporary Theology held at Montreal a number of years ago, when the question of the ordination of women was curtly brushed aside by no less a figure than Hans Kueng with the statement, that the question is *canonical*, not *theological*.

We cannot accept such a simplistic solution. The problem must be explored on the basis of the scriptures, the Church's history, the doctrine of theologians, the pronouncements of the Church. Obviously, dealing with an order, its nature and its institution involves theology at every turn. The most noted of the Church's theologians, such as Thomas, Bonaventure, Scotus, clearly held the position that women cannot by Christ's own law be admitted to priesthood. Thomas and Bonaventure were aware that some writers held that exclusion was merely a matter of *law*. No, says Thomas, it lies in the nature or institution of the sacrament (its validity). Surely the exegetical approach is theological. The argument that woman is subject to man and hence not suited to the dignity of high order is theological. And, of course, false. But we may not fault Thomas for his exegesis of Genesis (woman the temptress, woman made subject to man, etc.), unless we expect him to have anticipated modern exegesis and the concept of form criticism. The same may be said of all the writers of former times who, obviously, would be more fundamentalistic regarding the first chapters of Genesis than our current biblical scholars. (Some writers of the period did hold, however, that any one baptized was the subject of the sacrament of order, though they were clearly in the minority).

Of special interest is the thought of Scotus. The Doctor Subtilis insists that the Church would not have presumed to deprive all womanhood, without any guilt on their part, of a function which they would be able to exercise lawfully unto the salvation of womanhood and others, unless there were a *divine* injunction to the contrary due to the will of Christ. He too looks upon 1 Tm 2:12ff as an ordinance of Christ. Great lover of Mary that he was, Scotus makes the point that Christ did not even bestow any order on his own Mother, although no other woman could equal or even approach her in holiness. He too cites the argument from Genesis which makes woman, especially after the fall, subject to man.

We cite these points to make clear 1) that the problem was studied *theologically* by the great theologians; 2) that the exclusion of woman from holy order was not based *exclusively* on the actual inferior social status of woman in their time.

We must concede that the historic statements of many theologians both exalt and degrade woman. For this, however, we need not look to the past. Our theology, our Church practice, the law as operative today, the restrictions in the exercise of functions which are in themselves entirely open to woman, all clearly show that the Church order is *male oriented*. (For reference to the medieval theologians, cf. *Handbuch der Dogmengeschichte*, Band IV Sakramente Eschatologie, Faszikel 5: Ludwig Ott, *Das Weihesakrament*, Herder, Freiburg, 1969, p. 108f).

When we assert that the discussion is pertinent today, we have in mind the many problems involving women in private, social-political, economic life, the tremendous contribution made by women. Here we have a challenge which it would be pernicious to dismiss. The very fierceness of some proponents of women's claims must at least be faced. The use of political means to attain rights which depend on theological evidence is, of course, counterproductive. We insist also that the *spirituality of the Precious Blood is closely bound up with the ministry of women in the Church, and deserves to be considered.* We caution, however, that the admission of women to the priesthood would necessitate a totally special structure in the areas of priestly ministry. Should the present exclusiveness be abandoned, the Church would have to set up norms totally diverse from present norms in *de clericis*. This would be possible only through supreme prudence in guidance and direction under the full, warm light of the Holy Spirit. Mary, indeed, the Mother of priests, we now invoke you even in writing these few lines.

A NOTE FROM THE PAST

The theology of woman priests in the Church (we insist on the term) offers the reader a far more abundant literature than is usually recognized. The problem has been discussed for centuries. The theological assertion of what is considered the doctrine of the Church, or the *theological conclusion*, is fairly uniform. And, understandably, largely negative. The past theological exposition or speculation — especially when considered in the light of present-day exegesis, particularly of Genesis, our advanced knowledge of biology, the social status of women in our current civilization — seems to us totally unacceptable.

The biblical texts are primarily: 1 Corinthians, chapters eleven and fourteen; Ephesians, chapter five; 1 Timothy, chapter two; and from the Old Testament: Genesis, chapters two and three. We leave the study of these and other texts to the reader. It is our contention, however, that none clearly and summarily forbids the ordination of women to priesthood. We hold that no competent biblical scholar today would, after a scientific analysis, accept them as solid proof which his scientific biblical community would embrace.

As to the vast patristic literature, we hold with Father van der Meer: (Haye van der Meer, *Women Priests in the Catholic Church? A Theological Historical Investigation,* 1973, Temple University Press, p. 88), that despite the negative attitude toward what we choose to call the *thesis,* there is neither clear acceptance nor absolute rejection of the priesthood of woman on what he calls essential grounds.

Our appraisal of the medieval writers, to whom we have already referred, and the modern and present day theologians: the negative conclusion is overwhelmingly based on the traditional practice of the Church, but accompanied by a rather weak theological exposition and very vulnerable speculation. Even those who uphold an *affirmative thesis* have not fully elaborated their doctrine and placed it on firm and solid ground. The reason, of course, lies in the centuries old tradition of the Church's practice which left little room for open discussion. Yet we must stress the insufficient evidence for the exclusion of woman from priesthood, the weakness of the traditional argument, particularly when it is based on the notion that woman is *inferior* to man, has been the temptress (from Genesis) of man from the beginning, the implication of a certain moral hazard, even indecency in the mere acceptance of women to serve at holy Mass (*op. cit.,* p. 128).

The masculine bias is noted in such great minds as Thomas and Augustine (how he loved his mother, Monica!) who look upon the masculine sex as the nobler. Thus, Thomas in III, q. 31, art. 4, ad 1, says that Christ assumed human nature in the male sex because the masculine sex is the nobler (*quia sexus masculinus est nobilior quam femineus*). But he does a fine balancing act in the same article: Lest, however, the female sex be disdained, it was proper that he (Christ) take flesh from a woman (*congruum fuit ut carnem assumeret de femina*). In the same article he quotes Augustine: The liberation of man had to be made manifest in both sexes. Therefore, because he had to take on human nature as man (*vir*), which sex is the more honorable, it was proper that the liberation of the female sex appear from this that he the man (*vir*) be born of a woman. (*Hominis liberatio in utroque sexu debuit apparere. Ergo quia virum oportebat suscipere, qui sexus honorabilior est, conveniens erat ut feminei sexus liberatio hinc appareret, quod ille vir de femina natus est*). The passage from Augustine is cited from lib. 83, *Quaest. qu.* 11.

The primitive biological notion of conception, for which surely no ancient writers should be blamed, also contributed to the absurd notion of the inferiority of woman and the lower category in which she was placed.

Strangely this notion of male superiority was more firmly fixed in the religious and sacramental area than in that of the political-social, for queens were not without honor and acceptance and even accorded special ritual blessings. Throughout, one notices, such at least is this writer's view, a very considerable confusion that makes the whole presentation most unconvincing. To make out a case against the ordination of women from tradition, in the sense of the theological statements of authors, borders on the absurd.

A word on the authoritative statements of the Church, however, is deserving of attention and respect. We make two points: the Church surely has not defined formally by what is somewhat ineptly called the *extraordinary magisterium* that women by divine ordinance must be excluded from the priesthood. Nor do we feel that the ordinary magisterium of the Church as manifested in the constant practice of the Church is sufficiently clear, uniform and universal in favor of a thesis as the following: Woman by divine ordinance must be excluded from priesthood.

In fact, a degree of probability to the contrary may be found in certain practices of the Church. Women have in the past received and exercised rights, powers, functions which seem proper to sacred order (*diaconate*), though not to priesthood itself. We cite the following at random from van der Meer. In the eleventh century *deaconesses* were ordained or set apart by sacred rite that was entirely identical to that by which men deacons were ordained (p. 87). In certain places deaconesses were permitted to read the epistle, the gospel, to use the incense, give Holy Communion, wear the stole (*ibid*). As late as the last century in the Carthusian cloisters of women the abbesses sang the gospel in the high Mass on high feast days. Though this rite was later restricted and limited to the singing of the epistle, the stole seems to indicate that at a previous time the gospel was also sung. At their *consecration* the Carthusian nuns received stole and maniple (*ibid*). The consecration of deaconesses was not usurpation of privileges, for it was at times performed even by popes, a practice which continued on until the eleventh century (*op. cit.*, p. 8). At some places deaconesses distributed Holy Communion, and had the duty of bringing Communion to sick women. We also know that deaconesses in the Western Church brought Communion to women and boys, a practice which continued to the sixth century. Likewise up until the year 829 female holders of benefices brought Communion to the faithful (*op. cit.*, p. 101).

In some of the great medieval monasteries the abbesses ruled with what seems clearly to have been actual spiritual jurisdiction. This jurisdiction extended over both men and women, and even over clerics. Such a reality can scarcely be reconciled with the position of St. Thomas that since women are *subject* they cannot possess spiritual jurisdiction. Herford, in Germany, an imperial city, was originally under the dominion of the abbey of Benedictine nuns. In this monastery no bishop exercised any authority throughout the Middle Ages. The abbess exercised the power of jurisdiction over all the clergy, over the priests of the cathedral church, the rectors of the independent chapels. Papal authority forbade the bishop to celebrate solemn Mass in this monastery.

Herford is not a solitary instance. There were abbesses who exercised authority not only in Germany, but also in France, Italy and Spain. The abbess of Las Huelgas near Burgos in Spain had the authority to grant faculties for the hearing of confessions, exercise the care of souls and to preach. It seems impossible to make a fine distinction here between the actual granting of faculties or exercising spiritual jurisdiction and merely *nominating* individuals for these tasks. We note specifically that such acts are associated with episcopal insignia (*op. cit.,* p. 115ff).

Running through all the discussion of women priests is the stark contrast between the general status of women and their social position, as a whole, in former times, and the present position of women socially, politically, economically, today.

Van der Meer asks the question very flatly: Were theology and the Church dealing with a different woman than the woman of today? Insofar as much of any cultic role of woman was not separate from ordinary life, when Christ chose only men and the apostles chose only men, because only men were available or, perhaps, only men were thought of — should we, now that the disability of women has been removed and woman is no longer subordinate, retain the ancient subordinate position in the Church? We presume to hold that there was no *permanent* or *essential* reason for the exclusion of woman. Let us now rather think of Paul not so much as underrating woman, but as announcing that there is among us neither *male nor female* (Gal 3:28). An affirmative position seems justified.

A POSITIVE APPROACH

Though the writer foregoes the term *prove,* he does suggest the following as tenable for our direction and guidance in this delicate area:

1) The very evidence of spiritual jurisdiction and ordination of deaconesses suggests the sacramental or quasi-sacramental status and function. No convincing reason should lead us to continue excluding women from the further step, the priesthood, in the current development of the status, activity, and nobility of spiritual desire on the part of woman today.

2) The union of man and woman especially in marriage as fruitful union enriching the people of God materially and spiritually might be extended. Then the sacrament of marriage as symbol of Christ's union with the Church could be a model and pattern of a priestly Church in which neither man or woman is excluded from union with the Christ by priestly bond.

3) We ask: Should not priesthood turn toward *persons in community* transcending the restriction of sex? The unique talent of man and woman enriching and fulfilling each other could be used unto the advancement of the kingdom of God in the *kerygma,* the liturgy and all cult, the care and guidance of the people of God. Thus women priests would mean far more than a mere numeric increase. Rather they would enhance the priestly function and ministry itself. If the Holy Spirit inspires countless women through the summons to priesthood, if their vocation exists, and we have no clear and certain mandate from Christ to exclude them, no positive divine prohibition against accepting them, should we not harken to the call of the Spirit?

4) The very totality of redemption in Blood, the Blood in the eternal glory of the Celestial City, where Christ reigns as eternal priest, where none are married or given in marriage, suggests that all, male and female, belong to the Great High Priest, all who have chosen the call and bear the mark of that Eternal Priesthood.

5) The spirituality of the Precious Blood must embrace all the mysteries of Christ in his life, in the Church, in glory. It should look to the fullness of Christ as offered to all men, excluding none from any share in the ministerial efficacy of the Blood. In the sacramental life especially, the greatest and most fruitful efficacy of every state and condition should be made available. We feel no class should be excluded.

6) As to the discussion itself we must shun the angry argument, the political outcry, the sense of abuse: we think only of priests in the love of Christ the Priest.

A NOTE ON MARY

One of the hoary arguments for the exclusion of women from priesthood is the historic fact that Mary, Mother of God, Mother of the Church, Mother of Priests, was never chosen as Apostle nor as Priest. Our response is not that Mary was a priest, but rather that she was much more, more exalted than any of the *ministers of Christ.* She transcended the entire apostolic and ministerial order. We hold that Mary belonged to the Hypostatic Order.

This in no way infringes on the priesthood of Christ, for his total mediation centered uniquely in the priestly sacrifice on Calvary and in the Eucharist. All came to us through the hypostatic union. Mary as representing all mankind accepts the Son from the Eternal Father through the power of the Holy Spirit, indeed uniting him to all men in her blessed womb.

As his Mother she embraces and groups all men about her Son, the God-Man who offers all men with her to the Father. Such was her supreme mediatorial-priestly function which did not embrace a *ministerial* priesthood. However, in this supreme dialogue with God, Mary performed more than a ministerial function, though her action included them all *per eminentiam*. Some writers place Joseph also, as true spouse of Mary, and father of Christ by his bond with her (though it was not a physical fatherhood), in the hypostatic order (cf. Our Lady of the Precious Blood in these pages).

They pay to Mary the veneration of *hyperdulia*, to Joseph *protodulia*. The writer shares this view (cf. *AER,* March, p. 226, 1929). If Mary is the Mother of priests, we should exclude neither son nor daughter of hers from this privilege. For centuries indeed the Church shied away from conferring the title of Doctor of the Church on her noblest daughters, though they illuminated the entire Church with their teaching and inspired guidance. Finally today we honor St. Teresa of Avila as *Doctor* for her mystical doctrine and life illuminated the whole world. And she has granted this title to St. Catherine of Siena, who guided and enlightened the popes and the whole of Christendom in the melancholy days of the Western Schism. One is rather amused that the author of the article on Doctors of the Church in the *NCE,* written about 1966, considers it rather unlikely that any woman ever be made a Doctor of the Church. In but a few short years both Teresa and Catherine were raised to that lofty dignity by Paul VI. Perhaps this startling fact suggests caution regarding the possibility of the ordination of women as priests in the Church. (Paul proclaimed Teresa of Avila the first woman Doctor of the Church on September 27, 1970. Catherine of Siena was proclaimed the second Doctor of the Church about a week later, October 4, 1970).

A FINAL NOTE

Under no condition must our preceding pages be construed as opposition to any clearly definitive papal statement on this matter. Were we to assume that the very *substance* of the sacrament of order excludes women, we should indeed hold that women cannot be ordained to priesthood. It is our position, however, that such is not the case, but that the Church possesses the supreme power to expand and elevate the episcopal order in the Church enabling it to reach out to all her baptized members in the sacerdotal rite. The Church, we hold, can so expand the deeper and richer purposes, the goals, which are now demanded by the "priestly service" as to include a female priesthood in this broader acceptance.

As we probe more deeply the historic and theological evidence and find this power within the Church to suit all her needs in every age — which only the Sovereign Authority of the Church herself can determine or exercise — we may move prudently forward to lay the canonical basis for the priesthood of women. We dismiss the objection of those who admit the possibility of a sacramental diaconate of women, though excluding priesthood, by the clear statement that there is but one sacrament of order, giving power and grace *ex opere operato*. Any one who can receive the sacrament in the diaconate can advance to priesthood, and episcopacy (cf. D 959, 962, 966).

RAHNER'S PRESENT POSITION

In the May issue of Stimmen der Zeit (1977), Karl Rahner states his position in a critique of the *Declaration on the Question of the Admission of Women to the Ministerial Priesthood* (291-301). Since the article has reached our desk only recently, we can do no more than append a brief notice here. The dignity and profound theological approach warrant that the entire article be thoroughly studied.

A RECENT STATEMENT BY KARL RAHNER

In an article in *Stimmen der Zeit* of May 1977 which is a splendid model of theological essay, entitled *Vom Priestertum der Frau* (On the Priesthood of Women) Karl Rahner, S.J., explains the recent *Declaration on the Question of the Admission of Women to the Ministerial Priesthood* issued by the *Roman Congregation for the Doctrine of the Faith,* Oct. 15, 1976, with the approval of Pope Paul VI. Rahner limits his reflection to the declaration itself. His position is clear: the document is not a definition of faith, nor a statement of defined doctrine as such. But the theologian must respect it as a statement of the magisterium which has a greater weight than the argumentation it presents. But with this sincere respect, the theologian has the duty also to analyze the arguments its presents, weigh them carefully, and if they be flawed, reject them. The document as such is a statement of *human tradition* in the Church which has gone unchallenged for centuries as have other human traditions which subsequently no longer prevailed. He cites a number of similar instances, which particularly after Vatican II have been rejected by the Church. Toward this end the theologians must cooperate, conceding weakness, contradiction, which is found in the past, and patiently abide the time until, in full agreement with the magisterium of the Church, the obvious discrimination against woman in the Church will disappear. There must be a sincere regard for the "weak" consciousness of many members and parts of the Church, a point which we feel has not been sufficiently taken into account in many of the recent changes.

Rahner insists that the discussion must go on, can and must be expanded to cover all the viewpoints of many decades. We must be particularly concerned with the discrimination against woman in the Church. By a common effort we must seek to grant woman all that the Declaration concedes in principle, though the practice falls far short of this. Finally, Rahner points out that the declaration clearly demands that the Church must preserve fidelity to Jesus Christ. But he says, "in what does this loyalty regarding the problem consist?" For this reason, the discussion must go on. "With caution guided by mutual respect, with criticism for bad arguments which are found on both sides, and criticism against misplaced emotionalism . . . on both sides expressly or secretly, we must face with courage an historical transformation that is characteristic of the loyalty the Church owes her Lord" (pp. 291-301).

CHAPTER FIVE

THE PRECIOUS BLOOD SPIRITUALITY
SANGUIS CHRISTI
GUIDELINES OF JOHN XXIII

*As You Are Aware, the Devotion to the Most Precious
Blood of the Divine Redeemer is a Devotion Which Has
Always Been Very Dear to Us, And Since Our Election
to the Supreme Pontificate We Have Repeatedly En-
deavored to Propagate and Encourage Its Practice by the
Faithful Throughout the World (Letter of Pope John to
Father Herbert Linenberger, Moderator General of the
Congregation of the Most Precious Blood, on Occasion of
the Second Precious Blood Study Week, 1960).*

JOHN AND THE THREE OBJECTIVE DEVOTIONS
INDE A PRIMIS

The Apostolic Letter of John, *Inde a Primis,* officially singles out our
Precious Blood spirituality in the context of the *three primary* devotions
bearing a very special significance for the spiritual life. These the "Holy
See has openly approved and furthered."

It is supremely important that the Church's liturgy fully conform to
Catholic belief ("the law for prayer is the law for faith"), and that only
those devotional forms be sanctioned which well up from the unsullied
springs of true faith. But the same logic calls for complete accord
among different devotions. Those deemed more basic and more con-
ducive to holiness must not be at odds with or cut off from one another.
And the more individualistic and secondary ones must give way in popu-
larity and practice to those devotions which more effectively actuate the
fulness of salvation wrought by the "one mediator between God and
men, Jesus Christ, who is man, like them, and gave himself as a ransom
for them all." Through living in an atmosphere thus charged with true

faith and solid piety the faithful can be confident that they are "thinking with the Church" and holding fast in the loving fellowship of prayer to Christ Jesus, the high priest of that sublime religion which he founded and which owes to him its name, its strength, its dignity.
The Church's wonderful advances in liturgical piety match the progress of faith itself in penetrating divine truth. Within this development it is most heart-warming to observe how often in recent centuries this Holy See has openly approved and furthered the three devotions just mentioned . . .
Suffice it to recall the spiritual favors that our predecessors from the sixteenth century on have attached to practicing devotion to the Most Holy Name of Jesus . . . No less striking are the benefits that popes have attached to practicing devotion to the Most Sacred Heart of Jesus . . . Likewise the devotion to the Most Precious Blood, which owes its marvelous diffusion to the 19th century Roman priest, St. Gaspar Del Bufalo, has rightly merited the approval and support of this Apostolic See (translation by Francis Sullivan, C.PP.S., Messenger Press).

Contemporary theology has rethought much of the traditional doctrine on spirituality. The popular spiritual literature is issuing forth in floods. But most striking of all is the pastoral concern of our greatest theologians. For all his theological depth and erudition, Karl Rahner has a background of pastoral activity. We note his many radio addresses, his conferences to religious superiors, doctors, psychiatrists, chaplains, and varied other groups, his Theological Dictionary (in conjunction with Vorgrimler), his beautiful, brief essays, such as, *Watch and Pray with Me, Servants of the Lord, Shape of the Church to Come, Every Day Faith,* to mention only a few (for this phase of Rahner's work, cf. Herbert Vorgrimler, *Karl Rahner, His Life, Thought and Work,* Montreal, Palm Publishers, 1965). Another theological giant who has given us such gems as *The Way of the Cross, Love Alone,* is none other than Hans Urs von Balthasar who is noted for his new approach to theology — theology in its splendor. (Note also *Theologians Today: Hans Urs von Balthasar,* with its five fine essays).

The recent studies on the Sacred Heart and on Ignatian spirituality cannot fail to suggest how much of a newcomer our Precious Blood spirituality really is, despite the enormous sources now swelling to great proportions in recent Christological literature with its stress on redemption through blood in the biblical, traditional, liturgical context. The limitations are inherent in our very redemptive thought. We must grasp the current needs and trends, and structure corresponding forms into a *specific spirituality* without resorting to a rigid scholastic idiom which would chill the entire project rather than warm our hearts.

Even in its recent development the theology of Precious Blood spirituality reflected this paradox in exposition and proclamation. The biblical and patristic texts were gathered *en masse*. An amazingly rich museum of popular Precious Blood art disclosed widespread Precious Blood piety dating back for centuries . The most graphic form of religious imagery (*Schaureligion*) portrays the love of the faithful for the redemptive Blood (notably relics, shrines, pilgrimages awakened the deepest interest). The current Precious Blood art has kept pace with our other efforts (essays, biography, history, formation studies, and the rich yield of the archives related to Gaspar, Merlini, and Brunner) to awaken interest and promote piety. All this is an integral and creative background for our spirituality.

Meanwhile our theological exposition, and perhaps even more markedly the *kerygma*, repeated the Anselmian *juridical soteriology* stressing justice in paying the debt of sin with the Blood as *instrumental cause* of our redemption, *price* paid for the offense to the infinitely just God. Laborious were the studies on the material and formal object of the devotion, the importance of the sacred humanity in its more significant parts as related to the devotion's *ultimate object*: the *Second Person of the Trinity*. Most practical throughout was the *veneration and adoration* of the Eucharist, as sacrament and sacrifice. Significant too was the satisfactory aspect: suffering with Jesus for the salvation of sinners — although offering the Blood (the seven offerings, the Eucharistic chalice) seemed almost secondary. Possibly even more significant was the conception of the *Sanguis Christi*. To the writer's knowledge in only one or the other instance was the Precious Blood addressed in terms of *person*: this means, it would seem, a spirituality of adoration of one of the *partes humanitatis Christi*.

From this point of departure, our study turned laboriously to a more comprehensive and dynamic approach with the promise and hope of developing a far more significant spirituality of the Precious Blood. The providential patronage of John XXIII marked a turn in the study and practice. With the *Inde a Primis* came the beautiful *Litany of the Precious Blood,* the dedication of the second volume of the Precious Blood Proceedings to the noble patron. Gradually we go beyond the narrow concept of the *Blood adored* because of its bond of union with the God-head, the Blood which was the price of our liberation from sin. We think less of the juridical concept, paying an infinite price of ransom for an infinite offense. In broader, more biblical terms we reflect on *cultal* and *salvation history soteriology*. We deepen and expand the concepts of merit, satisfaction, sacrifice, and liberation. Above all we underscore the Thomistic theology of redemptive efficacy, the most comprehensive of all the concepts involved, in a sense embracing them all. And we see in the Blood, in the full light of the biblical texts, the summation of redemption: *totum opus redemptionis*. In this study we go one step further: we maintain that the term *Blood of Christ means the person of Christ in the entire redemptive work.*

Our statement is based on the biblical meaning of blood in both Old and New Testament. It goes far beyond the traditional sense found in our devotional literature and also in great part in our approved prayers. And, we may add, in our spiritual guidance.

SANGUIS CHRISTI

The cry of redemption rings in our ears as we proclaim the source of salvation: *Blood of Christ.* In the recent past our biblical scholars have mounted a massive study on blood, covenant, sacrifice, atonement, redemption, reconciliation, expiation, pasch, blood-life-soul, etc. Our Precious Blood Study Weeks and the flow of research from the European provinces of our Society have greatly enriched our sources. Now our systematic and biblical research presents an embarrassment of riches for the student of Precious Blood spirituality. In the following pages the writer singles out what most suits his special purposes, also embodying and expanding pertinent areas treated by him in previous studies.

First of all, we underscore the biblical meaning of *blood* and *Blood of Christ* in the context of his redemptive work. This means that the Blood of Christ is precisely Christ in relation to the shedding of blood. Both Old and New Testament support the dogmatic thesis: The Blood of Christ is Christ in his person as redeemer in his whole redemptive work. More specifically and comprehensively, it is a doctrine divinely revealed that mankind is saved through the *Blood of Christ.* Creeds and formulas of faith clearly document this basic truth of revelation and faith. This scriptural source is starkly proclaimed in the letter to Hebrews:

> But when Christ came as high priest of the good things which have come to be, he entered once for all into the sanctuary, passing through the greater and more perfect tabernacle not made by hands, that is, not belonging to this creation. He entered, not with the blood of goats and calves, but with his own blood, and achieved eternal redemption (Heb 9: 11-12).

BLOOD IN THE BIBLICAL CONTEXT

For the Hebrews (and other ancient peoples) blood is not a mere element of the body, a part of the whole. It is rather identified and bound up with man's life. As shown in the sacred rites and pronouncements of the Old Testament, this conviction is so significant in salvation history that the power and religious meaning of blood is to be taken and understood in this physiological context. To ignore this meaning would be to slight the inspired message itself. And, what is of special importance for our research, the revealed concept of blood in the Old Testament is clearly reflected in the New, so that *Sanguis Christi* and the other New Testament blood-texts are in perfect harmony with the Old Testament meanings.

Blood in the Old Testament is conceived of as a vital principle of man or animal. At times it is further specified by the *nefesh* contained in it. *Nefesh*, as life or principle of life of man and animal, is a *sacred reality* which is solely under the dominion of God. *Nefesh* identified with blood or contained in blood must rightly be viewed — on this point we have only man in mind — as the *total principle* of human life and activity. No human activity is excluded, not even the spiritual, a point which we must take into consideration when we study Old Testament blood texts which speak of blood with *nefesh* as the principle of human life. At least implicitly, such texts mean the principle of the entire life and activity of man, including the intellectual and volitional. Consistent with this attitude toward blood there were norms regarding its use or abuse. As to the prohibitions the sacred reality under the divine dominion may not be profaned.[6]

The same Hebrew conception logically explains the *sacrificial meaning and power* even of animal blood. As life (or containing life), sacred reality, under divine dominion, it is in direct conflict with the profane, the negative, the sinful. As belonging to Yahweh, it intervenes between Yahweh and his people (or the individual). It fashions a sacred bond uniting God and man who offers it to him. We cannot fail to discern that this sacred reality effects alienation from sin, as would be its function in the sacrifice of pasch and expiation. Equally obvious is its *unitive* function in the sacrifice of covenant or alliance. This basic significance of blood casts a very clear light on the value and sacrificial power of the Blood of Christ, to which we now turn.

In the New Testament *haima* reaches the peak of soteriological meaning in the death of Jesus. Not the mere material blood, but the *Blood shed* as *life* wrested from him violently! The *Sanguis Christi*, like the cross, most graphically expresses the death of Christ for our salvation (cf. Behm, *Theological Dictionary of the New Testament*, I, pp. 174-176). Note in this connection the great Precious Blood texts. What seems to me the most central, Col 1:20 is translated in the *Jerusalem Bible* as *by his death on the cross*, in the *NAB*, as *through the blood of his cross*, in the *Vulgate per sanguinem crucis eius*. The Greek has *dia tou haimatos tou staurou autou*.

The New Testament texts which refer to the *Sanguis Christi* (used at least 38 times) implicitly or explicitly relate to the primary sacrificial themes of the blood of animals in the Old Testament: *blood of pasch, of alliance* or *covenant, of expiation*. The basis of comparison in the sacrifices is clear:

that of Christ with those of the Old Testament. We rightly conclude that the *Blood of Christ itself* is the Blood of *alliance (covenant), pasch, expiation*: more specifically it is the Blood of the *new alliance, new pasch, new expiation*.

Moreover, the sacrifice of Christ is described in terms which in the Old Testament express sacrificial power. In fact, a common sacrificial terminology is taken over from the Old Testament Hebrew into the New Testament Greek. Such common terminology in Paul, and above all in Hebrews, warrants the conclusion — not at all farfetched — that the use of Old Testament sacrificial themes and terms refers to the death of Christ as a *sacrifice*. Therefore, it is evident that the sacred writers do look upon the death of Christ as a sacrifice in the light of the Old Testament sacred rite and idiom. Indeed, this death of Christ is the antitype of the Old Testament sacrifice of pasch, covenant, and expiation (cf. *Sanguis Christi,* A. J. Caetano de Cruz Fernandes, Roma, 1976 p. 83ff).

The sacrificial power of the Blood of Christ greatly surpasses the power of the Old Testament bloody rites. Only through Christ do we have the perfect destruction of sin, redemption of all mankind *once and for all*. Only in Christ's Blood is there the unique fulness of pasch, alliance, expiation, and the truly interior union of men with God, interior sanctity which is the sharing of God's own life. Christ is truly priest and victim, divine-human, who freely offers himself and is offered to his Father. His sacrifice is total, spiritual — those of the Old Testament were without reason, freedom, love, obedience — infinite in value, surpassing all merely human oblations.

Infinite perfection of sacrifice necessarily made Calvary acceptable to God the Father because of the divine person of the *priest* and *victim*. According to the texts of the New Testament the Father's acceptance is reflected splendidly in the glorious resurrection of Christ, as the intrinsically necessary complement of his death.

It follows that the description of the death of Christ and of its salvific powers frequently reflects the light of the resurrection as demanded by the intrinsic bond of death itself. Herein lies that unique significance of the New Testament texts on the Blood of Christ, which relate to the *total salvation* from sin, from the devil, from death. Such texts ascribe to the faithful Christian *justification* because of the *death* of Christ, and maximally *life* (supernatural life) because of the resurrection.

This unique sacrifice and its bond with the triumphal resurrection-ascension constitutes Christ the active *Mediator* of the *new alliance* even unto the eschatological consummation. Finally, *Sanguis Christi* on the basis of Hebrew anthropology and of the sacred use of blood, indicates *directly* the personality of Christ in the salvific act, whereas indirectly it connotes the *divine acceptance* of the same sacrifice of Christ, his triumph and the eschatological consummation because of the nature of this very same oblation (*ibid.*, p. 174ff).[7]

THE EUCHARISTIC BLOOD

In the few pages at our disposal it is impossible to give even the briefest summary of the immense discussion regarding the Eucharistic texts and the Last Supper. The thorniest problems center about the question of the Last Supper as the Passover meal. In the main we follow J. Jeremias in presenting the Supper as the Passover meal at which the Eucharist was instituted. Our note below refers to some of the differences of opinion based on the difficulties involved.[8]

The *Blood of Christ* passages in the Eucharistic context are our principal concern. We underscore particularly the concept of *salvific power,* evident in such terms as the *remission of sin.* Perhaps more striking is the *eschatological* resurrection couched in such lofty terms as *everlasting life.* In diversified wording the Eucharistic cup is seen to contain the Blood of the *new pasch, new alliance* or *covenant,* and *new expiation.* They clearly indicate nothing less than *integral salvific power.*

First, we note the paschal setting with the words of institution of the Eucharist in the historic context of the Pasch (cf. *DB,* John McKenzie, "Eucharist," p. 249ff). In the Gospel according to Matthew we have the account of the celebration of the Pasch and its preparation (26:17-19). Jesus is quoted: "I am to celebrate the Passover with my disciples." Mark adds the details of the man with the water jar and the upstairs room (14:12-16). Luke even gives the names of the disciples, Peter and John, who make the arrangements (22:7-13). The synoptic accounts agree in identifying the celebration and development of the Pasch in the twofold Eucharistic institution and the participation by the Apostles. Moreover, in the texts the theme of the *new pasch* and *new expiation* are intimately bound up.

In Matthew and Mark the Eucharistic Blood is the Blood of the *covenant* (alliance) to be poured out in behalf of many. Matthew adds *for the forgiveness of sins.* Luke says: "This cup is the new covenant in my blood, which will be shed for you," with the added injunction over the bread, "do this": "This is my body to be given for you. Do this as a remembrance of me" (22:19-20). We may add that the Greek term *ekxunnomenon* is often used for the effusion of blood in the Old Testament sacrifices of expiation:

> Surely we may conclude that *Blood of Christ* means: the personality of Christ in the act of sacrifice, which demands its complement in the resurrection. . . . and the parousia, the equivalent of the *entire new*

economy of salvation, most abundantly dispensed to individual faithful partaking of the Eucharist — from remission of sins to the glory of resurrection. How beautifully this corresponds to the testimony of John's sixth chapter on the Eucharistic Blood which gives to those who drink it everlasting life (cf. *Sanguis Christi*, p. 179 adapted).

It is this sixth chapter of John which stresses the life-giving power of the Eucharist. Here we have the sacramental significance, "since the blood is again the life which is communicated from Jesus to his disciples through the Eucharist" (McKenzie, *ibid.*, "Blood," p. 99).

Taken in its total context, we conclude, *Sanguis Christi* in its fullest sense embraces the whole new economy of salvation. It means that the personal Christ is rendered really present to us in the act of his sacrifice and dispensed integrally to the individual faithful with the new order of salvation. It follows that we now possess through the Eucharistic Blood integral salvation including what we shall eternally possess in the eschatological consummation. This position, we are convinced, reflects the *sensus fidelium* particularly in their devotion to the holy Mass in its relation to the Last Supper and the death on the cross.

THE CHILDREN REJOICE IN THE LAST SUPPER

In a little village between the Black Forest and Lake Constance in the parish of Kirchen-Hausen, Germany, Father Heiler introduced his children into the liturgical life of the parish. One of the means was the encouragement of the tots to draw pictures of the truths of faith narrated to them in their religious instruction. The response was very eager as the pictures produced by them for the Corpus Christi procession in 1952 clearly showed. On the altars in the village and in the fields were huge pictures proclaiming the great truth of the Eucharist.

One of these was a long picture of the altar of the Last Supper (cf. no. 4 in *op. cit.*). The picture has three parts and is pasted together from bright colored clippings.

Very graphically the central picture represents the Last Supper Eucharist. It has a background made of gold paper clippings, and is about four feet by five feet large. To the rear center of the table is Christ with the chalice, the twelve disciples around the table hold aloft the Living Bread, as large hosts, each waving it in his hand with great joy and emotion. They show the hosts in the bright light to all the world. In the very front is *Judas.* Instead of the host he clutches the purse with its price of treason. Only his face is pained and jaundiced, all the others are merry, almost laughing with joy.

In the center over the table between the Christ and the purse of Judas is the Holy Spirit descending upon the blessed group. Children from four to six years old produced the picture in memory of the First Communion of their brothers and sisters and cousins in whose celebration they participated. (cf. Schreyer, *op. cit.,* after page 136, no. 4.) The explanation of Schreyer, p. 166 ff, adapted here, offers the clearest evidence of the great interest of children in religious art and the influence they have in communicating religious ideals. Schreyer considers the work of the children as most fortunate in revealing the potentialities of future development of the pictorial presentation of the Church's life. The influence for good can be enormous.

PRECIOUS BLOOD SPIRITUALITY ALL-EMBRACING

The inclusion of the whole work of redemption in our Precious Blood spirituality goes far beyond the narrow juridical concept of *paying the debt* of sin incurred by mankind. (This concept had practically taken over the Precious Blood *kerygma* and very much of the reflective consideration of the passion and death). This writer in *The Everlasting Covenant* stressed, perhaps unduly, the five-fold manner of redemption of which Thomas speaks: by *merit,* by *satisfaction,* by *sacrifice,* by *liberation* (which is *redemption* in the more rigid sense) and by *efficacy.*

Merit is concerned with all the life-work of Christ on earth (all his free acts were infinitely meritorious). *Satisfaction* bound up with merit is always involved with hardship or pain. *Sacrifice* has been focused almost exclusively on the passion and death and, in past decades, explained on the basis of pagan and Jewish sacrifices. We shall instead place sacrifice and the great sacrifice of Calvary in its fullest Christian context. *Liberation* deals rigidly with the *paying of the price,* the Blood, freeing us from the bondship of sin. As already noted, authors here followed in the footsteps of St. Anselm, and indeed with a feudalistic bias. Finally, we deal with the redemption by manner of *efficacy* which includes the entire salvific work by the Savior.

Though there is patently much overlapping in the meaning of these terms, it is particularly *efficacy* which includes all. It is God's great *mercy-act* through his Son-made-man. It is time-eternity. It marks our Precious Blood spirituality uniquely. Only in this light do we speak of *eternal redemption.* Thus our relation to the redemptive Christ and his work is truly continuous and eternal (not merely something once done with enduring effects). It turns totally to Christ: in his earthly life (culminating in the cross, bloody sacrifice) ; to the Blood in the sacrificial-sacramental Church (resurrection, Christ-presence-action in the liturgy, in grace-giving) ; to the Blood of glory (eternal priesthood). The latter leaves much room for expansion, though Alfaro, Schierse, and others have given us remarkable insights (note also *Mystici Corporis,* no. 55).[9]

The comprehensiveness of such insight into Christian spirituality in its broadest outlines is evident from these lines of E. Larkin:

> The Christ in whom men meet the Father is not the Christ of memory alone, but one who lives on mystically and sacramentally in his followers (Acts 9:5; 1 Cor 8:11-13). The Church is Christ acting now, sanctifying man and offering men access to the Father (Eph 2:18). The Church is constantly reliving the life of Christ, especially the paschal mystery of *passing over* to the Father (cf. Jn 13:1; I Cor 5:7). Liturgically it makes present this passage, and historically its members recapitulate in their own lives the journey from sin to grace (*NCE* Vol. 13, "Christian Spirituality," p. 599).

We are deeply indebted, as Larkin clearly indicates, to the immense biblical and systematic Jesus-studies of our time, which have concretized and enriched the abstractive Christology of our handbooks. Most gratifying is the turn from the citation of selective texts for *theses* with theological notes in the manuals. Far from rejecting the ancient conciliar decisions and the majestic professions of faith which come to us down through the centuries, we reexamine them in the biblical context with the aid of the miracle of modern scriptural scholarship, with the freedom of the *Divino Afflante Spiritu.* More than ever before we have a believing, scientific and affective study of the Jesus who was truly and concretely human, steeped in history. New insights into his growth, his knowledge, his emotions, are now welcomed into our theoretic theology and the proclamation of the word. The literature is immense, gratifying, rewarding. In a measure even the bizarre Jesus reflection — despite its quixotic oddity — sheds some light on the profound attraction of his life, his words, his death. We repeat with wonderment the ancient axiom: God writes straight with crooked lines. We revel in the workings of his grace even amid the most bizarre situations of our puzzling modern life.

The Son of God assumed a truly human nature with all its finiteness, excepting only sin. He assumed all to redeem all. Truly he was an infant who cried and smiled, who learned to speak, to eat, to grow strong, to develop physical skills, though we insist there was no deformity nor indignity in the little home at Nazareth. But his toil was not free from hardship and sweat, nor was it free from pleasure in recreation and play. We think of him as sharing every phase and state of life uniting with him all men and women and every condition. The Eternal and Almighty was wrapped in human limitation. It has been said that the Whole was grasped by the

Fragment (cf. *TS*, Dec. 1971; The entire article, "Evolution Under the Sign of the Cross," by Leo J. Donovan makes provocative reading, p. 602ff).

Not only have the current biblical and dogmatic studies deepened our understanding of pertinent concepts relating to man himself (nature, person) in this evolving universe (Schell, Teilhard, Mynarek), they have enriched our ancient Christocentrism. Two points we underscore:

One: Christ, God's Son-made-man, is the center as *redeemer*. And our current Christology mirrors our anthropology. The *Why* or *Motive of Incarnation* is a central doctrine of revelation — stripped of the musty academic disputes between Thomists and Scotists with all their *futurabilia* as to what God would have done, IF!

We hold to one motive of creation: incarnation-redemption, discarding all priority of divine decrees. This world God, permitting but not willing the sin, decreed to create and redeem. The ancient disputes regarding what God would have done "IF" are mere possibilities with no relation to this world.

Two: we stress the recent enrichment of the ancient teaching of Thomas by accepting essentially the *Odo Casel* doctrine of the *mystery presence*. Thomas taught that all the actions and passions (*actiones et passiones*) of Christ are truly redemptive, causative of our salvation through the grace of Christ. These mysteries of the life of Christ are present and continue to operate in the Church. It follows that our Christian spirituality is basically redemptive spirituality, that is, Precious Blood spirituality rests in its very center.

The WHY of incarnation, both theoretical and practical, relates to man's freedom and his sin, and with it to the *scandal of the cross*. Involved is an entire complex of problems, which if we could solve would no longer be problems, for they are mysteries. If Jesus is God, how could he be man? If man, truly one of us, man more truly human than any of us, more sympathetic to our needs, how could he be sinless? Many ancient denials, well-meaning efforts to uphold a sinless Christ by denying that he was truly human, destroyed the very incarnation itself. The ancient response to any denial of the integral humanity was simply: if he was not integrally man, then man lacks integral redemption. Thus, if the Lord himself had no human soul, then we in our very souls were not redeemed. The mystery of his sinlessness conspired with his fully human tenderness to accept the sin which was not his own and atone for it with his Blood. Only the *sinless one* could bear the burden of all sin in atonement. The *innocent alone* can fully bear the burden of the guilty and effectively plead for mercy before

God. He the innocent one becomes our liberator. In him we see what God's love is and what we should be. What God in his infinite immutable nature could not be, lowly, suffering, dying, that he is in Jesus, his Son born of Mary. God is he whom we meet in Christ. God's mercy is incarnate in Jesus.[10]

PRECIOUS BLOOD SPIRITUALITY: OUTPOURING, RENUNCIATORY LOVE

Throughout this pioneer development of the Precious Blood spirituality one element is salient: the outpouring of renunciatory love, the courage of decision for God. As never before in its history, the world today is blanketed in the bleak night of the soul. Physical deprivation conspires with frustration of mind and heart. Millions suffer desperately, while other millions look on with indifference, frustration, unconcern, or at best hopeless sympathy. For *those who care* the hours of Christ in Gethsemani (in agony of blood as the disciples slept), the desertion of his friends as he died on the cross, the buffoonery which mocked the death of God's Son, the wrenched hearts of Mary and the few who still loved him — *for those who care,* these hours are our model and effective strength. Only here do we have the Precious Blood spirituality in its *heroic stage*: the greatest of love, love without the delights of love, without the tenderness of consolation. Love without the human joy and fruit of love! The supreme dedication!

Total giving, total outpouring, total dedication, is supremely symbolized in the *shedding of the Blood unto the last drop* in pain and agony. We call to mind the stern thought of Paschal, who pictures the Savior as pressing the last drop of blood from his *riven heart,* with the words: *I shed this last drop for you!* How often have we winced at the physical pain of the blood shedding, with scarcely a thought of the anguish of the soul of Jesus over the sins of men, as central to our spirituality. How weak our dedication which should disdain any pain and ignominy as we ponder the loneliness of Jesus turned over to the furious hate of his enemies on the cross.[11]

THE DESOLATION OF JESUS

According to the *JBC,* the words of Jesus often called "the cry of dereliction" are taken from the twenty-second psalm, verse two: In the *NAB* it is called the *Passion and Triumph of the Messiah.* Used in the early Church as the Psalm of the Passion, it has been called rather a prophecy than a cry of interior abandonment. Obviously it is not a cry of despair. (cf. *JBC,* "The Gospel According to Matthew," 43:200). But we think it does express the anguish of Jesus over the sins of men, supreme sympathy with the desolation of man in his sin, and with Israel in her rejection of her savior. In this light we study the biblical interpretation of Jesus' words on the cross: "My God, my God, why have you forsaken me?"

In the history of Christian spirituality — in the *kerygma* of the passion and the Precious Blood — the *Eli, Eli, lema sabachthani* of the *NAB* version of Mt 27:46 has been the point of departure for profound meditation on the passion in all its poignancy. The stress was laid on its significance for those who seem to be forsaken by God and in utter loneliness without God (In Mark 15:34 the *NAB* has *Eloi, Eloi, lama sabachthani*). Both evangelists refer to the *loud tone* or *voice* of Jesus. This is in harmony with the Israelitic psalm which rises to triumphal power in the divine praise. It must indeed be present in the prayer of Jesus on the cross. Nor should we ever lose sight of this triumph in our meditation on the intensity of the passion. Perhaps we must say, that when all seems lost, and God seems most remote, silent, inaccessible, it is Jesus with whom we pray and who pierces this dreadful silence and loneliness (cf. Ratzinger, *Introduction to Christianity,* Herder and Herder, N.Y., 1970, p. 223ff).

In accepting this beautiful interpretation of the passion prayer and its triumph, we feel that we may not ignore the meaning which many systematic theologians find in the same prayer. They find it basically the manifestation of interior desolation and anguish of Jesus even in relation to his Father. We have already noted the references to this desolation of Jesus on Calvary by Heribert Muehlen, when he speaks of the scandal of the cross and the distinctiveness of the person of Jesus and his deliverance over to sin by the Father. It is in this light that we present the following meditation on the *desolation of Jesus:*

A MEDITATION BY JAKOB BRUMMET

So inseparably bound up with the experience of suffering is God's silence that the only begotten Son of God himself willed to experience and bear it in the depth of his passion-mystery. We are shaken to our depth by the cry of desolation of soul: *My God, my God, why have you forsaken me?* (Mt 27:46). We do not, of course, grasp the abysmal depth of this word, but it does betray the fact that the Lord suffered for us all the ultimate in loss and dereliction. Precisely here is the term and halt, if that experience overwhelms us, in which God hides himself, as the soul wrestles in dreadful God-forsakenness. And all cries for help seem to fall back on the soul *apparently* unheard and unanswered. The Father does not answer, but he does accept silently the dying prayer of his Son: *Father, into your hands I commend my spirit* (Lk 23:46). Happy the man who in the midst of all *loss of God* can find refuge in such resignation. For him even the profoundest source of suffering will still become a *blessed abyss* (*Das Ueber Alles Ragende Zeichen,* Tyrolia Verlag, Wien, 1956, p. 72).

Blessed Abyss is the title of a book by Nanda Herbermann, quoted by Brummet in the following vivid description of her experience in a concentration camp:

I can truthfully say that behind the barbed wire fence and the walls of the concentration camp we encountered hour by hour the great boundlessness of God's love — And because I was permitted to experience in this hell the whole fulness of God's goodness, I can only bless those fenced-in years (*ibid.*, p. 73).

Obviously Nanda Herbermann belonged to those religious natures of whom Eugen Kogen ("SS-Staat") says: "They fled from their own obscurity trustfully into the light of God's fatherly kindness which is clearly discernible in the vision of faith even amid the tragic world of error and confusion. . . . Through suffering, misfortune, distress, catastrophe and crime there is a testing of spirits. He who believes in the Father in heaven stands firm. The others are shattered in the conflict with the realities of life. The young poet, Wolfgang Borchert, who died shortly after the war, presents a seeker after God in his drama, *The Man Outside*. Desperately he cries out: 'How have we sought you, O God, in every ruin, in every bomb crater, in every night. We have called out to you, O God! We have shrieked, wept, cursed . . . have you turned from us? Is there none to respond, none to answer our cry?' God is undoubtedly the great venture in the life of a man, a venture which day by day and hour by hour positions us anew in the world."[12]

Brummet concludes with the paradoxical insight of Father Lippert that God may well be *the great riddle, the great love and the endless suffering of a life.* Yet, without God we are fatally lonesome. We stress such horror of human experience not merely because it is the great reality of our present age, a reality we must relate to the *bloody passion and death*, but also because we must fault the current malaise which focuses attention on the *resurrection without the cross*.

Only too closely allied is this misconception of the paschal meaning to the notion that the thrill of drama and emotional uplift of spiritual life is the measure of piety, the norm of the obligation of common prayer, the sentimental syndrome of the liturgy. (One might cynically, but significantly, distort the ancient formula for such utter misconception of the meaning of prayer: *lex sentiendi, lex orandi*). Here too we focus attention on the glory of resurrection without the pain of the cross. The gifts of the Lover, even in the desolation of Calvary when most he asks for our love! One might ask what John of the Cross would have thought of the flippant, "Don't bother about the liturgy unless you feel it does something for you." His response, we think, would be: "Only in the dark night of the soul is the promise of the dawn."

PRECIOUS BLOOD SPIRITUALITY: INSPIRED GUIDELINES

Our redemptive theology, as we noted above, must seek a more comprehensive soteriology drawing from biblical and traditional sources for the greater enrichment of both the theology itself and the spirituality, though we do not neglect altogether the juridical elements. The reader is directed to the three volumes of Precious Blood Proceedings as a profitable source. They indicate the development, the progress in the study, and yet are only a beginning. We recommend the bibliographies throughout, and the wide range of readings from the various sources in the third volume.

THE TITLE: PRECIOUS BLOOD

The first letter of St. Peter, 1:9, calls the Blood of Christ *precious*. From the context it is evident that the inspired writer looks upon the Blood as *precious* since it is the price or ransom paid for our liberation from sin. The Blood of Christ is precious in the Old Testament sense that all blood belongs to God, is most suitable for sacrifice of expiation and consecration. But this Blood is uniquely precious : it is the *hypostatic Blood,* truly the *holy Blood,* belonging to God as most his own. Because of its union with the divine person, the human nature of Christ, the *Blood of Christ* has the personal value of the Logos himself: it is the divine Blood. (In relation to the text 1 Pt 1:19, note also the Old Testament texts as indicated in the notes of the *NAB*: Is 52: 3; 53: 7.10; and the New Testament texts: Rom 3:24f; 1 Cor 6:20; in addition cf. Ex 12:5).

This text of the title *Precious Blood* in St. Peter falls specifically into the category of *redemption after the manner of liberation* according to the Thomistic structure of the redemptive work as we have indicated above (cf. III, Q XLVIII, art. IV and V). To speak of our nature in its fallen condition, being liberated by the *priceless ransom* of Christ's Precious Blood is to place the *redemptive concept* in the category of *salvation history soteriology.* For the reference is to the liberation of the Hebrew people as recounted in Exodus (note chapter 12, with verse 5 referring to the lamb *without blemish*). The central event of Hebrew liberation through the blood of the paschal lamb was the most basic reality of Old Testament salvation history, type of the New Testament pasch: liberation through Jesus, the *spotless lamb.*

Paul's redemptive doctrine is so vast that we can do no more than glean a few essentials from the enlightening article by Joseph Fitzmyer, S.J., in the *JBC* (79). We mention only the effects of the redemptive work of Christ. Through his passion and death, through his Blood, and his resurrection (objective redemption) we obtain through faith and baptism (subjective redemption): a) reconciliation with God, b) expiation of our sins, c) redemptive liberation, and finally d) justification.

Our use of the term *objective redemption* is to be taken *horizontally,* the total work of Christ in his earthly life — his passion and death, his resurrection, his mystical presence in the Church, his eternal priesthood. The *subjective redemption* is the acceptance, the effect, in us, in grace and glory.

We shall attempt to touch briefly on these points of Pauline soteriology. *Reconciliation,* as we use the term in English, is probably the most comprehensible. We recall the beautiful English Christmas hymn which sings of *God and sinners reconciled.* Sin is offense, hostility toward God, barring man from intimacy of loving unity and peace with him. Paul calls the restoration of peace between sinner and God, admittance to the royal presence, *katallage.* It is achieved through Christ, through his death, his Blood. Fitzmyer notes how the work is ascribed to God the Father through the Son — it is *by his blood* (Rom 5:9). He refers to the commonly used English term at-one-ment which graphically underscores the simple significance of the reconciliation. We can only give the references to which Fitzmyer directs our attention: 2 Cor 5: 18ff; Rom 5:2; 10ff; Col 1:20ff; Eph 2.13ff.

The second effect is *expiation.* The term is difficult for us to grasp today. It indicates the source of reconciliation or pardon. Here Paul uses the Greek term *hilasterion* which might readily be taken to mean placating the wrath of an irate God. Much of our preaching and instruction on the passion and death has stressed wrath of God, with some excess in the concept of God in wrath against his own Son. Here our source thinks of it in the context of *wiping away* our sins, removing our defilement: the Father made his Son and the cross *instrument of expiation.* Advancing a step, he then has Paul to think of the *hilasterion* as the *mercy seat.* Old Testament propitiatory in mind, Paul may well have looked upon the cross as the New Testament mercy seat, Good Friday as the Christian Day of Atonement.

How significant is the *Sanguis Christi* in this context, for the blood-stained Jesus, red with his own Blood, is the Infinite Propitiatory removing our sins. Here our source refers to the Old Testament rites: the blood cleansed, purified, consecrated, expiated. The Blood of Jesus, in this is his life, is poured out freely — we recall the words of our liturgy in the first consecration formula: "Before he was given up to death, *a death he freely accepted.*" The Blood is poured out to free us from sin and unite us with God. Throughout, the Father, not in anger or wrath demanding justice, takes the initiative in love, gives his Son in love — the Son gives himself in love. And Paul in deep conviction, in the depth of his Precious Blood spirituality, identifies himself with the death of Christ — to rise from sin and live in and for God.

The third fruit of the bloody death, in the thought of Fitzmyer, is redemptive liberation. (This is one of the five categories of Thomas — *per modum redemptionis*). The ancient type of this liberation by Christ is the deliverance of the Jewish people from the slavery of Egypt. By the Blood of Christ we are liberated from the vilest form of slavery, the slavery of sin and Satan. Incidentally, in the history of this doctrine, the problem arose: To whom was the price or ransom to be paid. Some early writers, carrying the figure to excess, held that it was to be paid to the devil who held man captive. If this was ever seriously held beyond the point of graphic literalism, it soon disappeared and is now an antique in the museum of theological absurdities.

Obviously, the price was paid to God to whom the Blood was offered. By this liberation those who were freed from sin, from the shackles of the ancient law, from the penalty of death, now became a *divine acquisition*. As the ancient Hebrew people became the covenanted possession of Yahweh, so the redeemed-by-Blood became God's people, the new acquisition. As freed from slavery of sin they enjoyed the very bondage of Christ, whom to serve is to reign. They were under his law of love exulting in the freedom of the sons of God. Here the law is love.

The final fruit is *justification*. In our polemic, in much of the explanation of the *Handbuecher* on theology of pardon and removal of sin, this concept has been unduly expanded. Fitzmyer insists that it is not a basic concept of theology in Paul, except, perhaps, in the "polemic context of Paul's controversy with Judaizers."

If biblical scholars have cautioned against the hazards of the so-called juridical soteriology, it is not to deny its significance in Paul and in the whole systematic explanation of redemption. We may look upon justification in the sense of a divine verdict, a verdict indeed of acquital from sin and punishment, and be quite in accord with Pauline thought. Biblically we see Yahweh as the judge of Israel who is indeed upright and just. He is just in his verdict even in the bounty of his pardoning mercy. The first part of Romans is usually cited as the basis of Luther's so-called *Tower Experience*. Not the vindictive justice of God, but the merciful justice is revealed in the gospel which begins and ends with faith. The just man shall live by faith (cf. Rom 1:17).

The Council of Trent defined the Church's teaching on justification which we cite here at length:

Justification itself follows upon this disposition or preparation, and justification is not only the remission of sins (see 585, canon 11), but sanctification and renovation of the interior man through the voluntary reception of grace and gifts, whereby a man becomes just instead of unjust and a friend instead of an enemy, that he may be an heir in the hope of life everlasting (see Titus 3:7). The causes of this justification are the following: The final cause is the glory of God and of Christ, and life everlasting. The efficient cause is the merciful God, who freely washes and sanctifies (see 1 Cor 6:11) sealing and anointing with the Holy Spirit of the promise, who is the pledge of our inheritance (see Eph 1:13f). The meritorious cause is the beloved only-begotten Son of God, our Lord Jesus Christ, who, when we were enemies (see Rom 5:10), by reason of his very great love wherewith he has loved us (see Eph 2:4), merited justification for us by his most holy Passion on the wood of the cross, and made satisfaction for us to God the Father. The instrumental cause is the sacrament of baptism, which is the *sacrament of faith,* without which no one has ever been justified. Finally, the only formal cause is "the justice of God, not the justice by which he is himself just, but the justice by which he makes us just (see 584, can 10; 585, can 11), namely, the justice which we have as a gift from him and by which we are renewed in the spirit of our mind. And not only are we considered just, but we are truly said to be just, and we are just, each one of us receiving within himself his own justice, according to the measure the Holy Spirit imparts to each one as he wishes (see 1 Cor 12:11) and according to the disposition and cooperation of each one (*TCT* 563).

This doctrine on justification, essential to our Catholic teaching, is most pertinent to our Precious Blood spirituality. We insert the official teaching here for *two significant reasons.* As Catholic doctrine it has been the center of polemic discussion with most Protestants. In recent years, however, we have practically lifted this portion of Trent from the field of polemics. Today noted authors maintain that the Church's doctrine on justification does not differ essentially from that of Martin Luther for whom the doctrine of justification by faith was the very basis of the existence of the Church. This we stress very specifically later in our study, under the rubric: Our Spirituality, Supremely Ecumenical.

Our second reason: The doctrine of justification enriches the whole redemptive theology and its *kerygma.* As essentially bound up with the doctrine of grace, its fruitfulness in the Christian life has its eternal counterpart in heavenly glory.

REDEMPTIVE DOCTRINE IN AQUINAS: HIS ESSENTIAL THOUGHT

Thomas, as already indicated above, teaches that we are redeemed in a five-fold manner: after the manner of *merit;* after the manner of *satisfac-*

tion; after the manner of *sacrifice;* after the manner of *liberation* (redemption in a more restricted sense) ; after the manner of *efficacy.*

REDEMPTION THROUGH MERIT, SATISFACTORY MERIT

Whenever we speak of redemption in terms of *merit* and particularly of *satisfactory merit,* we must do so with certain reservations. On the one hand, the magisterial pronouncements (and the practically unanimous teaching of theologians) leave room for no doubt. We are saved by the *merits* (infinite) *of Christ.* It is to be regretted, however, that this concept of merit, as we already indicated, has almost preempted the entire field of soteriology since the days of St. Anselm down to our days, even though the term *merit* or *merit of Christ* is not strictly scriptural. Notker Fueglister, in *Die Heilsbedeutung des Pascha* says that the term *merit of Christ* is not found in the New Testament at least not explicitly *as a soteriological category.* The same holds for the term *satisfaction,* or *satisfactory merit.* Writing on merit in the *NCE,* C. A. Sullivan is in agreement, adding that the term is also rare among early ecclesiastical writers. We note, however, that the sacred pages provided the elements from which the concept was later developed. It is obvious, therefore, that *juridical soteriology* (particularly the explanation of redemption after the manner of satisfaction) should not occupy the center of interest in either dogmatic soteriology or practical piety.

The biblical explanation of redemption through merit points to the infinite moral value of Christ's bloody death in supreme *obedience* to the Father: herein lies the superabundant merit for pardon of men's sins.

> To sum up, then: just as a single offense brought condemnation to all men, a single righteous act brought all men acquittal and life. Just as through one man's disobedience all became sinners, so through one man's obedience all shall become just (Rom 5:18f).

No less does the great *kenotic* passage (cf. Piet Schoonenberg, S.J., in *Concilium* 11, "Who is Jesus of Nazareth", p. 47ff) clearly indicate the merit of the humiliation of Christ. He who is God becomes man, even as *man* leads a lowly life, becomes the Suffering Servant of Yahweh, humiliated unto death, only to rise in glory, whereby he is Savior and Lord:

> Despised and afflicted, God's Servant, though innocent, bears the sins of others. Stricken by God himself, he brings salvation to many. His passion and death, a most acceptable offering to God, more than compensate for the divine displeasure over the sins of men. Presented in the gospels as the fulfillment of the *Ebed Yahweh* (Suffering Servant) mystery, Jesus offers *satisfaction* to the Father in our stead. Supreme form of this satisfaction for sin is the utter self-giving to the last drop of Blood in the sacrifice of Calvary (*The Everlasting Covenant,* adapted, p. 115).

These salvific acts we rightly call redemption *per modum satisfactionis* in the Thomistic sense. We also place them under the rubric of cultal soteriology.

We have already spoken of the *ransom*, the price of blood paid to *purchase* — all at least implying our doctrine of *satisfaction*. Although we have already referred to Paul and *propitiation*, we add here a text from John and another from Paul, which indicate redemption *per modum satisfactionis*, again with the categories of Thomas in mind:

> My little ones,
> I am writing this to keep you from sin.
> But if anyone should sin,
> we have, in the presence of the Father,
> Jesus Christ, an intercessor who is just.
> He is an offering for our sins,
> and not for our sins only,
> but for those of the whole world (1 Jn 2:1-2).
> Through his blood, God made
> him the means of expiation
> for all who believe (Rom 3:25).

As already noted, satisfaction demands giving in the sense of suffering, self-alienation, renunciation. It aims at restoring or repairing the *injury* done to the honor of God by offense. *Merit* as such is reward for something done in God's honor for his glory, in love for him. The most excellent offering is one's total submission to God. This is merit indeed in all instances, but the painful submission to the last *drop of blood* unto death is the highest form of *satisfactory merit*. We stress these concepts because our systematic theology of redemption has clearly shown their relevance. Christian piety has marked them in the lives of the great saints, in their effort to *satisfy* for the sins of others as well as for their own. Moreover, the Church has officially stressed them. Note on merit: *D* 809, 836, 842, 923; on the so-called treasury of merit: *D* 550, *TCT* 817; on the merits of Mary and the elect, *D* 552, *TCT* 819.

For further reference, see the writer's *The Everlasting Covenant* dealing with the merit of Christ, chapter ten, and "The Satisfaction of Christ", chapter eleven. At the risk of monotony, we repeat that we here deal with traditional and systematic theology. Note the words of Edward Siegman, C.PP.S., in the *Proceedings of the Precious Blood Week II*:

> Negatively, we have seen that there is little, if any, basis in the Bible for a theology of redemption based on a theory of *juridical compensation, vicarious substitution, meritorious causality* or *propitiation*. Not that speculation along these lines is condemned or rejected. Revelation

is something living; while it contains mysteries that defy our adequate comprehension, they can grow in clarity in the light of the Church's reflection and experience and the study of theologians in categories other than biblical (p. 29).

An explanation of the concept of the *treasury of merits* of Christ and the saints is necessary for a twofold reason. There is a hazard of conceiving this treasury as a species of vast deposits in celestial vaults from which we can constantly draw as from a bank. Also that merit and increase of merit is statistical and computative, as would be the application of merit to the souls in purgatory. Rather, the term is a metaphor indicating the abundance of grace through the redemptive work of Christ. Note the incisive words of Rahner:

> The term came into use in the 14th century in connection with the theology of indulgences (D 550 ff, 740 a, 757 and *passim*), but the reality referred to is independent of this occasion. Indeed, the word itself only expresses by a different image what has always been made quite clear without its help; that God desires every aspect of the salvation of every individual by way of Christ, his infinite satisfaction and the "merits" he won on the cross (*D* 799, 2193, 2318 and *passim*), and by way of the whole Body of Christ, which draws from and in him the strength required for its own activity and causes this to redound to the *benefit of every member* (see 1 Cor 12:25f and *passim*). This total saving reality of Christ and his Body is called the treasury of the Church, insofar as it effects the obliteration of the temporal penalties due to sin, in particular by means of indulgences (*TD* "Treasury of the Church", p. 466ff).

Sanguis Christi: Redemption Through Sacrifice

In the proclamation, in all our instruction and spiritual guidance, we relate our redemption to the cross and the bloody sacrifice of Calvary. Largely because the Church has always held that the sacrifice of the cross is continued in an unbloody oblation called the Mass, and the Reformers, even those who never denied the Real Presence in the Eucharist, uniformly denied and repudiated the Mass, the Catholic-Protestant polemic centered around this doctrine. This violent polemic is largely responsible for the great concern of Catholic theology with the nature of sacrifice. For decades after the Council of Trent, which defined that the Mass was a true sacrifice, and the decades preceding Vatican II no other theological concept was so thoroughly studied and analyzed.

The first concern for Catholic theology is to show that Christ offered a true sacrifice on the cross for all mankind. On this basis we shall later turn to the continuation of the redemptive work of Calvary in the Christ-presence and Christ-action in the Eucharist, sacrament and sacrifice.

It is clear from the sacred pages that Christ offered himself to his Father on the cross as a sacrifice for all mankind. This is to say that Christ redeemed us after the *manner of sacrifice.*

For our biblical evidence space permits us to offer only a few pertinent texts. Especially significant is Ephesians 5: 1f:

> Be imitators of God as his dear children. Follow the way of love, even as Christ *loved you.* He gave himself *for us* as an offering to God, a gift of pleasing fragrance.

These words are paraphrased by Philip Seidensticker as follows: Christ *"has given himself for us as a sacrificial gift"* (*Lebendiges Opfer,* Aschendorf, Muenster, 1954, p. 146ff).

Notker Fueglister speaks of Christ giving "himself up for us as *gift and sacrifice"* (*Die Heilsbedeutung des Pascha,* Koesel Verlag, Muenchen, 1963, p. 278).

(Note in the above translation of Eph 5: 1f which is from *NAB* we have a change of person: Christ *loved you,* gave himself *for us.* The Jerusalem Bible has *loved you,* giving himself up *in our place. RSV* has *loved us* and gave himself up *for us.* Joseph Bover, S.J. in the *Greek* and the *Latin* has *us* in both places. The *NEB, NT* has *you* and *your behalf*).

Rom 3: 23ff in the *Jerusalem Bible* and in the *NAB* is also cited as indicating Christ's death for our redemption. We note Spilly's comment: "The Greek of this text is difficult to translate. The *NAB* is closer to the text than the Jerusalem. It does not say both *Jew and Greek* but *all men.* Paul is not only thinking of both groups but of all individuals as well" (cf. Fitzmyer commentary on Romans in *JBC* II 301-302). *Reconciliation* in Paul is usually *katallage;* here he uses *hilasterion,* "expiation." Moreover, the Jerusalem Bible does not specify *by his blood* which both the Greek text and the *NAB* do. The phrase *through faith* is obscure, but crucial to Paul's argument. The expiation is made effective through faith. Spilly shares the view of Fitzmyer that the most important aspect is what Jesus did, but the "benefits of it are shared in only 'through faith' " (Alphonse Spilly, C.PP.S., personal notes).

A COMMENT ON THE NATURE OF SACRIFICE

Our effort in this concise commentary on the nature of sacrifice must be placed in the context of the many decades of discussion and dispute whose larger purpose was to manifest the relation of the Mass with Calvary as true sacrifice. We are not merely concerned with a theological explanation of *how* Calvary was truly sacrificial or the Mass is truly sacrificial, though both are essential. We have in mind to explain the nature of sacri-

fice as such: what is the basic pattern into which both Calvary and the
Liturgical Oblation must fit? The following lines, taken with some adaptation from the writer's *The Everlasting Covenant* (p. 99ff), are placed here
as the more traditional doctrine, which the writer now greatly modifies
largely in accordance with the position of Joseph Ratzinger:

> Sacrifice is the most perfect act of religion. As the most exalted form
> of divine worship (*cult*), it is always (in any sinful world) also the
> supreme act of satisfaction for sin. Sacrifice is a *special act of external
> worship* (cult) in which a priest or official representative of the sacral
> community makes a material offering to God by some form of immola-
> tion or change — at least by withdrawing it from profane use and
> placing it in the realm of the sacred — in witness to supreme self-sur-
> render to the absolute holiness and majesty of God. The ends or pur-
> poses of sacrifice are: *adoration* or *praise, thanksgiving* for favors re-
> ceived from God, *petition* for new favors from the divine bounty, and
> *satisfaction* in various forms in any state or order involved in sin. The
> great diversity of sacrificial rites in religious history makes definition of
> sacrifice difficult. Some theologians hold that the offering must be
> *immolated* or *destroyed* in recognition of God's supremacy over life
> and death of his creatures, whereas others demand only that the offer-
> ing be withdrawn from profane use and placed in the sacral sphere in
> recognition of God's holiness and sovereignty. If we limit the *destruc-
> tion* theory to certain types of sacrifice, and demand no more generical-
> ly than *some change* or *immolation* (at least the withdrawal from pro-
> fane use, etc.), we should find a broad basis of agreement in our
> definition. In the Old Testament the holocausts were destroyed.
> Though this is usually called a *total destruction,* the fragrant odor was
> conceived as ascending to God.
> Essentially bound up with certain sacrifices is the sign of the divine
> acceptance in the eating of the sacrificial meal, the sacral communion
> with God. In all sacrifice, but particularly in the sacrifice of the New
> Testament, we must look upon the external religious rite as a most
> solemn sign attesting to the full submission of heart to the all-loving
> God.
> Though man by his very nature is bound to the practice of religion
> which includes this supreme form of divine worship, the character of
> the sacrificial sign and the deputation of the priest or official represen-
> tative of the community is to be determined by God himself. The com-
> munity itself is sacral by the very bond of sacrifice, as the sacrificial
> rite by its inmost nature is social.

To the last man the 16th century Reformers repudiated the Mass as a
sacrifice. Theologically the repudiation was based on the unique sacrifice
of Calvary. Christ in his Blood offered himself "once for all" (Heb 9:11)
and "achieved eternal redemption" (Heb 9:12). Martin Luther firmly held
the Real Presence, the Eucharist as true sacrament of the Lord's Supper. His

denial of the sacrifice, we think, was due to the uniqueness of Calvary, to his notion that the Catholic Mass in its actual practice was really "the work" of the Mass priests, whereas man is justified by faith alone, not by works, to which we add the very inadequate explanation of the Mass by Catholics in that period.

The sordid commercialism which might well be called a *traffic in Masses* had an impact on Luther and many of the Reformers, which, we feel, could not fail to influence even their most basic theological thinking. Surely it helped to create a hatred for the concept of the Mass among millions of the dissidents. It might very well have accounted for the alterations in the Anglican "form of ordination" and, perhaps, of the "intention" of ordaining prelates. These points are now being restated in the discussion on the "validity of Anglican orders." We must note that recent restudy of this entire matter has served to create a much more favorable opinion regarding their validity. Two works by John J. Hughes, S.J., *Absolutely Null and Utterly Void,* and *Stewards of the Lord,* are largely accountable for the more favorable attitude. We suggest further study in an ecumenical spirit.

Liberal Protestants, of course, would reject what they would call a realistic concept of sacrifice in favor of some type of symbolical or ethical offering of one's work and one's self to God. According to Behm, writing in the *Theological Dictionary of the New Testament* I, pp. 174-176, late Judaism had accepted a "weakened and spiritualized" concept of sacrifice which appears to have been largely symbolical "of personal and ethical processes." The same writer holds that the conception of the Blood of Christ was largely a metaphorical expression of Christ's self-offering, obedience to God, demonstrated in the crucifixion.

These concepts, however, run counter to the entire Catholic tradition and the official teaching of the Church's magisterium. According to John L. McKenzie, many theologians have doubted that the sacrificial character of Jesus' death is referred to in the gospels and in Paul: according to these writers it was "first explained by the author of Hebrews." McKenzie himself maintains that "sacrificial terms are rare in the Gospels and in Pauline literature." And he adds that "there are good reasons for believing that Hebrews makes explicit what was believed and taught in the primitive apostolic instruction." It is clear that the distinguished biblical scholar holds that Hebrews does teach the "priesthood and sacrifice of Jesus." He also points out that the "sacrificial character of the Eucharist" is indicated in 1 Cor 10: 16-22 (*DB,* art. "Sacrifice," p. 758).

The *EDB* finds the doctrine of the sacrifice of the cross in Paul in many passages, in Hebrews, and indicated in the gospels (Mt 20:28; Mk 10:45). (Article "Sacrifice," col. 2087-2088). The *EDB* sees in the words of the institution "the sacrificial character of the Eucharist," (art. "Eucharist," col. 699).

A BROADER CONCEPTION OF SACRIFICE

In a recent article in *Stimmen der Zeit,* Jan. 1974, p. 3-16, entitled *Erloesung als Befreiung* (*Redemption as Liberation*), Hans Kessler attempts an enrichment of the incarnational doctrine suitable to our time, with a concept of sacrifice drawn strictly from Christian sources, a concept which seems to this writer to be truly biblical and more in accord with the idea of God's infinite mercy. Kessler relies much on Joseph Ratzinger's *Einfuehrung in das Christentum.* This we now take up using the English translation: *Introduction to Christianity.*

Kessler begins with the defined proposition of faith taken from the I Council of Constantinople: Christ was crucified for us. He maintains, however, that the council did not define the sacrificial character of the death on the cross. He insists that we may not deny this truth because the Council of Trent presupposed it in her definition of the Mass as a true sacrifice (D 940, 948). The theologian has a certain leeway in explaining the nature of Jesus' death, which faith teaches was for our salvation. Even admitting its sacrificial character — as we must — we still have not explained nor has the Church determined with precision what we mean when we say: the death of Jesus is a sacrifice.

He raises what seems to this writer serious objection to the post-Tridentine explication (including what we have presented in the previous page as the position we once held). He cites Bartman as characterizing the explanation as *suspect.* Throughout he is convinced that the non-Christian (pagan and Jewish) explanations should not be our sources in a definition of Christian sacrifice. There should be one supreme source, Jesus' own death and the biblical context in which it is placed. Moreover, he specifically raises two points for us to ponder in relation to the usual definition found in our *Handbuecher:* 1) The concept seems to imply that the *sacrifice* has what might be considered a causative influence on God through the act of man. 2) The so-called external act of sacrifice wields a "primary determination on the gift itself" which should rather be wrought through the "formal element of the inner religious act." Then he proceeds drawing largely from Ratzinger, to show that the non-Christian point of departure must give way to the Christian: What Christian sacrifice is can be determined solely from Jesus and his totally unique work. At this point we take up the *Introduction to Christianity* of Ratzinger:

> I. Precisely the reverse of nearly all world religions in which men
> seek to *appease* and *conciliate* the divinity by expiatory acts, is

the *NT* presentation of God as *coming to man* in order to bestow favor upon him. Through creative mercy, active righteousness, God sets crooked man straight. "This is truly something new, something unheard of — the starting point of Christian existence and the center of *NT theology of the cross*: God does not wait until the guilty come to be reconciled; he goes to meet them and reconciles them. Here we discern the true direction of the Incarnation, of the Cross . . . In the NT the Cross appears primarily as a movement from *above to below*."

II. "Worship too, man's whole existence, acquires in Christianity a new direction": "thankful acceptance of God's gift" . . . *Eucharistia* means "man's permitting himself to be endowed with gifts" . . . "permitting ourselves to be endowed with his (God's) own gifts and thus recognizing him as the only Lord . . ." "Christian sacrifice does not consist in a giving of what God would not have without us, but in our becoming totally receptive and letting ourselves be *completely taken over by him*" . . . "Letting God act on us — that is *Christian sacrifice*."

III. But the NT texts — and the expiatory acts of Jesus — also disclose the "upward movement of mankind to God." This demands closer scrutiny and interpretation of the Cross, according to the NT. At first the Apostles thought the total enterprise of Jesus — whom they expected never to be overthrown — was utterly wrecked. Though assured by the resurrection that he was indeed the Kyrios, the "point of the Cross had to be learned slowly." This was wrought by OT texts and the Cross was explained by the "OT cult theology." Hebrews connected the death of Jesus with the OT ritual: God wanted not the sacrificial activity of men, the beasts, the creatures — which were all his already — what he willed was what man *alone* could give: the *yes* to God, "in which man gives himself back to God."

IV. Rejected were all pre-Christian 'substitutions,' the priestly tribe of Levi itself; no longer did the ancient rites prevail. A new liturgy, a cosmic liturgy, a priest from the non-priestly tribe of Juda, in a sense a *layman*, put to death for a *political crime*: into the real temple, i.e., before the face of God, Jesus stepped to offer himself. "He took from man's hands the sacrificial offerings and put into their place his sacrificial personality, his own *I*. The text says he wrought this with his own blood" (Heb 9:12); "this *blood* . . . is simply the concrete expression of a love of which it is said that it extends to the end" (Jn 13:1). "It is the expression of the *totality* of his surrender and of his service; and embodiment of the fact that he offers no more and no less than himself. The gesture of the love that gives all — this, and this alone . . . was the real means by which the world was reconciled; therefore the hour of the cross is the cosmic day of reconciliation, the true and final feast of reconciliation. There is no other kind of worship and no other priest but he who accomplished it: *Jesus Christ*."

V. "Christian worship consists in the absoluteness of love, as it could
only be poured out by the One in whom God's own love had become human love; and it consists in the new form of representation included in this love, namely that he stood for us and *we let
ourselves be taken* over by him . . . It demands that . . . we accept the love of Jesus Christ that "stands in" for us, let ourselves
be united in it, and thus become worshippers with him and in him.
. . . According to the conclusions which we reached above, the
Christian sacrifice is nothing other than the EXODUS of the FOR
THAT ABANDONS ITSELF, a process perfected in the man
who is all EXODUS, all-surpassing and self-surrendering love.
The governing principle of Christian worship is consequently this
movement of EXODUS with its *two-in-one* direction towards God
and fellow-man. By carrying humanity to God, Christ incorporates
it in his work of salvation. The reason why the EVENT on the
cross is the bread of life "for the many" (Mk 14:24; Mt 26:28;
Lk 22:19) is that he who was crucified has smelted the body of
humanity into the *yes* of worship. It is completely 'anthropocentric,'
entirely related to man, because it was radical theocentricity, delivery of the *I* and therefore of the *creature-man* to God. Now
to the extent that this EXODUS of love is the *ec-stacy* of man outside himself, he is stretched out infinitely beyond himself. He is
torn apart as it were, far beyond his apparent capacity for being
stretched. To the *same extent,* worship (sacrifice) is always at the
same time the cross, the *pain* of being torn apart, the dying of the
grain of wheat that can only come to fruition in death. But . . . this
element of pain is a secondary one . . . The governing principle of
the *sacrifice* is not *destruction* but love. And even this principle
belongs to the *sacrifice* only to the extent that love breaks down,
opens up, crucifies, tears — as the form that love takes in a world
characterized by death and self-seeking" (Joseph Ratzinger, *Introduction to Christianity,* Herder and Herder, New York, 1970, p.
214ff. Translation by J. R. Foster. The German original, *Einfuehrung in das Christentum,* Koesel-Verlag, Muenchen, has this
doctrine on p. 232ff. The above has been adapted).

Ratzinger's concept of love of God and neighbor in his explanation of
sacrifice is particularly significant, attractive, and most suited to our Precious Blood spirituality: redeemed by the loving outpouring of Blood on
the cross we are held to the most exalted love of neighbor, whose salvation
we must seek as our own — in and through union with the Christ of
Calvary. United-with-all-others-in-the-selfless-love-which-honors-God-himself,
we attain the highest existence, fullest liberation and compassionate union
with all men. We cannot truly embrace man in worthy human love except in
turning upward to God in-and-with Jesus, the perfect MAN. Utterly vapid
is mere human love without the love of God.

Ratzinger's term in German *der Exodus des Fuer* is translated the "Exodus of the For," which seems crude in English. The translator is determined to express the idea of *total outpouring of self, total leaving of self, total self-abandonment* in loving self-giving to God. Only the pouring forth of blood *to the last drop* expresses this concept in sacrificial actuality: The cross was indeed and is the Christian sacrifice.

In the writer's *Everlasting Covenant* and in all his previous explanations of sacrifice, he rigidly limited the sacrifice of Christ to his bloody passion and death on Calvary. (Obviously we are now prescinding from the mystical sacrifice of the Mass). One of the difficulties involved in such an explanation was that it seemed to eliminate the earthly life of Jesus from the sacrifice as such, limiting it to the other categories we have already referred to. According to the explanation just taken over from Ratzinger the entire earthly life of Jesus is most intimately bound up with Calvary and is truly a part of his sacrifice for our sins. Calvary is thus the tremendous climax. Unblushingly we place the Ratzinger context as theologically more acceptable than our own. This we now consider outmoded, though it does serve as a background for Ratzinger.

LIBERATION: A FINAL NOTE

So much has been written in this post Vatican II age about religious freedom, about freedom in the Church, and politically about the rights of the oppressed even to resort to violence (some insist there is a theology of violence which would justify revolution through armed uprising), that we feel we should add here a few paragraphs about the spiritual fruits of the liberation from sin and its slavery. These lines are adapted from the writer's *The Everlasting Covenant,* p. 169ff.

Salvation history is the unfolding of the grand design of the liberation of man from the slavery of sin and Satan. The Old Testament preparation for the final redemptive work of Christ on Calvary centers in the annual commemorative of the Passover. The Hebrew people are religiously formed and constituted by the historical reality of the Passover and its religious commemoration. The celebration kept alive the divine covenant and the reflection on God's redemptive love in saving his people. Yahweh constantly reminds them of that *original Exodus* from Egypt (Ex 13:3). They who had been enslaved must show qualities of mercy and kindness to others (Ex 22:20). The enslaved kinsman when dismissed shall be weighted down with gifts. Yahweh's deliverance of his people from the slavery of Egypt was prophetic pattern of the New Testament intervention through Christ, who alone could shackle the Spirit of Evil.

In the New Testament throughout, sin is clearly pictured as serfdom and alienation from God. Satan is the strong man (Mk 3:26f) who has chained man (Lk 13:16), enslaved him and subjected him to his evil power (Acts 10:38; 26:18). It is a sinister force, in a personal sense, which dominates (Rom 5:21) and enslaves (Rom 6:17), alienating man from God (Eph 2:13). Great is the conflict between the Kingdom of God and the Kingdom of Satan. Through Christ's Blood we are rescued (Col 1:13). The slave is freed. The spiritually dead are given life. Those in darkness have seen the light. The entire human race once enslaved is now liberated. The slaves have become the sons of God. All human liberation, economic, political, social, must rest on the *first redemption after the manner of liberation*. It is beyond our present purpose to discuss the contemporary liberation movement in our social order, but it is a serious distortion to establish a social-theology in priority over the liberation from sin.

SANGUIS CHRISTI: REDEMPTION AFTER THE MANNER OF EFFICACY

Our redemption is wrought by God through the God-man in time and eternity. As already indicated, we call this the objective redemption (viewed *horizontally*). Viewing all this as God's action, the effect in us (grace, glory) is the *subjective redemption*. As explained, the *total objective redemption* is wrought through the *Blood of Christ*. Only thus do we understand and proclaim: without the shedding of blood there is no pardon of sin. Especially important in the relation of redemption after the manner of efficacy to the work of God in Christ, is the *resurrection,* too often neglected when we speak of what Jesus actually wrought for our redemption-salvation.

Two Pauline texts establish the link of passion and death with resurrection-ascension, the first from Romans, the second from first Corinthians:

> The words, "It was credited to him," were not written with him alone in view; they were intended for us too. For our faith will be credited to us, also if we believe in him who raised Jesus our Lord from the dead, the Jesus who was handed over to death for our sins and raised up for our justification (Rom 4:23-25).

This we call the classic text of the death-resurrection doctrine of St. Paul: both death and resurrection are *effective* in the work of man's redemption (removal of sin, restoration of supernatural life). For the exegesis of this important Pauline pronouncement, we should seriously study the paper of S. Lyonnet, S.J., *La valeur soteriologique de la resurrection du Christ selon saint Paul*, Greg. 1958, Vol. XXXIX, 2, p. 295ff (cf. also the writer's *The Everlasting Covenant*, p. 181 ff).

As to our second text, Gerhard Delling cites what to his mind is the oldest "summary *(Zusammenfassung)* of the decisive primitive Christian utterances of faith known to us," 1 Cor 15: 3-5, in which the salvific meaning of the cross is bound up closely with the confession of the Risen One. This relation (*Zuordnung*) which we also find confirmed expressly elsewhere in the New Testament leads Delling to the thesis: *There is no theology of resurrection without the theology of the cross.* But obviously there is also no theology of the cross without theology of the resurrection (Review of Gerhard Delling's, *Der Kreuzestod Jesu in der urchristlichen Verkuendigung*, in *TR* 1972, no. 5, col. 372, by Gerhard Schneider).

We note the text:

"I handed on to you first of all what I myself received, that Christ died for our sins in accordance with the Scriptures; that he was buried, and, in accordance with the Scriptures, rose on the third day; that he was seen by Cephas, then by the twelve" (1 Cor 15:3-5).

THE RESURRECTION: A NOTE

The resurrection of Jesus as unique historic reality is a basic article of apostolic preaching and of the Christian faith. It is not directly discernible and demonstrable, for Christ arose in a glorified body. Even the Apostles, Thomas clearly teaches, were able to see the risen Savior, whom they knew to have died, only with the eyes of faith. For our part we can and do show that this apostolic faith-conviction of the Apostles and the many others who were witnesses, was worthy of acceptance. Christ did not prove his resurrection, such is the teaching of Thomas, by arguments grounded on human reason, but he did present evident signs which made their *faith credible* for themselves and the proclamation. Our belief, in turn, is based on this faith and preaching of the Apostles. We prove that it was well founded on both historical and psychological grounds. It is truly a "corporeal" resurrection.

It is far beyond our present purpose to offer any critique of contemporary studies in this area: Christ's resurrection is totally unique, in a glorified body: the same Christ who died drenched of his Blood on Calvary, was buried, arose again. The historic Jesus of Nazareth is the Lord *Kyrios* risen from the dead. This is the ancient faith. Any attempt to separate the Jesus of history from the Lord *Kyrios* in whom we — and the Apostles and the early Christians and Christians of all times — believe, would destroy the ONE REALITY OF OUR REDEMPTION. Cross *and* resurrection are the one *Easter event,* the Center of Salvation (cf. III q. 55, art. 2 and 5, also cf. *EDB*, "Resurrection of Jesus Christ").

The resurrection is the seal of divine approval on the death of Christ, it inaugurates the new and celestial mode of Christ's existence. In one striking sentence Kessler, in the article already cited, enunciates the great article of our faith: "Jesus did not — such is the conviction of the primitive Church — remain in death. Rather, indeed, he was taken up into the finality and incomprehensibility of God" (p. 13). Since it inaugurates this new mode of Christ's existence, it would mean a new manner of life for us. Here again the Church's prayer is the norm of our belief and our life. The encyclopedic article referred to above concludes with the thought of the Paschal preface referring to Christ, who "by dying did away with our death and by rising again restored our life" (*ibid*).

We conclude this brief comment on the resurrection with the thought that we must accept the TOTUS CHRISTUS. To close our eyes to the historic Jesus, to stress only the *proclaimed Jesus* is to risk what has been aptly called *kerygmatic docetism*. It would mean disdain for the true humanity of Jesus and its salvific meaning for us. We repeat: our salvation has its origin in the HISTORIC CROSS. We must live in its shadow until the Second Coming (cf. Walter Kasper, *Einfuehrung in den Glauben*, Gruenewald, Mainz, 1972, p. 48). The reader will do well to read Kessler, *op. cit.*, p. 13ff, on the three basic aspects of the redemption in relation to the resurrection: the Christological (the Crucified One is eternally confirmed), the ecclesiological (Christ lives in our kerygmatic-sacramental-practical salvific action), the eschatological (expectation of the Second Coming and our resurrection: *I believe in the resurrection of the dead and life everlasting*).

Only in this great mystery of the resurrection of Christ can we begin to see the meaning of human existence, itself a mystery. A total absurdity would be man's existence without the corporeal resurrection of Christ, for the meaning of man's existence would be extinguished in death. To accept the cross but deny the corporeal resurrection of the crucified Christ is to embrace that very absurdity. The faith affirmation of this mystery of resurrection is also an affirmation of our faith in the Church insofar as our acceptance of the apostolic faith cannot be grounded on any experience of our own. Only in the great mystery of the suffering and death of Jesus — the great sacrifice of the Bloody cross, accepted by the Father in the glorious corporeal resurrection — can we, sustained by the apostolic witness and constant divine tradition, reach out in hope to the risen *Kyrios*. Our entire nature is turned in hope for union with the One who has gone before us, "necessarily the first" (Rahner, *ET*, 1430ff).

A Critique From Current Christology

This critique is our reflection on Walter Kasper's, *Jesus the Christ* (Paulist Press, N.Y. 1976), a highly complex and perceptive theological work dealing with every area of *Christ-thought*. Only recently has it come to our desk, as we make bold to draw from it: All Christian churches, all Christians, turn to *a person* to explain their own religious convictions, to find solution for their deep problems in life and religion. The obviously basic question in this inquiry is:

> Who is Jesus Christ?
> Who is Jesus the Christ, for us?

Jesus is the Christ, as the most basic affirmation of Christian belief means: One sent by God, the Messiah anointed by the Spirit, the salvation of the world, the eschatological fulfillment of history. Incarnation, in purpose, in effect, means reconciliation of God and world through a unique oneness of God and man in Jesus who is God-man. Reconciliation means liberation, and liberation means reconciliation, primarily a divine gift to us, and secondarily a human task for us. Our Christological concern for our time: how do true God and true man in one person (and the theological explication) relate to today's diverse philosophies and attitudes? Indeed, how, it is asked, can true unique man be God and lay claim to absolute unsurpassable significance? (p. 15-17).

As Catholic-Christian thinkers amid the most diverse views, we hold to a living tradition with remembrance of Jesus in a vast extensive horizon confronting philosophy, especially metaphysics, (p. 15-17-18-19-20) i.e., existence as such. Almost spontaneously the Christian becomes a metaphysician because of his faith, with recourse also to social sciences, to sociology as such. Obviously a determined or specific historical Christology with limits and bounds, facts, sequence of time and space, must be universally responsible Christology attuned to human questions, needs, problems, aspirations today. Because final ultimate reality has been revealed only in Christ, faith in Christ radically questions all closed systems which claim to impart real meaning to existence, to concrete human history.

The study of Christology historically suggests the significance of viewing Christ in his dynamic relation to us. It is quite clear that belief is directed to the object believed. To recognize Christ is to recognize his bounty. We are concerned with Christ in himself and Christ in relation to us. What is Christ in himself, what is he for me?

We should not permit ourselves to be maneuvered between an ontological and a functional Christology. Our present concern: where and how do we meet Jesus the Christ today (p. 24).

Our starting point is the confession of faith of the Church community clinging to the conviction: "Jesus is the Christ." Center and content of a

Christology claiming to interpret this faith turns to the cross and resurrection of Jesus — to transition from the earthly historical Jesus to the *Kyrios* of faith and glory — it extends forward to parousia and back to incarnation and eternal pre-existence: this means that God assumed a human nature with its history and destiny. In Jesus, salvation history opens up to and embraces all history (p. 187).

PROBLEM OF MYTH, DEMYTHOLOGIZATION

The present age, since the Enlightenment, challenges all religion with the demand for a study of myth and the need for demythologization in religion. Myth is a form of understanding proper to an out-of-date epoch of history, the primitive era of the childhood of mankind. Since men were not and could not have been aware of the real cause of things, they saw supramundane causes and powers at work everywhere in the world and in history. Since the Enlightenment, liberal theology has sought to discard all supernatural religion, all revelation, prophecy, miracles, and grace which are to be exorcized from religion by a process called demythologization. Such is the extreme, destroying faith. Our first question: What is the thoughtful response of Christology in Catholic Christian theology? Walter Kasper maintains that a critical demythologization is possible, perhaps even necessary in some instances. He gives the one example: he feels that very many of the faithful look upon Jesus as a god who came to earth vested as a kind of Father Christmas, who speaks through a mask as a stage actor. Little concept is here of perfect man, intellect, free will, growth, development. Here demythologization is called for. The problem is most difficult. It is no easy task to explain the human nature of Jesus, but we must seek to study it for an authentic belief in Christ. Somewhat more difficult is what Kasper calls the positive aspects: divine revelation uses human language which reveals something only when it reaches the hearer, when he understands it. In Jesus Christ, human existence as a whole becomes the grammar of God's self-expression. Christological statements are statements about man. The knowledge and study of man must give us an initial understanding of what has happened in Jesus Christ. But how is theological discussion possible and meaningful? One must avoid the extreme of making Christology merely an excessive anthropology cancelling the underivable originality and novelty of Jesus Christ. We must show Jesus Christ as the place (*locus*) of both divine and human freedom. If we cross the barrier between an acceptable anthropological interpretation and an unacceptable anthropological reduction, the demythologization converts dialectically into its opposite and Jesus of Nazareth becomes man mythologized (cf. Kasper's critique of Rahner's Christological-anthropology, p. 48 ff).

THE EARTHLY JESUS

Jesus really existed. He was born, lived with Mary and Joseph, worked and played, studied and prayed, publicly preached, worked miracles of loving mercy and finally was crucified. He died and was buried. The gospels — for all their abundant materials on the life of Jesus — are rather the witness to the faith of the disciples in the earthly Jesus and the risen Christ. Clearly every "uncritical fundamentalism is ruled out as pseudo-biblical." We are quite aware that Jesus is a "figure of unparalleled originality." Hence the basic challenge: Who was, who is Jesus of Nazareth? Not John the Baptist, not monastic ascetic of *Qumran*, not professor or theologian, not programmed reformer proclaiming overthrow of kings or emperors, but a teacher with ultimate authority, a prophet, the last and greatest of prophets. Gentle to children, respectful to women, seeking to serve rather than be served, he disdained no service, not even the most menial. Above all he proclaimed the Kingdom of God, of love, opposed to the forces of evil. Totally incapable of deceit, in utter candor, hating all hypocrisy, he the most human of humans, especially in his love for sinners, proclaimed the nearness of the Kingdom of love for all. Indeed he could speak for God, since he was truly unique Son calling God his Father. All others become sons of God, as with him they pray: Our Father. The Kingdom — which is at hand — is the Kingdom of his Father's love communicated to all. It comes to power, for his love alone reveals itself as the meaning of life. World and men/women find fulfillment only in love, which is the supreme perfection of justice.

In this real world, human beings have divorced themselves from the love of God by sin, self-seeking: everything falls to pieces, until the ultimate source of all reality, God's love, re-establishes itself and comes to power; the world is restored to order and salvation. Then men can live with one another: the coming of the Kingdom of God's love means salvation of the world and of each individual. This is the tremendous consequence of our preaching (p. 86).

GOD'S PLAN . . . JESUS' CLAIM

The miracles of Jesus in their diversity reflect the reality of divine power in Jesus. Many miracles reflect the faith in the fulfillment of Old Testament type now evident as the divine plan unfolds. We do caution against too rigid a conception in the modern historical, or shall we say, the clinical sense. Accepted in faith, the miracles reveal the divine presence, the divine message in him who rightly claims to be the *Son of God* (cf. p. 109 and pp. 163-196 with biblical texts. See below: Our Confession: Jesus the Christ is the Son of God). Very significant: in the gospels "we find God called 'Father' no less than a hundred and seventy times" (p. 80).

THE DEATH OF JESUS

This historically certain event took place in all probability on Friday of the Jewish Passover as all four evangelists attest. The Sacred Meal was either the Paschal Supper or a farewell supper. We date it April 7, 30 A.D. Though Kasper says the words "of institution" are not rigidly the exact words used by Christ since they are "liturgically stylized," this does not detract from their profound truth and reality. Note his words on the Eucharist: "The supreme realization of human existence is the Eucharist" (p. 213). As to the death by crucifixion, Kasper quotes Cicero: the idea of the cross should never come near a Roman citizen . . . it should never pass through (his) thoughts, eyes, or ears (p. 113). (Also note what Kasper says on p. 118 regarding Jesus' recitation of Ps 22, in connection with what we have already said on this point in the previous pages).

THE RESURRECTION

Here we have actual encounters with Christ in the Spirit. Faith did not establish the reality of the resurrection. The reality of the resurrected Christ, obtruding in spirit upon the disciples, established faith. Here we have a species of believing-seeing. Since the Easter faith — Jesus is the risen Christ, the *Kyrios* — rests on the witness of the Apostles, then the only access we have to it is that witness as handed down in the Church, the community of believers. Only in and through this witness is the risen Christ, through his Spirit, a present actual reality in history. For historical reality is never independent of the fact that it is known in history: Jesus a "permanent presence in history through the witness of the Apostlic Church" (p. 140). Pungently Kasper says: "What Jesus lived before Easter *ontically,* is expressed *ontologically* after Easter" (p. 110).

OUR CONFESSION: JESUS THE CHRIST IS THE SON OF GOD

Since Jesus of Nazareth revealed and communicated himself once and for all, uniquely, unmistakably, definitively, and unsurpassably, as the Son of God, our confession of Jesus Christ as Son of God manifests the specific and essential in Christian faith as a whole. Christian faith, therefore, stands or falls with our confession that Jesus is the Son of God (p. 163). (cf. above: God's Plan . . . Jesus' Claim).

HELLENIZATION IN OUR CHRISTOLOGY

Walter Kasper: "In virtue of its eschatological-universal claim, Christianity could not avoid entering into discussion with the Greek philosophy of the *Logos* and being." This "also asserted a universal claim: there was question not of self-surrender but of a self-assertion of Christianity. Essentially this was nothing less than *aggiornamento* of the period, of the hermeneutically necessary attempt to express the Christian message in the idiom of the time and in the light of the way in which the questions were to be raised" (p. 178). The creeds of Nicaea and Constantinople were surprisingly exact in hewing to the line between "legitimate and illegitimate hellenization." Arianism was illegitimate hellenization. And, as against Arianism, Nicaea represented de-hellenization. But here again a caution: It is understandable that the theology of the early Church did not succeed in grasping at once, in all its consequences, the basic decision made in Nicaea and Constantinople. This would have demanded a complete remolding of all the categories of ancient metaphysics.

In consequence, metaphysical, ontological reflection found its way into theology and finally largely supplanted scriptural thinking in terms of eschatology and salvation history. Thus Christianity lost much of its historical dynamic and perspective for the future. Here lies the very considerable grain of truth in the thesis of the de-eschatologizing of Christianity as the precondition and consequence of its hellenization. This brought about the stress on the immutability of God, his freedom from suffering and sacrifice or passion (*apatheia*), something not at all in harmony with the intention of Nicaea and Constantinople.

The great problem for the Greek mind was the concept of a God who became man to suffer and die (p. 178ff. Note entire p. 179). We conclude with an ecumenical rubric: it is particularly significant that Martin Luther did not view the cross in the light of the philosophical concept of God, but rather God in the light of the cross. We underscore this statement in the Heidelberg disputation of 1518: "No one is worthy of the name of theologian who perceives the invisible things of God as understood through the things that are made, but only one who understands the visible and concealed things of God as perceived through the suffering and the cross" (p. 180).

CHRIST'S SUFFERING: VICARIOUS SATISFACTION

The student of Precious Blood theology will find it significant that Kasper enriches the concept of redemption through vicarious satisfaction rather than merely accept it from traditional systematic theology. Our author insists on a theology of representation with a biblical basis. He underscores the texts, "for us", "for the many", Christ died "for our sins" (1 Cor 15: 3-5). In these contexts *hyper* has a triple meaning: 1) for our sake, 2) for

our good, our benefit, 3) in our place. All are implied and intended at
one and the same time expressing Jesus' *solidarity* with us as the very center of this human existence. "Paul develops and deepens this theology of representation." According to the Apostle, a real exchange is effected in and
through Christ . . . It is, therefore, by his own choice that Christ becomes
identified with us (p. 216). "Jesus takes on himself our guilt-entangled history but, through his voluntary and his *vicarious* service, imparts to it a new
quality and establishes a new beginning" (p. 218). "The idea of representation offers a total view of the biblical conception of history. *Adam* represents the totality of mankind. In him, the blessing or curse of all is decided"
(p. 218).

Our readers cannot fail to be impressed by Kasper's explanation of St.
Anselm's doctrine (cf. p. 219ff) which is unusually thorough by comparison
with our text book statements. No less valuable is his explication of redemption by liberation. Only in Christ are we liberated *to human freedom*
through grace giving us the fulness of existence. We note particularly that
here we are concerned with the very nature of finite human existence, not
merely with fallen man. This redemption, as liberation, agrees with what
we have sought rather limpingly to explain. Kasper insists that the doctrine
is truly biblical. We are concerned with a true act of divine grace (cf. p.
205 f). Striking is Kasper's statement regarding original sin which he finds
very significant as an important elaboration of theological thinking, though
he considers the term unfortunate. There is need for a less awkward re-
statement of the basic doctrine. Few theologians will differ on this point.
Though many writers have practically destroyed the doctrine in their explanations, others have provided an explanation which seems artificial and contrived; others again have offered well-founded and meaningful solutions in
this difficult area.

Chalcedon and Hypostasis

As to the work of Chalcedon and the distinction between nature and
person, the use of the significant word *hypostasis,* Kasper rightly stresses that
by this use of the word the great council safeguards unity in duality, duality
in unity of God and man. We are grateful to him for insisting that we have
here not hellenization of the Church's doctrine but rather de-hellenization in
confrontation with Monophysitism (p. 237). Nor is the word a product of
Greek background: the independence and originality of personality was only
discovered and "conceptually formulated in wrestling with the fundamental
data of the history of revelation. One of the most important contributions
of Christianity to human civilization, this concept meant the emergence of
a new understanding of reality as a whole" (p. 240). We append a few strik-

ing concepts from this great work with the regret that we can by no means do it justice, directing our readers to the arduous task of studying its pages. Jesus Christ in his living personality is salvation, salvation of our whole being. It is new being, new existence in the whole man (p. 207). God alone has and is life (p. 255). Jesus uniquely is the bearer of the Spirit (p. 256).

Such is the critique we suggest for our own Christology in the study on the Spirituality of the Precious Blood.

JOY IN OUR SPIRITUALITY

No writer in English has sung the praises of the Precious Blood with such lyric beauty as Father Faber in his great prose poem, *The Precious Blood.* The beauty of his thought is only equalled by the almost ecstatic rhythm of his style. With the rhapsody of this devotional classic still ringing in our ears, we cannot fail to reflect on the joy which should be ours who have written so long on the theme and attempted, be it ever so frailly, to practice the devotion in the Society of the Precious Blood. For this reason we place here at the end of our first part, a closing essay on *The Joy in our Precious Blood Spirituality.*

St. Thomas places joy (*gaudium*) among the human emotions (*passiones*) as *delight* according to *reason*. In the mind of the Angelic Doctor joy and sadness finalize all the passions (I II q 31, art 3 and q 25, art 4). That joy is no less one of the *fruits* of the Holy Spirit is evident from Galatians 5:22, where *joy* follows immediately after *love*. The *gifts* listed by Paul stand in contrast to the evils flowing from the flesh which rob man of his inheritance in the Kingdom of God.

Obviously spiritual joy can be found only in man's relation to God, the supreme joy being found in the eternal bliss in the vision of God. In this life, the Old Testament proclaims, man finds joy in many earthly events, weddings, harvesting of crops, triumph in combat, though these are always related to God and the salvation which comes from him. This is evident in the many jubilant prayers, psalms, and canticles, in the feasts and sacrifices. Particularly beautiful are the symbols of joy and delight in choice earthly good (wine, oil, life, long progeny, peace and tranquility, etc.). But here again all joy depends on God (cf. Jer 7:34). In the New Testament the concepts of joy relate principally to Christ and the message of redemption and herein lies our joy in the Precious Blood spirituality.

Joy as religious treasure is totally and utterly bound up with the person of Jesus Christ and salvation granted through him (p. 380, Vol. I *BTW*).

The New Testament is filled with references of joy through Jesus beginning with the jubilant angelic announcements: to Mary, to the father of John, to the shepherds. Joyful are the canticles of the *Benedictus* and the *Magnificat* as given in St. Luke's infancy narratives. Heaven rejoices at the conversion of sinners. The persecuted rejoice that they have been able to suffer for Christ. Greatest indeed is the joy of all Christians in receiving the *glad* tidings from the lips of Christ's Apostles.

In our Precious Blood spirituality we find joy in sorrow for sin, joy in suffering with the Crucified in the anticipation of the glorious resurrection. The *Sanguis Christi* — as the person of Christ in the total work of redemption — is the source of all joy — in the divine word freshened by the Blood — in the unity of the redeemed as the people of God, one in the Savior — in the sacramental-sacrificial Church — in all the mysteries of Jesus' life-death-resurrection in the Church. But above all in the joyous expectation of the Second Coming! In the communion of saints there is joy of the *family of Christ* on earth, in purgatory, heaven.

Our Precious Blood spirituality, particularly in its heroic aspect — reflecting the forsakenness of Jesus even by his friends, the mockery of his enemies, the disdain for his grace — will cultivate this paradox of joy in sorrow and suffering. Paul who seems to have labored most and suffered most, is filled with joy *without bounds* despite his many afflictions (2 Cor 7:4). Paul finds his joy in his suffering for the Colossians (1:24). He rejoices over the joy of others, "The joy of Titus" (2 Cor 7:13). James advised his readers to consider it "pure joy" to encounter every kind of trial (1:2).

As we note elsewhere, Bonaventure found in the very horror of Christ's suffering and death, the distorted features, the wrench of agony and pain, the inner beauty and splendor of the Jesus whom we love. Not in his suffering, but in our sharing it, we find the joy of supreme love. Similarly, Bonaventure's Francis rejoiced not only in all nature which proclaimed God's love, but in the Blood and wounds of the Savior. Strange troubadour of Christ, deep down his joy flowed from a Jesus-suffering-sympathy with human suffering, which without the pain and patience of Jesus would fill any one with horror. One cannot brush aside his acts because of the implications of contagious disease and modern hygiene. Of that he could not have been aware. Important spiritually is this: only the Jesus-love could enable the refined and delicately nurtured Francis to embrace lepers, wash their sores, rejoice in the wounds the Crucified shared with him. [see: Mystical Heights.]

For us in our Precious Blood spirituality it is the love of Jesus — how glibly we trip along with the phrase *for his sake* — which should bring us the deepest joy of spirit. It is love without the delights of love. The full meaning must be placed in our love truly *for his own sake*. Our joy must be immensely fruitful in sympathy for the lowly and deprived in a dreadfully unbalanced social-economic order. This means impelling force for the *spiritual revolution* with the inward strength to shun physical violence in favor of spiritual violence for reform. It must make us different, as Francis was different, welcomed, sought after, loved as he was loved. Only this joy can transform us into true followers of Christ, saints who in some measure share the agony-joy of the Francis who truly loved Christ (cf. Walter Nigg, *Great Saints*, Regnery, 1948, p. 24ff).

The source of supreme joy must be the Eucharist, in the sacrifice which is the real symbol of the death and resurrection, in the partaking of the Body of the Lord and drinking of the cup of salvation. Here joy must unite us, perhaps most deeply in small family groups on special occasions, baptism, marriage, jubilee, celebration of vows. This must encourage us to further the beautiful practice of celebrating the Eucharistic liturgy in homes. One calls to mind the touching account of Luke in chapter 24 on the encounter of the disciples with Jesus on the way to Emmaus, their hearts burning within them as he explained the inspired scriptures, their eyes opened at the breaking of the bread. Such must be the joy we find in the *Table of the Lord* which is indeed the *Opfermahl* and *Mahlopfer* (sacrificial banquet and banquet sacrifice), in the reading of the sacred scriptures at the Mass, and in the sacred homily. We of the Precious Blood spirituality must find herein our special joy in encouraging our youth, our weary and fatigued, our lonely and aged to share in the Eucharist, as we joyfully break for them the bread of life and offer them the cup of salvation. Deeply enriching our spirituality is our love for the Heart of Jesus from which flows the Precious Blood.

CHAPTER SIX

PRECIOUS BLOOD SPIRITUALITY THE SANGUIS CHRISTI HAS WROUGHT: CHURCH, SACRAMENTS

The Church is Creation, Foundation, Center Wherein the Virtue of the Sanguis Christi Continues to Reside. It is Impossible to Study Its Grandeurs Without Being Led at Almost Every Step Into the Magnificence of the Sacraments; and Then Again the Sacraments are the Structure of the Church.

(cf. Father Faber, *The Precious Blood*, p. 289)

Recent theology has related the salvific work of Christ in carrying out the divine will that all men be saved (1 Tm 2:4), redemption through efficacy, to the Church in her very essence. She is the people of God in whom Christ is present with the word of truth in the inspired scriptures, the divine tradition, teaching office; present in her pastoral office guiding the lives of men; present above all in her sacraments. As to the latter, we may speak of her as the Primordial Sacrament, Sacrament of the Humanity of Christ, which is the Sacrament of the Word.

The Gospel according to John gives the striking account of the piercing of the riven side and the flowing forth of "blood and water" (Jn 19:34). According to the *Mystici Corporis* (Paulist Press, no. 29), the "Church was born from the side of our Savior on the cross." This, the encyclical teaches, is the unanimous patristic doctrine, particularly that of St. Ambrose. According to the *Mediator Dei* (*NCWC*, no. 17), the sacraments flowed from the Savior's pierced side. (We are not here concerned with the medical explanation which has been dealt with recently. cf. *JBC* "Gospel According to John," 63:172).

The Church born on the cross was proclaimed on Pentecost with the coming of the Holy Spirit in the first apostolic sermon, the discourse of St.

Peter (Acts 2:14ff). The Holy Spirit was to be sent to all mankind through the risen Christ whom Peter now proclaimed as Messiah:

> This is the Jesus God has raised up, and
> we are his witnesses. Exalted at God's
> right hand, he first received the promised
> Holy Spirit from the Father, then poured
> this Spirit out on us. (Acts 2:32-33).

When asked what his hearers were to do Peter answered:

> You must reform and be baptized, each one of you,
> in the name of Jesus Christ, that your sins may be forgiven;
> then you will receive the gift of the Holy Spirit (2:38).

All mankind can now attain its eternal destiny through the divine-human mediator, Jesus Christ. But, as we have already indicated, mediation specifically relates to the *redemptive Blood*:

> Remember that, in former times, you had no part in Christ and were excluded from the community of Israel. You were strangers to the covenant and its promise; you were without hope and without God in the world. But now in Christ Jesus you who were once far off have been brought near through the blood of Christ (Eph 2:12-13).

The letter to Colossians links baptism of *immersion* with the *death, burial,* and *resurrection.* Even more vividly does Paul in Romans relate the death and burial with baptism and resurrection unto glory with the renewal of Christian life.

> In baptism you were not only buried with him but also raised to life with him because you believed in the power of God who raised him from the dead (Col 2:12).
> Through baptism into his death we were buried with him, so that, just as Christ was raised from the dead by the glory of the Father, so too we might live a new life. If we have been united with him through likeness to his death, so shall we be through a like resurrection (Rom 6: 4-5).

The Church, which we have thus entered by the first of the seven sacraments, leads us as the Church on pilgrimage to glory. This Pilgrim Church at the great grace-giving, redemptive junctures, according to Karl Rahner, offers to redeemed mankind the unique sources of grace which we call the sacraments of the Church and Christ. Often they are called the *sacramenta separata* in the relation to the Church as Primal Sacrament as noted above.

Though baptism is the first sacrament, the Eucharist is principal and central in the grace-laden system which is the Church. Through the Eucharistic sacrifice-sacrament she is constituted and built up as the Society of Worship, whereby God is worshipped and men are brought to salvation. The very heart of the redemptive work, the continued presence of the Christ-action in his Holy Spirt is the Eucharist. Each member of the Church bears the mark of baptism in its greater fulness through the other sacrament of initiation, confirmation. As numbered in God's *priestly people* (cf. 1 Pt 2:9), they are more ready to offer and receive the Eucharist and outwardly reach to all the redeemed to share with them the *Sanguis Christi*. Now the reception of the other sacraments assumes the nature of a right and a duty, according to its nature, the human need, and the divine call.

We note regarding the Eucharist a continuity which must be paralleled in the life of the Christian. The sacrifice-sacrament as the center of our lives must be shared far more frequently than the other sacraments. At all times the Christian must die to Christ in order to live with him. The *mystical death* of the Christ who is in glory is symbolically presented in the Eucharistic liturgy, the Mass, through the separation of the species of bread and wine. The sacred offering is both food and drink (bread and wine). According to a profound theological view the reception of the Eucharistic species (*Communion*) as integral completion of the sacrifice represents the acceptance of the sacrifice by the heavenly Father. The visits, the processions, Communion to the sick, all relate to the sacrifice, to the permanent presence-of-Christ-in-the-Church.

Because of its special holiness, a unique sacrament, *penance,* prepares the sinner for the Communion. According to Semmelroth, this sacrament is the tribunal before which the sinner, repentant, receives the verdict of absolution which removes the *sign of accusation* from baptism whereby the sign of *priestly capacity to join in the mystic offering is restored.*

Marriage, sacramentally linked with Christ and the Church, makes the Church fruitful in its fruitfulness. It involves sacrifice, expiation, submission, mission to celebrate the Eucharist in sacral and sacred fellowship! Physically, socially, and spiritually it is the basis of all fellowship in the Church. More closely linked with the Eucharist is the sacrament of order in its various steps or orders, in which official ministry of word, guidance, sacrament culminates in the liturgical Eucharistic cult.

Finally, the ultimate situation — again we follow Semmelroth's pattern of thought — is the approach to death. Death is life's crowning event, the summation of life turning to final and definitive encounter with God or, horror, definitive perdition. Uniquely significant is the sacrament of the anointing of the sick. We do not wish to think of it in the harsh sense of sacrament of the dying, but of the sick and aged who have an awareness of death with the loving faith and hope which places one's whole life in God's hands. Often we pity those who die a *solitary death*, unassisted and unattended, but every death in the deepest sense is solitary. Each one must die alone, yet those with living faith and hope in Jesus, die with him, for he who taught us how to live, to pray, also taught us how to die. To those with such faith who place their whole life in submission to God, the redemptive Christ through the priest of his Church comes with the unique sacramental grace of Christ's dying. Sacred is the bond between the anointing of the sick and aged, who "begin to be in danger of death" (*Constitution of the Sacred Liturgy*, nos. 73, 74, 75, *DOV*) and the Holy Viaticum, mystic Food for the final journey. The order, frequency, and manner, of reception are explained in the light of Jesus himself leading us to glory in the resurrection.

> Though he was in the form of God,
>   he did not deem equality with God
>   something to be grasped at.
> Rather, he emptied himself
>   and took the form of a slave,
>   being born in the likeness of men.
> He was known to be of human estate,
>   and it was thus that he humbled himself,
>   obediently accepting even death,
>   death on a cross! (Phil 2:6-8)

Linked with him sacramentally as we have shown above, we will die with him and share his glory. Only Karl Rahner could have struck the final note on *death*: the dying of Jesus embracing all being, our living, our dying:

> Part of the innermost being of the world is what we call Jesus Christ in his *life and death,* that which was poured forth upon the whole world at the moment when the vessel of his body broke in *death* and Christ really became, even in his humanity, what of right he always was, the *heart of the world,* the *inmost center* of all created being (*TD* Death, p. 118).

THE MYSTERY OF OUR DEATH: A NEW NOTE

Both our current theology and scientific research have recently been *newly* concerned with the attitudes to be assumed toward death. An updated theology of death is surely called for and now it is being studied in the context of research and the guidance of those who approach death. For this reason we add the following pages to this chapter which has dealt thus far with the Church and the sacraments.

We premise the discussion with a brief reference to the very significant volume of *Concilium,* Vol. 94, which is devoted to The Experience of Dying, edited by Norbert Greinacher and Alois Mueller (H & H, 1974). Note the diversity of the contributions and the points of view: One is by Elizabeth Kuebler-Ross on Dying as a Human-Psychological Event (p. 48ff), another, by Alois Mueller, deals with Care of the Dying as a Task of the Church (p. 126). Signifcant is, Towards a Theology of Dying, by Gisbert Greshake (p. 80ff).

The *TR* no. 2, 1976 has two reviews that merit careful reflection: Jesus' Unique Death (*Jesu ureigener Tod*) by H. Schuermann, reviewed by Gerhard Schneider; Life After Death, reviewed by Jacob Kremer, a work on Paul's argument for resurrection from the dead according to 1 Cor, chapter 15. The writer was especially impressed by the incisiveness of the former work. The death of the cross had to have its own "thesis." Christ's death must have a unique meaning found in Jesus' own actions, his intention, his manner of enduring the supreme torture and his yielding his spirit to God.

Amazingly Ladislaus Boros relates to the death situation the encounter with Christ, the ultimate decision, the meaning of the universal salvific will (cf. 1 Tm 2:4), the universality of grace, sacrament, membership in the Church. He has a unique and striking definition of purgatory as "becoming truly ourselves" and the "meeting with Christ" as "judgment." In contrast to our view of death as weakness, hopelessness, and utter incapacity, he says that "death makes it possible for a man to act for the first time fully as a person." Though we need not accept his position in its entirety, the reader must see in this chapter on *Last Things* (p. 49ff) a deep enrichment of our Precious Blood spirituality and never cease to ponder its profound necessity and universality in the order of Christian spirituality (cf. *Christian Prayer*, Ladislaus Boros, Seabury, 1976).

Our theology has always been concerned with death as related to sin, the fall of man, redemption through Christ, the sacraments, our final destiny. For obvious reasons our moral theology dealt seriously with the *actual moment of death* (as perplexing then as now). New and startling is the current problem dealing with the transplantation of vital organs from *dead* to *dying*: When does death occur and leave us guiltless in the removal of vital organs? The old and somewhat simple approach to the use of extraordinary means to sustain life takes on a far more complex meaning in the context of technological sustaining of life. It is meaningless without the exercise of basic vital activity and with the added hazard of external control of life itself (e.g. euthanasia) by the State. Theologically, the moral concern was directed to the evil of taking human life directly except on carefully defined conditions (e.g., just war, self defense, just punishment).

Our dogmatic texts highlighted the four last things: death, judgment, heaven (purgatory), hell. The sombre significance of death was evident in every species of grotesque art, mournful tunes, constant preachments, but also in magnificent literature and art, such as Gray's *Elegy Written in a Country Churchyard,* Tennyson's *In Memoriam,* Bourdeloue's *Eulogy at the funeral of Louis XIV,* the *Burial of Count Orgaz* in the Church of Santo Tomé in Toledo in Spain, the splendid cemeteries (Genoa, Rome) with their monuments to the heroes fallen in war (Madrid: Monument to the Fallen). Probably the most melancholy of all the problems was that of original sin and the fate of infants who died without baptism. The most divergent explanation disturbed our theology from the theory of natural happiness to actual torture (Gregory of Rimini, *Tortor infantium*). We do not have space for further detail.

All this is still far from a true theology of death. We feel that such a study would involve the primitive concepts of death and afterlife, the Old Testament and New Testament concepts of death and the future life, the relation of death to sin, and of both to the death and resurrection of Christ in a far more profound and ultimate sense than in all our past study. Much of this is indicated in the preceding pages. Here we wish to stress the widespread current interest in death in the context of instruction and guidance particularly for the aging, the stricken with fatal illness.

Alongside the tender and loving presentation of death which we find in the *cinéma vérité* (cf. *America,* May 15, '76, under the title "The Word: Love and Death") there is the recent research into death and resurrection from death, and the assertion of what has been claimed as "being called back from death." Here we meet with the conviction that the border line has been passed, the border line beyond death. We refer to the account in the Chicago Tribune of May 23, 1976: A number of patients after resuscitation "testified" to a most agreeable experience on their entry into the *afterlife.* One of the researchers, Dr. Elizabeth Kuebler-Ross of the University of Chicago, is quoted as saying she is convinced "beyond a shadow of doubt that there is a life after death . . . Hundreds of cases of this kind have now been *scientifically verified.* We've just been afraid to admit it."

Karl Rahner, whose great work on the Theology of Death (*Zur Theologie des Todes, QD,* no. 2, Freiburg, Herder, 1958) has been widely acclaimed, briefly discusses a feature of the Kuebler-Ross book in his *Christian at the Cross Roads* (p. 84ff, The Theology of Dying, Seabury Press, N. Y., 1975). He presents a profound insight into the dying person's acquiescence in death, which is the fifth stage in Kuebler-Ross stages of reaction to death on the part of the person who knows that he or she is to die. We feel that the theologian might welcome such scientific research as a backdrop to the fact of revealed truth: death ushers man into the eternal afterlife, with heaven, hell, and purgatory. Moreover, the *moment of death* concept in relation to man's eternal destiny, the final movement of divine grace, the providential guidance of mankind, the salvation of infants who die without baptism, all these points and others can be profoundly enriched in this new scientific atmosphere.

As is evident from what we have said thus far, death relates to sin, if not merely in the natural and physical order, surely in the supernatural redemptive order, to the death and resurrection of Christ. Many theologians today hold that death itself is the source and context of a final decision for God or perdition. We are inclined to agree with Father Wright, S.J., writing in the *NCE* (Vol. 4, p. 692, art. Death, Theology of) that at the moment of passing into the immutability of eternity the soul makes a final decision, and that this act is not an entirely free option, but rather a summation of life's many free decisions, finalizing and fixing them forever, either unto God and eternal joy or unto self and eternal perdition. It is free only in the sense that it is culmination, summation through ultimate *turning to* or *from God.*

Here one is reminded of the much neglected teaching of Aquinas that every human being, at the point of moral maturity, is given the grace to turn to God and direct his life to his final end. Should he repudiate this grace and turn from this final end, he would be guilty of sin and deserving of perdition. Should he turn to God, he would receive the grace and favor of God directing his life to him. The grace is given to all mankind even where the *gospel has never been preached* (1, 2, Q 89 art. 6, and elsewhere).

The *final decision,* according to our source, is under the impulse and attraction of grace and corresponds "qualitatively" to free decisons made in life. Thus there is involved a loving concern of God who "wants all men to be saved" (Tm 2:4). The final decision is at the "first instance of the soul's permanent state." It is the ultimate or final fruition of all free, virtuous decisions of life. And, finally, in view of the Council of Trent's declaration that final perseverance is far more than a mere grace but rather a *great gift* (*magnum donum*) (D 826), we may hopefully assume that God closes this human existence and begins that other life by a supreme dying-Jesus-redemptive grace — in a sense the ultimate fruit of the Precious Blood.

We are far from assuming that there is a final "option" by which the total past life can be disregarded. But there is room for those who die without baptism through no fault of their own. We may rightly assume that the problem of the billions who die without baptism — enormously increased by our present knowledge of the long existence of the human race — does weigh heavily in favor of this sympathetic study of the *moment of death.* One is tempted to wonder out loud how the *all men* in 1

Tm 2:4 could be made to refer only to a very small fraction of the human race. Nevertheless, we do make the statement with caution and deep respect for the authority of the Church.

Above all we should not dare to display indifference toward the grave obligation of parents and pastors to provide for the baptism of infants in strict accordance with the Church's traditional practice. Moreover, our *kerygma* must proclaim the intimate bond of the "moment of death" with the total life which must prepare us for the final end. We may go a step further. We think we must accept the moral teaching that none of our deliberate acts can ever be morally indifferent. Hence, life has its tremendous meaning precisely in the light of the "moment of death." Our joys are anticipation of the eternal bliss, our sorrows are to be borne in the light of the cross and the final glory. As all the sorrows of Christ pointed to passion and death, his joys and triumphs (Thabor) to the glory of resurrection, so too must we unite our joys and sorrows with his. Our dying in Jesus must mean our resurrection with him in glory.

Cold and bleak, indeed, is the life that turns toward death as the end-all of human existence. Man without meaningful death is of all living creatures the most miserable. No meaning, however, can be found except in Christ, in the Christ-life, and in Jesus dying. All the sacramental life of the Church, and in it our own sacramental life, is completed and perfected in our death. All our virtuous acts, our progress in grace and virtue attain their consummation in the moment of death. Finally, as we go forward to meet Christ in glory, we shall enter the glorified company of the blessed. Then, indeed, love and death are one. Even now we reach out to the countless sick who suffer in terminal illness, all the dying in the world, praying that they die in the Jesus-love. Always, the profound Christ-experience of passion and death makes him the source of our victory over the death which is sin, and the moment of death the eternal consummation in glory.

We conclude with the thought of Karl Rahner regarding the *moment of death*. The great theologian suggests that we need not concur with the many theologians who today make of the precise moment of death a total decision, a definitive Yes or No in every possible instance. Rather he suggests that "the temporary is quietly taken from men and the silent infinity of God is offered, in which it becomes relatively easy for the person to turn the last deed of his life to his eternal salvation" (*ibid.*, p. 186). He expands his hope to the inclusion also of the "anonymous Christians" (*ibid.*). We personally think of it as applying especially to the countless tender infants who died without explicit baptism. How great indeed is the loving power of the SANGUIS CHRISTI. Glory be to the Blood of Jesus!

CHAPTER SEVEN

THE PRECIOUS BLOOD SPIRITUALITY
THE HUMAN FIGURE: THE SYMBOLS
THE LAMB   THE CROSS

On the Cross the Lamb Is Lifted
Where His Life Blood Shall Be Spilled

In this chapter we take up the complicated task of reflection on the presentation of Christ, the God-made-man to the eyes and hearts of mankind to whom the apostolic word of salvation has been preached. In the primitive Church it was the symbol *XR* (from the first two letters of *Christos*) which represented Christ and paradoxically concealed the reality. Even more striking was the *fish* designed to express to the initiated and conceal from profane eyes the figure of the Savior, (*ICHTHUS,* an acrostic meaning *Jesus Christ, Son of God, Savior*). Jesus was also represented as the Good Shepherd with the lamb on his shoulders, as indicated in his own words. But the lamb with a flag and "surrounded by a cruciform nimbus" (cf. old *CE,* art, "Symbolism," Vol. XIV, p. 376c) readily created the hazard of ignoring the true humanity of Christ. In consequence the Quinisext Synod "forbade the representation of the lamb" as a substitute for the "body of Christ on the cross" (*NCE* art, "Lamb of God," Vol. 8, p. 340c). (Incidentally the *XR* has been historically related to the cross likewise). Since we devote the greater part of this chapter to these two basic biblical-real symbols of the Redeemer and redemption, the lamb and the cross, we must premise our reflection on the various forms of the Redeemer-figure in the many diverse presentations where the gospel has been preached to men.

We note, first of all, that among the Fathers of the Church some have pictured Christ as mean and lowly, others present him as majestic and inspiring in appearance. Again he was presented in areas and times as bearded, and elsewhere as beardless. Today most commonly he is presented with long hair and beard. As to his actual appearance, however, both Irenaeus and Augustine agree that we do not have an authentic knowledge of his bodily form and features (*Christus in Aller Welt, Christ Throughout the World,* by

Joseph Jobé, Econ-Verlag, Wien, 1962). Jobé in this striking work presents pictures of Christ from practically every nation in the world, together with an illuminating text on the theme, from which we select a few points. He says we have no really authentic picture of Christ, no description of his appearance, no actual biography. We do not know the color of his eyes, or of his hair, the sound of his voice. Yet this man, born in a cave and put to death on a cross, who preached love and salvation to all mankind, has created a never ending interest in all phases of his life expressed in paintings from all peoples and all times.

Early legends tell of pictures of Christ. Noted is the so-called Abgar picture of Edessa which is connected with the apocryphal letters to Edessa. According to the *Legenda Aurea* the painter sent by the king to paint Christ was blinded by the radiant face of the Lord, who then took a fragment of his cloak, pressed it to his face leaving his sacred image on it. Only later was the image taken to Abgar, and later to the Church of San Silvestre in Capite in Rome. Deeply moving is the story of the veil of Veronica which we have in our present work, the great drawing of Rouault. Less known is the story of the painting of St. Luke and the sculptured head by Nicodemus. (We are not referring here to the Madonna of St. Luke much venerated in Saint Mary Major in Rome). All these are beautiful legends, the tender manifestation of simple loving faith and a desire to have the image of Christ, the Holy Face, impressed in men's hearts.

The Trullan Synod, to which we referred above, officially encouraged the painting of the picture of Christ when it restricted the use of the symbol. It decreed that the Lord is to be presented "not as a Lamb but in human form. The full greatness of the Divine Word must be made apparent also in the shell of our human lowliness. The painter must lead us so that we call Christ to mind, how he, suffering in the body, dying for our salvation, obtained the redemption of the world" (*op. cit.*, p. 8). We refer again to the volume of Jobé, it is richly illustrated with pictures of Christ from all phases of his earthly life to his passion and death on the cross. There are selections from every area of the world: the Christian countries, the mission lands, China, Indochina, India, Indonesia, Oceania, the Gold Coast and other parts of Africa, Japan, Korea, Vietnam, Brazil, America. This highly diversified book is well worth our study in our Precious Blood spirituality, in which we honor the Christ of all seasons, all places, all his earthly life and glory, in our pilgrimage to the Christ in glory.

Unique is the Christocentrism in the picturing of Christ — not only nations, peoples, tribes have pictured him as seen through their own culture and racial features, but great artists and sculptors mingle with the simple folk, even the most primitive, in telling their story of faith. Every means of expression, painting, weaving, carving, stark simple lines, all tell of the universal faith in Jesus, the universal Savior, the center of space and time. Often the most fantastic art forms, expressionistic, cubistic, totally alien to our notion of the normal mode of expression have, after deeper and longer study, revealed a deeper meaning of hidden faith and love. Something of this we shall find in our pictures in this study.

Of no other human form can we say it has been the universal object of men's desire, center of loving veneration. Even those who have debased him, hated him, written the most revolting things of him as the manifestation of lust, deceit, ugly ambition, unwittingly proclaim him, for the dead are encrusted mummies, ashes, dust, objects neither of love nor of hate. But two thousand years find the millions still loving him, often strangely, fantastically, and perhaps millions still reviling him as those who clamored for his death on the cross. The reason can only be — of Jesus alone can it be said: he is no longer dead, raised on the cross, laid in the tomb, he has risen again. He lives forever, will be forever loved or hated, loved unto glory and salvation, hated unto death and perdition. We pray that deep down even those who turn to him fantastically (e.g., in Jesus Christ Superstar) through his grace shall see the true light of HIS FACE. And those who turned from him unto perdition, will turn back embraced by his love.

We of the Precious Blood spirituality
beg of you, Jesus, to imprint on our
minds and hearts, YOUR TRUE IMAGE,
which is the glory of the Father in
your Holy Spirit. Amen.

THE LAMB   THE CROSS

Though it is true of Christian spirituality as such, our Precious Blood spirituality especially has two central symbols based obviously on the *Sanguis Christi* itself. We touch upon them only briefly. They are, as is evident from the above pages, the *lamb* and the *cross*. Lamb and cross are bound up with the ancient and continuous prayer practice of the Church. Manifestative of her whole life-style, their use from the very beginning clearly indicates that without the lamb and the cross, her whole spiritual life would be sadly impoverished. As we indicated above, they have a splendid theology of their own, biblical, historical, liturgical, a rich and luminous spirituality.

Lamb and cross, though diverse, are most intimately bound together in redemptive history, in all salvation history. Lamb reflects beauty, tenderness, providence of God, nature, the historic pastoral life of the Hebrews and other ancient peoples. Biblical, the lamb relates to the worship providentially leading to the climax of all salvation history in Jesus, the Lamb of God who takes away the sin of the world. The cross, though it had a deep meaning even in non-Christian cult and culture, became the supreme religious symbol in Christianity when this cruel instrument of torture was made the instrument of redemption through the agony and passion in Blood.

The eschatological triumph proclaims the eternal efficacy of the sacrificial death. The Lamb that shed his Blood on the cross reigns in splendor in the heavenly Jerusalem. Celestial chant proclaims the fruit of the Blood, its glory and power. His is honor, adoration of all creatures, especially of the chosen hosts of the undefiled, "The first fruit of mankind for God and the Lamb" (Rv 14:4). The sublime theme of the Book of Revelation is the *Blood of the Lamb*. With his power he has opened the seven seals. Those who have endured great tribulations have washed their robes in his Blood. Standing in majesty and splendor, he is given honor by all creatures, who are to be shepherded by the Lamb. In his book of life are written the names of those who have not worshipped the beast. He is Lord and king, light and splendor of the heavenly Jerusalem.

Throughout we cannot fail to note the splendor of the language of the revealed word. As Schnackenburg points out (Rudolf Schnackenburg, *The Truth Will Make You Free*, H. and H., New York, 1966, p. 48ff), this is evident in many passages of the Bible, in Deuteronomy, in the Gospel of John, in the Mission Command in Matthew, in the Book of Revelation. In the liturgy much of this solemn language must stimulate us to a love for the grandeur of the divine truth and worship.

THE LAMB OF GOD: THE SUFFERING SERVANT

The relation of Jesus to the *Suffering Servant* and the *Paschal Lamb* is indicated in the account of the conversion of the royal Ethiopian minister by the deacon Philip (Acts 8: 26ff). The study of this Deutero-Isaiah background in the New Testament reflection underscores the most obvious parallels: the meekness and submission to suffering (he was *"like a lamb led to the slaughter"* Is 53:7) ; and the gentleness of the lamb and the pure texture of its fleece to the purity and innocence of the Suffering Servant (*"He had done no wrong nor spoken any falsehood"* Is 53:9). The first letter of St. Peter speaks of a lamb whose blood is *"beyond all price: the blood of a spotless, unblemished lamb"* (1 Pt 1:19). The very title *Lamb of God* applied to Christ takes on a profound victimal sense in the light of the prefigurative lambs in the Old Testament sacrifices, the daily offerings of atonement for sin. Here also the Servant of Yahweh poems picture the Suffering Servant as a lamb (Is 53:4ff).

A Comment from Joachim Jeremias

According to Joachim Jeremias, the early Christian community expressed three things in describing Jesus as *amnos*: the patience of his suffering, his sinlessness, and the efficacy of his sacrificial death. The background is probably the Suffering Servant and the Paschal Lamb. Under *arnion* rather than *amnos*, he notes that the statements of Revelation concerning Christ depict him as Redeemer and Ruler, and in so doing bring out all the most important elements in his title as Deliverer.

The Lamb has been slain; his Blood flowed in atonement for sins. But the Lamb triumphed over death. He is omnipotent and omniscient. He takes over government of the world by opening the book of destiny in the heavenly council, receiving divine adoration, establishing the rule of peace on the heavenly mountain, overcoming demonic powers, exercising judgment, and making distinction on the basis of the book of life. As victor he is the Lord of lords and King of kings, celebrating his marriage festival with the community and ruling his own as partner of the throne of God. The Greek terms *amnos* and *arnion* are translated into Latin by *agnus* and into English by *lamb*.

(This all too brief summary of the thought of Jeremias is taken from the *Theological Dictionary of the New Testament*. The comment is based on a study of the first volume, pp. 338-341. The writer has presumed to condense the original study of Jeremias presented by Alphonse Spilly, C.PP.S.).

The Lamb in John's Gospel

John plunges his theological thought into the realm of eternity defining eternal life as *prolongation* of the supernatural verities of faith. Under the symbol of the *Lamb* the Precious Blood is similarly extended. It is an apocalyptic symbol. What John saw in vision are truths which he conveys through this picture. Though the symbol of the Lamb is only one among many in the Book of Revelation, it occupies an extraordinary position, pervading the whole book. The frequent use of the Lamb enabled John to transmit the larger complex of his Christological and soteriological teaching through this one symbol: a most convenient symbol to express the doctrine relating to the *Blood of Christ*, for the Blood of the Lamb gives it profound and proper meaning.

The Baptist introduced John to Christ in the words used so commonly in our prayer — "Behold the Lamb of God" (Jn 1:36). The note in the *NAB* suggests that the Baptizer may have had in mind the "great apocalyptic lamb who would destroy evil in the world" (Rv 17:14). The evangelist,

Lamb

By Albert Wider, Widnau, Switzerland, from
"Continente" kindness of Father Loipfinger
(cf. page 101).

Apocalypse

By Franz Nagel, St. Joseph Church, Schweinfurt,
Germany, kindness of Gertrude Rupprecht-Schuering
(cf. page 103).

Cross of Horror

By Germaine Richier in Notre Dame de Toute Grace, Assy, France (cf. page 112).

Veronica
By Rouault, "Miserere," Kunsthalle, Glockengiesser-
wall, Germany (cf. page 149).

Jesus in Agony
Grotto, St. Joseph's College, Indiana (cf. page 127).

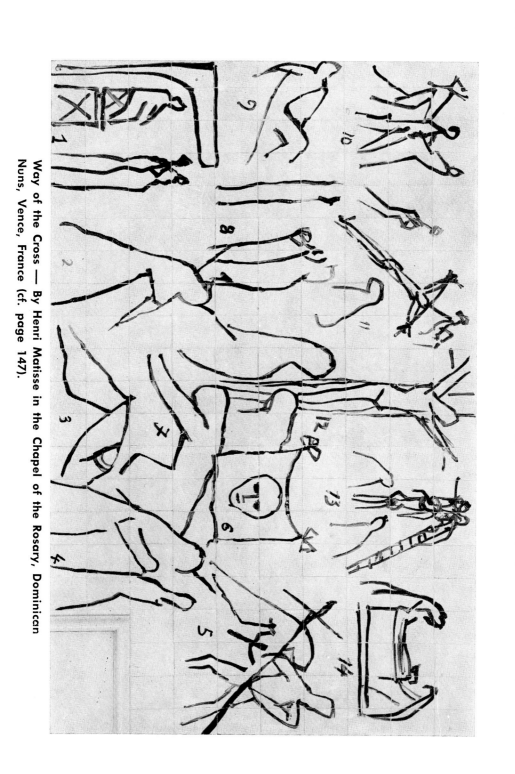

Way of the Cross — By Henri Matisse in the Chapel of the Rosary, Dominican Nuns, Vence, France (cf. page 147).

Cross of Beatitude

By Lioba Munz, O.S.B., in St. Alban, Cologne, Germany (cf. page 113).

Angel of the Father, at top of the Cross of Beatitude.

The Resurrection Scene on the Cross of Beatitude.

according to the same note, may have thought reference was to the Paschal Lamb "and/or" to the Suffering Servant (Is 53:7.10). But surely the title must have clung tenaciously in John's memory, and ultimately may explain his predilection for the image. Undoubtedly its meaning matured and deepened gradually, coming to full realization only after the death of Christ. The image by which John had come to know his Redeemer now became a fitting symbol to introduce Christ to his readers.

When Revelation was written, Christ had already been glorified. This is why John combines both the glory and the suffering of the Savior in one symbol. Customary in John, references to the sufferings of Christ never present them as humiliating experiences. The death always moves in a realm of glory and exaltation. For John, then, the sacrificial death is a reality which is not to be considered apart from the glory coming to Christ through it. *Death of Christ* and *glory of Christ* are joined inseparably as cause and effect. The symbol of the lamb proclaims this double reality: *sacrificial death of Christ* and the *glory attached to it.*

In the grandiose vision of Revelation John sees the enthronement of the Lamb. He sees the Messiah as "the lion of the tribe of Juda" (5:5), and then shifts from lion to lamb, "standing, as if slain", impossible picture, but a clear apocalyptic idea. The background is the Old Testament and the apocryphal apocalyptic literature. The lamb as slain could have its origin in the sacrificial lamb of the Passover, though it was more probably inspired by the Messianic prophecy of the Lamb in Is 53:7. The Servant of Yahweh is the lamb led to the slaughter, offering himself in sacrifice for the sins of his people. And this John wants to convey about Christ pictured as a Lamb, as if *slain.* But he is triumphant, *standing,* with seven horns expressing complete power, for seven was symbol of completeness or perfection. The detail of the horns is derived from the apocryphal *Book of Henoch* where the Messiah is a lamb with great horns leading the people of God to triumph. The Lamb also has seven eyes, a detail borrowed from Zec 4:10, where the eyes of the Lord range through the whole earth. They are symbolic of God's omniscience and wisdom in governing the universe. John also calls the eyes the "seven spirits of God" (Rv 5:6). They symbolize the Holy Spirit. Summing up all, the *Lamb is the triumphant, powerful, sacrificial Christ.* Associated with him is the Holy Spirit whom he sends forth into the world. And the saints proclaim the Lamb in the source of his power: it is the *redemptive Blood* (Rv 5:9). Blood is source of the Lamb's triumphant power, symbol of the triumph of the saints.

The second vision presents the saints (Rv 7:9-17), the multitude with white robes and palms in their hands, washed in the Blood of the Lamb.

They have reenacted in their own lives the twofold phase of the life of the Lamb. Their suffering is indicated by the great tribulations through which they have passed, their victory symbolized by the white robes and the palms. But it is in the *Blood of the Lamb,* not their own blood, that their robes have been made white. The multitude recognizes this as they sing: "Salvation belongs to our God and to the Lamb" (Rv 7:10).

There are other visions of the Lamb in the Book of Revelation, all orientated to the triumph of Christ and his followers. In their totality they embrace all of John's reflections on the Blood of Christ: In this one symbol of the Lamb his teaching is summarized: the Blood and water from the riven side represents his redeeming Blood and the Holy Spirit. The Blood is redemptive Blood, for the saints sing of redemption with Blood (Rv 5:9). It is the source of the Holy Spirit for the seven eyes symbolize the Spirit (Rv 5:6). Note the return to the image of water. The Lamb leads Christians to the fountains of living water. Then paradoxically the Lamb is the shepherd leading the saints to the fountains of the water of life (cf. Rv 7:17). Washing in the *Blood of Christ* and redeeming with that Blood are singled out in the canticles which honor the Lamb (cf. Rv 5:9; 7:10.4). Most significant is light: redemption signifies and effects transition from darkness to light. The splendor of the heavenly city needs neither sun nor moon: God's glory illumines it, and the Lamb is the lamp (Rv 2:23). The Blood of the Eucharist effects the union of the Lamb and the redeemed whose marriage supper is in the heavenly city (Rv 19:7ff).

John calls the apostles, "apostles of the Lamb" (Rv 21:14). That the *Blood of Christ* held a lofty place in the *primitive catechesis* is clear from other New Testament writings as well as from John's. In them the title, "apostles of the Lamb," finds its full justification. John and the other apostles were successful in their pleas that *Christians honor the Blood of Christ*. It is quite plausible that the hymns to the Lamb in the Book of Revelation were songs of the primitive Church. John seems to have inserted them here and there in the book, placing them on the lips of the Church militant and the Church triumphant.

We turn in nostalgia to this picture of the primitive Christian community at prayer gratefully adoring the Blood of the Redeemer. The Christians of the first century sang: "Thou wast slain, and hast redeemed us for God with thy blood . . . Worthy is the Lamb who was slain to receive power and divinity and wisdom and strength and honor and glory and blessing" (Rv 5:9.12). (The above was taken, much abbreviated, from Robert Siebeneck's, *The Precious Blood and Saint John, PBP* I, p. 65-87. The entire article and particularly the notes deserve the most careful study).

THE PASCHAL LAMB

As the Old Testament blood of the paschal lamb freed the Hebrews from the great plagues and Egyptian slavery, so Jesus, the New Testament Paschal Lamb, freed all the world from its sin (Jn 1:29). In the first letter to the Corinthians, Paul calls Christ our *Passover* who has been sacrificed (5:7). More significant is the priestly epistle to the Hebrews, particularly chapters 10 and 11.

Pertinent is the statement of Nikolasch:

Moses prescribed the first pasch and the sprinkling of the door posts with the blood of the lamb in faith. Thereby the first-born of Israel was saved. But the future and hidden, the true Paschal Lamb, which Moses had seen with the eyes of faith, is Christ. Henceforth the hearts of Christians will be sprinkled with the Blood of this Lamb and thus delivered from evil conscience, from evil spirit (Heb 10:22).[13]

We have noted elsewhere that the institution of the Eucharist is placed in the context of the Jewish pasch, the climax of ancient Passover, celebrated by Jesus in fidelity to tradition. Reference to the *cup* reflects the Old Testament covenant and the liberation from sin and slavery. Type emerges into ultimate reality, the true Lamb fulfilling the type and prophecy of the Old Testament.

The historic litanies, the most solemn of liturgical prayers, extol the Lamb of God. Solemn are the chants at ordination and consecration, the doxology (in the Eucharistic liturgy): *Domine Deus, Agnus Dei, Filius Patris, qui tollis peccata mundi,* the touching Eucharistic Communion prayer with the plea for pardon and peace. And the paschal *Exsultet*:

This is the paschal solemnity in which that true Lamb is slain by whose blood the door posts of the faithful are hallowed.[14]

THE ARTIST'S APOCALYPSE

The modern artists revel in the splendor of the Johannine vision. Lothar Schreyer includes two in the work we have already referred to, one by Franz Nagel (between pages 96 and 97) in splendid color, the other by Herbert Boeckle (No. 17 after page 136) often called the *Seckauer Apokalypse*. The author explains the latter at length in his long chapter 13: *Das Christusbild und die eschatologische Verkuendigung (op. cit.,* p. 217ff).

In order not to expand our text unduly we shall stress here the apocalyptic figure of Franz Nagel, which is in the Church of St. Joseph in Schweinfurt, Germany, with a comment drawn from the explanations of Schreyer. These latter, however, go beyond the splendid work of Nagel. The apocalyptic figures refer to the end-time, the Second Coming, the final judgment. Elsewhere we have spoken of the great dragon and the Woman of the Apocalypse who represents the Mother of Christ and of the Church. Central is the Christ in glory, robed in white, the Head of all the redeemed. Such is the Nagel picture. Here too the Lamb has the sacred nimbus indicating the seven eyes. Blood flows from its side and down to the earth. Usually there are four special figures: man, lion, steer, and the eagle. Man refers to the incarnation, the lion to the grandeur and majesty of Christ the King, the steer to the sacrifice and priesthood, the eagle in flight to the proclamation of grace and divine favor spread out to all. High above is the Holy Spirit who indicates the glory and splendor and light, which are the fruit of holy lives. Throughout all the assembled united with Christ, the heavenly Priest celebrates the celestial eternal liturgy high above the barren altar below. There is the greatest diversity in the work of artists, some of the modern suggesting our current technology. Space restricts us to these few comments, as we recommend the study of the picture itself in the light of the Book of Revelation.

[The author regrets that he has not been able to reproduce any of the illustrations in color for the obvious financial restrictions on this work with its limited number of copies].

A Final Note

In some of our great churches the Lamb loomed up in tremendous majesty. It inspired thousands of pilgrims who viewed the ancient St. Peter's at Rome with awe. The basilica of Cosmas and Damian in the Roman Forum suggested to Neunheuser: it is "a genuine theophany . . . comprehending in multiple symbolic content all the mysteries of Christ in one single triumphal vision" (quoted in *The Everlasting Covenant,* p. 275). Imitated in a thousand churches, it has drawn the pious attention to him "who was lifted up for our salvation."

Probably no painting of the Lamb has so entranced the devout pilgrim as the Mystical Lamb in the Belgian cathedral of Ghent, by H. and J. Van Eyck. Unforgettable is the writer's visit to this sacred chapel to venerate the altar of the Lord. The great Eucharistic theologian, Maurice de la Taille, S.J., thus succinctly describes the masterpiece of sacred art:

The Altar of the Lamb

The sin spread over the whole human race of men, from the First Parents, the Lamb washes away through its Blood. This Blood caught up in the Eucharistic chalice he gave to the Church, as he was en-

throned on high, the Eternal Priest according to the order of Melchisedech (*Mysterium Fidei*).

In view of the length and complexity of our discussion on the cross,
we insert here a few pages on the *Icons*, which as we shall see share
something of both lamb and cross, and yet should not be placed under either
heading of lamb or cross. For this reason we speak of them as unique images.

THE ICONS: UNIQUE IMAGES

Icons in the Byzantine liturgy must be considered much more than
images of instruction or the basis for a veneration of God and the saints.
They are looked upon rather as theophanic, in some deep mysterious way
sharing God's epiphany. This is revealed in all salvation history culminating
in the incarnation and the redemptive work of the *Kyrios* and ending in the
parousia. Julius Tyciak tells us:

> In this theophanic structure there is the mystery of the Church as the
> presence of the Lord and his divine salvific work. In the Church and
> her liturgy the coming of the Lord takes place and the parousia looms
> up . . .

As to icons, the same writer speaks of the mystery of the

> icons as a manifestation of transcendent worlds and expression of the
> Christological mystery.
>
> (*Heilige Theophanie*: Reflections on the Cult of the East,
> Paulinus Verlag, Trier, 1959, p. 7).

Above all, the liturgy manifests the mystery of the Church. In it there
pulses her heart beat. The liturgy is her vivifying self-manifestation. Salvation itself under the veil of mystery is contained in her sacred liturgy.
Through the salvific acts of the divine *economia* the Church manifests herself as the great universal fellowship of the glorified world. Thus the Church
herself is a mystery in that dual sense of the intellectual and cultal (cf.
ibid., p. 9).

> The icon fashioned in prayer and fasting is a kind of theophany. In
> it we meet the mystery of the God who stoops down to us. This mys-
> tery and as well the intelligible meaning of the icon is best disclosed
> by the liturgy. For the liturgy is indeed the making-present of the
> divine salvation among us. And the multiple forms and modes, the
> sacred sounds and rhythms, the pictures, the words and symbols par-
> ticipate in the mystery idiom. They proclaim the hidden realities of
> a world beyond, which reaches out to us in sacral service. In the midst

of this manifold living reality (*Organismus*) is the *icon* as manifestation, speech, countenance of a divine reality which reveals itself only under the veil of mystery. And indeed the liturgy has dedicated a special feast to the mystery of the icon (*ibid.*, p. 19f).

Tyciak speaks of this feast as commemorating the victory of the forces of orthodoxy over the Iconoclasts. Its meaning is strictly *Christological* and *soteriological*. Moreover it is comparable to the Feast of Corpus Christi in the Latin Church. The liturgical hymn sung on the great feast reveals the meaning of the veneration of the icons:

> The Word Unlimited, of the Father, was limited insofar as He became man and united the image of man, who had fallen, with the divine beauty and led it back again to the original condition (*ibid.*, p. 20).

The writer continues:

> The icon is a manifestation, fashioned in form and color, of the true hypostatic unity of divinity and humanity in Christ. It participates in the *incarnation* and through it the divine glory (*doxa*) looms up. At the same time it leads man back into the original, divinely given beauty. Hence it is itself a salvation-history sign (*ibid.*, p. 20ff).

The icon is a divine "Mystery" — "Cultal Mystery" — uniting the heavenly and the earthly, the divine and temporal.

> What is wrought in the sacramental forum, the presence of the divine salvation, is reflected in the icons, above all in the sacral realm of the cultal structure (*Kultbau*), though it enters also into the private sphere of everyday life. It has nothing to do with magic . . . The relation of original with representation is in no way to be grasped in any material or psychological sense. It lies beyond all categories of this perceptible reality and transcends it. Only believing man experiences in a mystical communication the salvific relationship of icon and the original reality (*Urbild*). Only the *empiricism of faith* has entry. Therefore only the blessing of the icon makes the "icon" (*ibid.*, p. 21).

Significant in all this is the invocation of the Holy Spirit by the Church. Hereby the icons become bearers of the "divine energies." As members of the Mystical Body, the men of "believing heart" are affected by all the movements in the Church. By her blessing of the icon the Church places all who venerate them in the circle of her own loving prayer world. The believer, the viewer, the man of prayer is united with the celestial world visible in the icon, as it is audible in the Sacred Scripture.

> In the theology of the icon there reigns the living Christian thought, that through incarnation of the Son of God all things are consecrated.

In that the Son of God assumed man as *microcosm* in personal unity with himself, he sanctified therewith the *macrocosm*. In man all levels of being come together, he gathers all together. Therefore the holy Fathers harkening to Paul say that Christ came in order to embrace *ALL* under one *HEAD* and to renew it in himself. Hence, the icon is to be understood only from the *theiosis*, the divinization of the world. The glorification of the world rests on the totally and exclusively non-Platonic incarnation in the Johannine sense (*ibid.*, p. 23).

The icon is a kind of "sacramental" sign of our encounter with the invisible world. Not at all governed by the rules of art such as relate to perspective or plastic effort, the icon seems flat and lacking in depth. The chosen colors are usually red-gold, sun-gold, and turquoise, which express the glorification beyond the earthly and establish the living relation of the transitory world of the here and now with the heavenly realities.

Significant for our study is the relation of the icon to the redemptive order: "Salvation history taken in its entirety, the world of the renewed cosmos, of grace and sacraments, is the actual image of the invisible which radiates from the countenance of Jesus Christ, the great WORLD ICON," (*ibid.*, p. 25). In recent times Bulgakow has constructed a cosmic and salvific approach to the mystery of the icon:

The Son of God is the Image of the Father as uncreated Wisdom. Created Wisdom is the ALL-MAN, the SOPHIA, the created icon of God. This was renewed in Christ, as the uncreated and the created Wisdom met in the incarnation unto personal union and thus again restored the WORLD ICON eternally loved and beheld by God. Beyond the Wisdom doctrine, which appears as a more imaginative than logically unambiguous expression of thought, looms the grandiose thought of the Predestination of Christ. He is the primordial image (*Urbild*) of the total cosmos, in whom all is created and redeemed. This is described in the comprehensive cosmological-Christological vision of the letter to Colossians: "He is the image of the invisible God, the first-born of all creatures. In him everything in heaven and on earth was created, things visible and invisible, whether thrones or dominations, principalities or powers; all were created through him, and for him. He is before all else that is. In him everything continues in being" (I, 15-17), (*ibid.*, p. 26).

These pages on icons should profoundly enrich our reflection on images in our liturgical worship and our whole prayer life, and thus deepen our spirituality of the Precious Blood.

THE CROSS

The cross in the most varied forms is found even in non-Christian culture and bears the most diverse meanings, such as power of the sun, redemption, predestination, death, life, paradise, etc. Its symbolic use appears in both primitive and advanced civilization and in such widely diverse areas as India, Etruria, and Peru. The national significations, we are told, "are not abrogated but rather deepened and purified by the development of Christian symbolism" (*NCE*, art. "Cross", Vol. 4, p. 473). In Christian history the cross has become the central symbol of the Christian faith and the proclamation of the mystery of the redemption. In the Christian context an instrument of the most exquisite torture becomes an integral part of the biblical message of salvation, committed to us in the apostolic preaching.

Biblical Meaning

In the gospels the term *cross* is almost exclusively the cruel instrument of passion and death. The gospels give the account of the *way of the cross* and the crucifixion (cf. Mt 27, Mk 15, Lk 23, Jn 19). For Paul the cross is the whole redemptive mystery centering in Christ's bloody death. In 1 Cor 1:18 when he speaks of the "message of the cross" he means the total Christian message with its tremendous paradox (absurdity-wisdom-weakness-power). If through the cross and the death on the cross, Paul is crucified to the world and the world to him (Gal 6:14), then every Christian must also die with Christ in baptism in order to rise to a new life (Rom 6:3ff). The cross with its death is the source of our life. The whole redemptive thought may be summed up in the poignant term *theologia crucis,* with its marked stress of the passion and death in Christ and in us.

In the distress and anguish of our times, we ponder this *theologia crucis* when God remains hidden to so many. In most instances we feel that they are what Rahner would optimistically call "anonymous Christians." We think, he feels that they do not truly and totally deny God, though God is hidden from them. For such our Precious Blood spirituality and its *kerygma* must proclaim a unique *theologia crucis.* We ponder Paul, 1 Cor 1:17ff, for our theme. For the Jews who demand *signs* and the Greeks who search for *wisdom,* the impotent helpless God-incarnate (*stumbling block to the Jews and folly to the Gentiles*) was indeed for all men — Jew and Gentile — the power of God and wisdom of God.

For Martin Luther, the sinner (all of us) can grasp God only under this paradox. God's power is manifest in the omnipotence of the cross. His grace is revealed in his wrath, his benevolence only in trial and plague. God hides himself in incarnation and cross and precisely thereby manifests the basic law of his presence in the world. This is not the very essence of God, which is mercy and love, but rather his reaction to man the sinner. Faith in constant combat pierces through the paradox to the loving God. Today man in his existential anguish and his quest for God must seek him and can find him in the incarnate Son, the impotent God-man who is indeed the power of God and the wisdom of God. Our Precious Blood spirituality in its *kerygma* and its prayer and in its meditation must — with loving faith and hope — find through the cross, its impotence, its condescension, that infinitely profound wisdom and power, for the omnipotent God speaks to us through the weakness and folly of the cross.

DEVOTION TO THE CROSS

The devotion may assume many forms, but historically there are *three* principal areas of cult and interior devotion: the honor to the *True Cross;* the veneration of the *sacred images* of the cross fashioned in the most diverse ways; and the *sacred use of the cross* as sign and gesture in prayer blessing (of self, objects, in sacramentals, sacraments, liturgical sacrifice, etc.) and daily life and worship.

THE TRUE CROSS

Historically, the finding of the True Cross profoundly influenced the devotion to the holy cross throughout Christendom. No other relic of the passion and death could be so precious as the crude wooden cross on which the Savior had been suspended for hours and which was stained with the priceless Blood of our redemption. The beautiful liturgy of its feasts, especially the Good Friday veneration awakens a deep love for the Savior who died on the cross. The sorrowful mysteries of the rosary, the stations or way of the cross, and many other prayer forms directed to the cross, all are calculated to create a love of the cross.

The Feast of the Exaltation or Triumph of the Cross, celebrated on Sept. 14th has the most glorious hymns in all the Church's prayers. Throughout, the Church has in mind the cross as a real symbol of our redemption. And her veneration, especially on Good Friday, is called *adoration,* or *latria,* which is paid to God alone. But this veneration is usually called *relative latria,* for we direct our worship through the cross to the God, the God-man who died on the cross — who is worthy of the infinite honor in worship. (As to the many accounts on the finding of the cross, cf. *NCE*, Cross, Finding of the Holy, Vol. 4, p. 479).

CROSS AND CRUCIFIX

The cross — as we speak of it here — is an image or figure of the True Cross on which Jesus died. Historically and artistically (symbolically) it has assumed countless variations in Christian history. The *crucifix* — also with

many variations in Christian veneration — is the cross with the image of
the Savior suspended upon it. Both may be presented in a diversity of media,
from crude and simple wood or stone (forms or lines) to the elegance of
precious metals and gems and artistry. The cross or crucifix in the history
of the Church's devotion to her Savior presents many facets, e.g., the body
of the Savior may be depicted as triumphant, as suffering in great agony,
as fully clothed, or bearing only a loin cloth, but all have essentially the same
theological basis and significance: liturgically and religiously they reflect the
redemptive death. Kerygmatically, they are on the level of popular instruction and edification. The purpose of the image is to proclaim who dwells in
our mind and heart.

The history of the cross has had its period of great splendor —
represented by the glorified cross, by the rich mosaic of Santa Pudenziana
of Rome and San Apollinare in Classe at Ravenna, and the gold cross of
Justin II — and its period of violent persecution, often resulting in the
destruction of superb beauty (cf. *NCE*, Vol. 4, art. "Cross," p. 473ff).

The use of the cross as private and public adornment, as object of veneration in our public places, or as symbol of faith and reverence in churches
and in public worship (e.g. processional crosses) testifies to our loving devotion to Christ who has redeemed us with his Blood. The cross is the instrument of instruction, object of religious veneration, and witness to the
Christ who is in our heart.

SIGN OF THE CROSS

Tracing the cross on one's forehead was customary as a private act of
prayer or devotion already in the second century. In the fourth century it
"came into wide use in the liturgy." A signing of the lips is indicated in the
eighth century. Our large sign of the cross customary today dates back to
the fifth century. In the Eastern churches the use of two or three fingers
indicated the two natures in Christ, the three persons in the divine Trinity.
It expresses diversity of meaning especially in the liturgical services, means
dedication to God, points to sacred deeds and meanings (in Mass, etc.), begins and concludes sacred functions: the cross is truly the beginning and end
of all things. We note, ecumenically, that Martin Luther advised the Christian to begin and end the day with the sign of the cross (cf. Dr. Michael
Buchberger, *Aufbruch zur Einheit und Einigkeit im Glauben,* p. 38, Herder,
Freiburg, 1948).

A COROLLARY

In many sacred places in the world honor is paid to the Precious Blood
through the veneration of sacred relics, instruments of the passion, or other

objects connected with the Savior's life on earth or with marvellous manifestations of the Eucharistic presence. We mention only the Precious Blood Shrine with its relics and pageantry at Bruges in Belgium, the sacred Veil of Veronica, the Lance, the Cup (claimed to be displayed in the Cloisters in New York), the miraculous hosts, etc. We call attention to the extensive research made by Charles Banet, C.PP.S., which is only too briefly treated in our Precious Blood Proceedings. In a series of articles in *Il Sangue della redenzione,* William A. Volk, C.PP.S., treats the *Precious Blood in the Liturgy,* including the *Sanctuaries and Relics of the Precious Blood.* To our mind the most fascinating and convincing of all the relics is the *Shroud of Turin* which is discussed in an extensive literature of its own, as noted in the article on Holy Shroud, in the *NCE,* Vol. 13, p. 187ff.

(The traditional teaching on the *triduum mortis,* the period after Jesus' death preceding the resurrection, holds that the Logos was separated neither from the body nor from the blood. At resurrection soul, body, blood, were all reunited. Such particles of flesh or blood which remained on earth are no longer united to the divinity, but must be considered sacred relics to which a *relative latria* is due as we explained above. Cf. *Precious Blood Proceedings,* Vol. I, especially pp. 109ff, 229ff, 235ff, 244ff. We present this traditional view, but do not take up the controversial resurrection teaching of certain present day writers).

For the doctrine on *descent into hell* as found in professions of faith the writer refers the reader to *NCE* Vol. 4, art. *"Descent of Christ into Hell,"* p. 788ff. cf. also Ratzinger, *op. cit.,* p. 223. He relates it to the death of God, the silence of God, and the utter loneliness of man. The Christ who descended into hell "established the nearness of God in the midst of abandonment by God" (p. 227).

THE CROSS: HORRIFYING AND BEATIFYING

It is horrifying that men condemn the God-Man and put him to death. Even more horrifying, this act is a *sacrifice* which men have offered their God. Nor does the free consent of the God-Man-Victim, or the fulfillment of the divine plan by which the God-Man offered himself as a sacrifice to expiate man's sins remove the horror. We are permitted to experience the incomprehensibly divine-human love, and in it, in the making present of the oblation on the cross, we behold the *mystery of the cross* which we may express in words and fashion in concrete perceptible images. In faith we seek through images of human oblation to point out the divine-human sacrifice. Only in horror of soul can the true reality assume form and be manifested. By faith what we view in horror becomes vision of blessedness, if redemption through the Savior's sacrifice moves us, and faith and conviction of the triumph of Christ over sin and death penetrates our mind and heart.

Between being-cast-down through the death of Christ on the cross and being-raised-up through the triumph on the cross, we experience in faith, the tension of the here-and-now, on earth. This is the *passover* of Christ, the Pascha, the summons and the support for imitation of Christ, hope for coming home (*op. cit.*, p. 186). All this is suggested by the *two crosses*.

CROSS OF HORROR

Shock and scandal was aroused by the huge crucifix of *Germaine Richier* (born 1904, died 1959) in the Church of Notre Dame de toute Grace in Assy, France(the story of the church's construction itself and the cooperation of the most noted artists is fascinating, cf. Schreyer, *op. cit.*, p. 149ff). Confronting us is a figure scarcely resembling anything human. With passionate gesture of submission the arms are stretched out in inexpressible suffering. The body is numbed, withered, scorched to red bronze, like the figures strewn on the streets of German cities after the bombings of World War II. Visitors were horrified, the episcopal authorities were practically forced to remove this *scandal of the cross*. But strangely enough, the sick, of whom there were thousands in the area, pleaded for their Christ: "He is our Christ, piteous and merciful." Eventually by direction of the Holy See itself the cross was returned (*op. cit.*, p. 188f).

P. Pie Régamey, noted authority on the new art in France, insists that after the first shock a more moderate and reflective mood viewing the work in total context should lead to a more meaningful impression: *massive* radiance proclaims the great triumphal movement, the glorious bronze, the imposing dimensions, and the solemn dignity soon lead to a grasp of the deeper meaning. Sharply the critic notes that we are faced here with the paradox of every crucifix: to reconcile the *tragedy* with the *glory*. If we ponder the Germaine Richier crucifix in the light of Jesus' great cry of victory,

No one takes it (my life) from me;
I lay it down freely (Jn 10:18).

If we marvel, as we should, how the artist succeeded in reconciling the shame of the cross with the regal sacrifice of Christ, then we cannot fail to recognize in this work of art one of the most convincing interpretations of the great mystery which our faith ponders and which no form of sculpture can ever exhaustively present (*ibid.*, p. 188).

In the light of this cross the sin of mankind which the God-Man took upon himself is burnt up, annihilated, and the human nature of Christ is glorified in the ultimate sacrificial gesture of the love-embrace. Those who pray before this crucifix may and can ponder it only in the totality and unity of cross and human image. Here pictorial proclamation, our object of interior and exterior meditation, manifests the transformation of the self-giving and self-offering, earthly-corporeal human image into the glorified human image of the God-Man. Here is the mystery which manifests itself symbolically in the transformation into the Cross of Light.

Paschal triumph is not possible without the devastating shock of the death on the cross. As the human image is corporeally demolished by this shock and death dissolves the human body, and the terrifying proclamation in image attests thereto, so also do the proclamations in word regarding the death on the cross. In fact in the new word-art of the 20th century, which is called *expressionistic* or *abstract,* human words are literally shattered, torn to tatters, as we note in such works as Erich Przywara's *Karfreitagsliturgie* and Paul Claudel's paschal poem (*ibid.,* p. 189f).

CROSS OF BEATITUDE

Only from the terrifying vision can the beatifying vision of the Crucified emerge and draw us to the goal, the mystery of Christ, the support of prayer, progress on the way to the perfection of the heavenly Father (cf. Mt 5:48). Profoundly moved by the suffering of the Sinless One who took upon himself the guilt and sin of men in order to redeem them from guilt and sin, men endure their own suffering in the suffering of Christ. Such realization is a call of grace, which hurls men into the night of sense, of understanding, of will, even annihilating them until they become conscious of the love of God in the very realization of alienation from creatures. Admission of guilt turns to sorrow and penitence. In the life of the soul the shattering experience of annihilation is transformed into the certainty of sorrowful participation in salvation through the crucified Savior. In hope man now sees in the cross of death the sign of life, with the vision of blessedness.

If experienced inwardly, this transformation is proclaimed outwardly in the Cross of Beatification by those who possess the charism to preach and fashion the cross of Christ. Words and works are signs of salvation, witness of divine love, gift of grace to the world in order that the world in its experience of shock cease to yield to skeptical doubt but rise to exultant hope in the death on the cross, hope in the glory of resurrection. Such was the charism of the Benedictine nun, Lioba Munz of St. Maria at Fulda to whom we owe the gemmed Cross at St. Alban at Cologne (1958, cf. no. 9, *op. cit.,* p. 191ff). The beauty of the cross with its precious jewels radiates the beauty of the world renewed in Christ. Embraced in symbol is the world of stone, of plants, animals, men and angels.

The noblest metal, gold, shines like the sun. Precious crystals glow in deep rich clusters in contrast to the dark ebony of the tree of the cross. The animal world appears to adore at the crib of the Son of God. The world of man makes its submission through the Virgin and Mother Mary: *Ave Maria.* In the center is the figure of the *Kyrios enthroned* in the midst of the crucified and transfigured world. At the *foot of the cross* in sharp relief is the Annunciation to Mary. Her's is the great beatitude: *gratia plena,* full of grace: By the word of the angel there nestles in her hands, in her bosom the Dove of the Holy Spirit. In dove-white robe the angel appears shadowed round with the green of mysterious hope, wings dipped in the color of sacrifice, burnished in the flames of heavenly love. In his left hand he bears the Cross of Triumph, as the right points to the Virgin entirely veiled in the blue light of faith, Maid of the Lord and Bride of the Holy Spirit.

The Nativity Scene, at the end of the cross beam to the right of the Lord, tells of the birth of the God-Man in the golden night in the circle of the blue light. The Mother in the rich warmth of faith and sacrifice looks on the Child swaddled in bright cloth in a stone crib with the ox and the ass huddling close, for animals see the Redeemer and will share salvation.

To the left the Resurrection Scene proclaims the victory over sin and death. The grave is empty: the Victor has arisen. The holy women will wander about with their spices, all excited on this golden morn. They will follow him into the blessedness of the celestial realm to which the mighty angel still sitting at the tomb raises his left hand as with the right he clutches the cross of the risen Lord.

From above on the Cross of Blessing the angel of the Father seems to dash downward binding with beatifying gesture the world redeemed with the heaven of God. The world redeemed is led home through the great Restorer and Renewer of creation. In the golden radiance of the heavenly sun the Lord *Kyrios,* enthroned, raises his right hand in blessing, his left holds the Book of Life, resting on his left knee. He rests his feet upon a sphere, dark, blossoming with stars, olive-green, red-brown and blue-green, the stone in the center a brilliant opal. At the head of the *Kyrios* to right and left pure rock crystals turn attention to the glassy sea of the Apocalypse.

The Cross of Earth has transformed itself into a four-rayed star of heaven. Facing the faithful is the movement of the triumph of the incarnate God aloft to Son of God and *Kyrios* enthroned above the redeemed earth and the new heavens. Facing the celebrant at the altar is the most profound mystery of the incarnation: Christ the High Priest unveils before him the tremendous reality, that he, the incarnate God as *Kyrios* remains on God's throne as the Lord of sacrifice and the Oblation itself. He remains ever the Crucified with the marks of his wounds, arms ever extended, always to offer himself.

The great aureola (often called the *gloria*) glimmering in the burning carneole reflects the splendor of the glorified flesh. Thus is made visible the resurrection of the flesh, the exaltation and transfiguration of human nature through Christ in the bliss of Christ who shall die for us to the end of the ages. The four rays of the cross directed into all the world glow with the clarity and tenderness of the divine love symbolized by the splendid quartz and crystal.

The cross is suspended in the sanctuary (*Altarraum*) before a wall of stones from demolished walls, rebuilt from wreckage, which truly symbolized the wreckage of our crumbling world. Here hangs the Cross of Benediction, the Sign of Light, before which we pray: *Ave Crux, Spes Unica. Hail, O Cross, Our Only Hope!* We pray these four words before the cross which shocked and terrified us at Assy and also before the beatifying cross at Cologne. The man of today lives in tension between the two: terror and blessing. It must be his hope that the horror and terror awaken in him the anticipation that the cross of blessing be opened to him in love. Only the grace of the Crucified grants this prayer: May the Crucified harken to it as we kneel before the Lord of the cross. (Synthesized and adapted from *op. cit.,* pp. 186-195).

CHAPTER EIGHT

THE PRECIOUS BLOOD SPIRITUALITY
MEDITATION   PRAYER

*All Christians Must Spend Some Time Daily in Prayer
and Reflection on the Divine Truth. Such Prayer and
Reflection Must Lead to That Deep Interior Union with
God Which Is Breathed into Our Hearts by the Spirit of
Love, Who Is the Bond of Union Between Father and Son.*

A WORD OF INTRODUCTION

SOLITUDE IN SILENCE: THE ATMOSPHERE OF PRAYER AND MEDITATION

The Christian experience looks to *sacred silence* as essential to the ideal
of prayer and meditation. In the sense of environmentalism it shuts out
the clamor of the crowd, the nerve-shattering hum and hiss of the machine,
auto, plane. But in the sense of *sacred silence* linking the Christian to God,
we have the union with him in prayer. He calls to us in this sacred silence
and we respond with constantly increasing depth of love through prayer and
meditation. Only in such silence (solitude) can the Christian truly enter
into himself.

There are times when the Holy Spirit moves us to silence and solitude: in preparation for accepting the call to sacred order, to the holy vow,
to new resolutions in great crisis in our spiritual life. But also, to the silence
preceding the sacred liturgy, the reception of holy Communion, or the other
sacraments. There are times set apart for silence by the Church herself in
the holy rule of religious communities: some held to perpetual silence as
unique example for the Christians who can conceive of nothing too sacred
for chatter. The very term often used for the special, deep silence of religious
communities is awe-inspiring: THE GREAT SILENCE — *Silentium Magnum.*

We may look to the eternal silence of God as that endless eternity before
he uttered the word of creation through the Word. We may and should look

to the *silence of Jesus*: the silent nights of communication with his heavenly Father. Above all we must ponder the *silence of Gethsemani* which enclosed the Prayer-to-the-Father-for-Unity, and was followed by the dread silence of his patience in the scourging, the crowning with thorns, the standing alone in shame on Calvary. This silence and this prayer in agony, we may call the *great canon* of the Sacrifice-of-the-Cross. Throughout all of this, we think of the *world's gesture,* half in contempt, half in pity: BEHOLD THE MAN. Our hearts must cry out to him in silence too deep for words. We behold the *Man,* the *Perfect Man* with all our love.

We ponder the silence of Mary and Joseph. According to Luke (2:51), Mary kept in her memory the scene of Jesus in the temple. She kept in her memory all his agonies which were also her own. We ponder and recall our American Precious Blood tradition, of almost perpetual silence amid work and prayer. A lesson today!

But silence is linked not only with prayer, but also with speech in charity, for silence can be rude and offensive, can be linked with pride of self-priority. The silence of sacred atmosphere, of prayer and meditation is also the silence of gentle speech that gives others no pain. With this silence is the firm word against injustice, praise for justice and truth. Our Precious Blood spirituality makes this silence its own.

As devout reflection on the realities and truths of faith, *meditation* arouses fervor and promotes holiness. It should always be in the context of prayer, vocal or recitative, interior and free, individual and practical. To be effective it must go beyond occasional spontaneous reflection — though this is profitable and desirable — for method and plan are of its essence. But both method and plan should not be merely external, artificially contrived, much less externally imposed. Imagination, memory, emotion, intellect, all enter. But always the interior man in his relation to God must be basic. Meditation assumes many forms according to the diverse spiritualities and attitudes of groups and individuals. The context of the Precious Blood meditation is apparent from these pages. Obviously the Precious Blood prayer pattern will be reflected in the Precious Blood meditation.

The meditation will be Christocentric. The themes — we insist on many themes —are to be pondered largely in relation to the life and death of Jesus, to his total redemptive work. As we have already indicated, and shall again point out in relation to Precious Blood prayer, the reflection on the Trinity, the *theologia* must penetrate into the *economia,* the incarnation-redemption. The ultimate in all meditation is strikingly expressed by G. Ruemke:

God is the Ultimate Ground of our being, the Ever-Sought-After-By-Man. The human countenance of God is Jesus of Nazareth, who died the *death of hope for us*. In the depth of the existence of every individual there glows the light of God: the Holy Spirit. Therefore humanity is a community which is one in God, for salvation is for all (G. Ruemke in *TR* no. 6, 1972, col. 482).

In our Precious Blood meditation we ponder how Christ comes forth from God bringing the God-life to man, his human-divine life, blesssing all human activity with the mercy of his grace. In meditation, the Precious Blood meditation, we reach out to this Jesus-life enlightened by his Spirit. We seek to make all stages of his life our own. We ponder the thought of Aquinas, to which we refer frequently in these pages, that the acts of Jesus' life (and his sufferings) are efficacious unto our salvation and for this we constantly pray. His presence in his Mother's womb sanctifies every infant-waiting-to-be-born, his infancy sanctifies all infancy, his childhood all children, his manhood all men and women. His work makes all work sacred, his joys become our joy, his tears bless our sorrow, his play our play and recreation, his rest and sleep our repose, and finally his agony the agony of our suffering, his dying our death. On all this we ponder in our meditation. Union with Jesus is not merely the memory of what he has done for mankind — though it must surely be this — nor is it a past cause of a present effect and no more. It is the now-with-us in the Jesus-presence-and-action in the Church and among all mankind, in and through his Holy Spirit.

We call the reader's attention to the profound insight of Walter Kasper (*Einfuehrung in den Glauben*) which can be expanded in personal application: the meaning of Jesus must be, indeed, the meaning of Jesus for me. Unique is the redemptive act; that which is for all men is as totally for me as though I alone were saved. Taking up the concept of St. Thomas More as the Man for all Seasons, we think of Jesus as the Man for all men/women, the meaning for all meaning. How tremendous the concept of every group of men and women pondering Jesus as the ideal (supreme helper) in every stage, state, event of their lives! The meaning of Jesus would become the meaning of their lives. What shall we say of his love for Mary and Joseph, of his obedience to them (when we find obedience difficult and almost impossible), of his utter submission to God his Father, his guidance by the Holy Spirit whom we seem to forget in proportion to our very need for his help?

We speak so flippantly of *doing our thing*. He did the *supreme thing*, the redemption of our world. That too is our purpose, the one-and-only. What shall we say of making ourselves, all things we say and do, *meaningful* through the Jesus meaning? The early Christians spoke of their life as the *way*. All we do is in this, the *Christian way*.

Such is our functional Christology, stressing less the ontic, nature-and-person, than the purpose of Jesus, God-man, sent to us. Bringing the Trinity into our whole lives, we can offer the chalice of Jesus-Blood to the Father in the very sharing of its fruits with our fellow men in a supreme Jesus-love. We must dare to open a totally new mode of existence, flowing directly from our Catholic-Christian faith, from our Precious Blood spirituality. It will enter us into the heart of Jesus as into the hearth of his Blood. This and all things we would ponder — and do — in Jesus' name.

A CONCLUSION

Like prayer, meditation always reflects the call of God, the offering of his grace, and our response. The response directed even to the physical sufferings of Jesus has made these the object of meditation of many saints. Pondering the physical sufferings of Jesus, however, must direct our gaze to what is even more important, the interior suffering, the soul-searing dread in the agony in the garden, the desolation in the mockery of the cross. These we must relate to the anguish of our minds in solitude and forsakenness, particularly in our old age and final illness. In every instance the thought of the passion must lead to the profound piety of the saints. For our age, for every age, the Precious Blood spirituality must be linked with the inner sufferings of the Christ, with the broken heart from which flowed his Blood.

The thought of our union with Jesus has never been expressed so tenderly and realistically as by Newman:

> Christ himself vouchsafes to repeat in each of us in figure and mystery all that he did and suffered in the flesh. He is formed in us, born in us, suffers in us, rises again in us, lives in us; and this not by a succession of events, but all at once: for he comes to us as a Spirit, all dying, all rising again, all living (*Parochial Sermons*, V, 139, quoted in *Inscape* p. 72).

Meditation on the passion and death of Jesus is the basis for the contemplation in which the soul casts aside the world and worldly things to enter into immediate and tranquil union with God. Infused contemplation is a great gift of divine grace by which God communicates himself directly to the soul through his incarnate Son and in his Holy Spirit. Even though we conceive of grace as Uncreated Grace, this mystical union with God is not in itself the Beatific Vision, although even in the Beatific Vision the glorified Christ does enter not as medium but as *disposing cause* in the soul in glory.

The thought is Rahner's: because Christ redeemed all creation in an infinite continuous love, Christian mysticism does not mean a rejection or denial of the world, but rather an embracing of the world in a most intimate, immediate, personal encounter with "the personal God" (*TD*, art.

"Mysticism," 301ff). The way to genuine mysticism is surely arduous and its final stage is indeed the purest vision of God possible in this life, for it is not through figures, pictures, images, but direct "seeing" though it be encompassed in the dark night of the soul.

The Precious Blood spirituality through its meditation and contemplation, God granting his grace, leads to this union with God. Such is the deeper meaning of Christ, his function in relation to his Father and the Holy Spirit. We begin with the deep realization that the incarnate Son, our Redeemer through his Blood, is the perfect revelation of the Father, and only through him are we taken up in a new life communicated in the Holy Spirit — all this is basic to our Precious Blood spirituality which we must all seek to practice in the very beginning of our Precious Blood meditation.

PRAYER

Our dear Lord gives us his own beloved prayer in which we unite with him in addressing his Father, who is our God, as *Our Father*. We find the account in both Luke (11:1ff) and Matthew (6:9ff). We are almost shocked at the Lucan account, for it is so casual. One day Jesus was praying in a certain place. Gently the disciples waited so as not to interrupt him, then one of them asked, "Lord, teach us to pray, as John taught his disciples." We should much like to know — the pious are often most curious — where it was that the Lord was praying, who of the disciples made the simple request, which all of us should make, *teach us to pray*. And what was the special prayer of John the Baptist? The entire scene is so casual, prayer is taken for granted, as that we eat and drink, go about properly clothed in association with our fellowmen. But most of all that Jesus, the Man Who Prayed, should teach us *how to pray*.

All this suggests the one basic question for this little rubric on prayer: WHAT IS PRAYER? Up to now, we think we may say, that theology has given us no simple definition of prayer comprizing all its essential elements, though men deeply experienced in prayer have treated it in depth and breadth. At all times men of every faith have made prayer an important element in their lives. But prayer is a deep mystery involving man's most profound relation to the transcendent God of revelation who has called us from darkness to divine inaccessible light, who has redeemed us from slavery of sin and led us to divine friendship itself. The mystery of prayer, according to Rahner, finds in nature no analogue. It is not reflected in figures of nature or nature's world. It flows from the divine summons, and calls man to the friendship of familiar intercourse with God. Hence, we do have what we might call two classic definitions of prayer: to speak to God, to raise heart and mind to God. Though intimate and love-filled, it means surrender to the absolute transcendent love itself.

Prayer lies at the heart of man's true existence. Resting in sacrifice, it is the noblest act of man, basic to our religion by which we honor God. In prayer we turn to the God who revealed himself through his Son, enlightened us with the Spirit of Jesus who taught us how to pray. Because God has reached out to man, offering him the covenant of his love, has built his tent among us, prayer is never merely external; it is always most profoundly personal and intimate, and also communal. In the Old Testament Yahweh called Abraham, made him the father of a great people, and in his deliverance of them from Egypt formed with them a covenant made with their father.

This covenanted people in its relation to Yahweh became a people of prayer, of sacred law, of divine promise. Their grateful consciousness of the mighty deeds of Yahweh prompted them to turn to him in their needs, to look forward to the final triumph of the One-Who-Was-to-Come. Their prayer, found in inspired writings, consists largely of the Book of Psalms which praise the greatness of the Lord, thank him for his help, admit guilt and weakness, and beg the Lord for help in all needs.

In the New Testament the covenant by which God fashioned his people in the prior covenant through the blood of animals became the new and eternal covenant sealed by the Blood of God's own Son. All men, redeemed through his Blood, became the covenanted people. The New Testament prayer centered them in God's own Son, in the prayer of Jesus: in the desert, in the Sermon on the Mount, in Gethsemani and Calvary. In our name he spoke in the familiarity of infinite love for us and with us to the Father. All prayer of Christians, henceforth, is through Christ the Lord.

We think of our prayer as *ascent to God* and *dialogue with God* and usually list adoration or praise, thanksgiving, petition, and propitiation as forms of prayer. Though these points are very simply stated there is a vast history of prayer and prayer-practice in the Church bound up with holy lives and the guidance of the Church and her theologians and religious leaders. Always there is the reflection on the revealed truth and the sacred forms. In a recent work dealing with prayer in its continued developments and continued existence, Josef Andreas Jungmann, S.J., presents us with an enlightening account of prayer throughout Christian history (*Christliches Beten im Wandel und Bestand,* Verlag Ars Sacra, Munich, 1969).

For our study two things are particularly meaningful: *First,* the Christian prayer throughout the ages has been in constant development; changing forms reflected dogmatic or doctrinal attitudes. *Secondly,* the changes also suited the moods and needs of the times, of the Church and religious structure. It must follow that we in our present age, which differs so radically from all previous ages, must reflect the changes in our prayer and prayer forms. The very history of prayer is itself a model of instruction. Jungmann himself concludes his work with the reference to the profound shock to which our present-day Christian prayer has been exposed. What we would call the laws of science now dominate the world. God himself has been pressed unto the "rim of reality." There is present an attitude of scepticism which passes prayer by as "superfluous," and as it "undermines the foundation of faith" also undermines the "desire for prayer." As many of us in recent times, Jungmann deplores the presumptuous, arbitrary striving for novelties on the part of some which has resulted in a sad religious impoverishment. But, in a note of optimism he also sees an enlightenment of spirit on the part of many, with prayer arising from steadfast hearts. How many today truly look up to the Christ who taught us to pray, who has gone before us, through whom we praise the Father in his Son and their Holy Spirit (*op. cit.*, p. 166ff). We add with Madeleine Delbrêl that the "godless tumult of our industrial world is a constant provocation inciting us to prayer" (*TR*, 1976, no. 1, Col. 72).

Oratio Continua

We are admonished to *pray always*. This continuous prayer is not to be understood in an absolutely literal sense (some bizarre-minded men did actually take the words literally). We suggest that the sacred injunction implies a certain totality in our prayer, the fulfillment of all the precepts of prayer, the turning to prayer on all occasions of trial or crisis in our lives, the involvement of our whole selves, mind and heart and to a degree our bodies in prayer. (Jungmann has many insights into the gestures connected with prayer, the raising of our hands, the various bodily postures, standing, kneeling, etc. Actually kneeling at prayer is rather late in the history of prayer). The great saints lived in an atmosphere of prayer through a consciousness of God's presence. Though we should constantly seek to imitate the saints, we should not be too disturbed, as older people often are, because of "distraction" in prayer. But we can always grow in the spirit of prayer, enter into the deep silence through which we communicate with God and reach out to him as he reaches out to us. We must live our prayer through prayerful life.

Prayer must be the source of the deep love for our fellowman, for all prayer as Jesus' prayer embraces all mankind, but most of all those who are near and dear to us. Parents should join their children in family prayer, and mothers especially should teach their children how to pray. A final caution: in the words of a very outspoken missionary in our Precious Blood community, prayer must never be merely the *spare tire* for an unanticipated emergency. In this ecumenical age it is well to remember that we may and should pray frequently with our separated brethren, many of whose leaders were profound men of prayer (cf. *Oratio Continua* on the prayer life of Luther and Calvin, *Das Gebet* by Friedrich Heiler, one of the greatest books on prayer written in our time. See also *TD*, art. "Prayer"; *Handbuch Theologischer Grundbegriffe*, Gebet; *Encyclopedia of Theology*, "Prayer"; *NCE*, Vol. 11, art. "Prayer").

THE PRECIOUS BLOOD PRAYER

The Precious Blood prayer formulas as approved by the Church do not constitute a massive volume of words and pages. In most constant use are the *seven offerings* and the newly approved *litany*. We also include the rosary and the way of the cross, as both meditation and prayer, which especially in America have formed so much of our public and private prayer life. But as in all prayer, we must go beyond, far beyond even the most sacred formulas, for all spirituality includes also the *spontaneous* prayer of the individual and in many instances of the group, spontaneous private and spontaneous common prayer. We feel, also, that the various groups should compose special Precious Blood prayers adapted for group occasions.

The Precious Blood prayer linking the Precious Blood societies, should also reach out to all who practice the Precious Blood spirituality. First of these are all called by the Precious Blood vocation and the members of the Precious Blood Confraternity. Noble is the bond of the works of zeal performed by all *zealous men and women of the Precious Blood*. Profoundly the Blood of Christ unites all who turn to it through grace and desire forming a bond in Christ and his Spirit. It should be the function of the Precious Blood societies to promote the spirit and practice of this prayer beyond all societal limits. Those least able to work, to engage in pastoral tasks, the sick and enfeebled may find here the special vocation of zeal in the Precious Blood. Their example: the *missionary* saints who never left their monasteries.

All prayer includes the sense of discipleship, with Jesus, with our families, with our group leadership. We indicated this in the previous pages on prayer. When our Lord gave his disciples the Lord's prayer he indicated clearly that we must pray with Jesus. Him we join in praying to the Father. Our Precious Blood prayer, all prayer indeed, is a mysterious and transcendent experience under the influence of the Holy Spirit who prays with us.

The Spirit too helps us in our weakness, for we do not know how to pray as we ought; but the Spirit himself makes intercession for us with groanings that cannot be expressed in speech. He who searches hearts knows what the Spirit means, for the Spirit intercedes for the saints as God himself wills (Rom 8:26f).

Prayer as the most sublime of human activities must engage the whole man. But it is neither activity of man alone or the Spirit alone. Though today man is concerned with this world alone, with man and the world he fashions, only by prayer can he transcend this world and through Christ reach out beyond. Only prayer can unite all that man is and does — all his joys and sorrows, his total experience, his needs and wants — to him who is the *Infinite Other, God.* Prayer as union with Christ spiritually forms the Christian community; it strengthens, heals, enriches self and community. Most surprising of all it alone truly *humanizes* man, for creature is most perfect creature when most closely linked to Creator, through that perfect bond of union with God, the God-man, the Christ who is both God and man.

Our Precious Blood prayer must raise mind and heart to God in all times of great crises. When all seems to collapse about us, our home, our family, our friends, we must unite with Christ and call to the Father. We know that in the Old Testament in the great times of trial, especially in the time of exile, God summoned his fallen people to the profoundest form of sorrowful prayer and led Israel back to himself. Individuals, even kings, at the time of the sinfulness of the people, called to God and were saved by prayer (Jonah, chapter 3). David in his sin rebuked by God, through Nathan acknowledged his evil deeds and prayed to God (2 Sam, chapter 12).

In all our Precious Blood prayer we respond to the summons of God in union with Jesus whose prayers are always answered. Is he not God's own Son, anointed by his Spirit? Is not God always present, united with his blessed humanity in the hypostatic union? At all times in his life Jesus responded to his Father's will, as a child in the temple, in his retirement in the desert, on every special occasion, in the great hours of special prayer. His whole life was prayer response to the Father, especially so in the great liturgical prayer after the Last Supper, which we have already referred to as the Canon of the Official Sacrifice of Calvary. We must unite with him in our Precious Blood prayer, because we alone are assured that we shall always be heard when he prays with us and we with him. Hence we pray to the Father, through his crucified Son, in his Holy Spirit.

PRAYER: A CRITICAL NOTE

The historical differences in spirituality are especially evident in the diversity of prayer forms, structures and attitudes, and most of all in the contemporary abrupt and bold approaches. We see this in the language, the structures, the practices and even the postures, the critical assumptions. Note the use of the rosary, the way of the cross, the breviary and even the variations in the Mass itself. As in our total spirituality, here also we cannot dispense with the bond with Christ, and what we might call the hard core of tradition, especially so evident in the inspired word and the whole revealed truth. If we have courage for the new and varied — so essential to the contemporary attitudes, needs, demands, appeals — we may not discard proper loyalty to the old and tried of the past. We must always *keep in touch* with the concrete person of Jesus and the total historical action, the redemptive Jesus in the whole work of redemption. This we have sought to stress throughout our study. We may not accept the new, no matter how tremendous its value, at the price of the loss of the past heritage with its great figures and realities. We should remain cautious in our criticism of both past and present, though indeed we must be critical in an objective, prudent sense — with a conciliatory attitude toward present spiritual trends, and with the lessons of the past in full view — in shaping a Christ-centered synthesis for a life mastery suitable to our own age.

By way of practical stress for our own communities of the Precious Blood we may not dispense, as communities or individuals, with what we call the Church's official prayer — and by this we mean the communal recitation of the canonical hours at least on occasions such as community gatherings. Still less may we dispense with the *common community* prayers or exercises. The concelebrated Mass becomes community liturgy in the various houses, again especially on the feasts of the community calendar. These sacral communal means we deem essentially a part of the bond of the Precious Blood spirituality in the religious societies of the Precious Blood. We place no limit on individual and group prayer in every area of these societies and their spiritual inspiration.

THE PRECIOUS BLOOD LITURGICAL CALENDAR

A joyful community celebrates with the universal Church the great redemptive feasts, common heritage of all Christian spirituality, but it also enjoys the privilege of a special liturgical calendar. The followers of Gaspar, now their one canonized saint, celebrate his feast as a *solemnity*, with special canonical hours and Mass, on October 21; the feast of the Most Precious Blood also as a *solemnity* on July 1. (We ask again that it be restored to its former position in the calendar of the universal Church). *Mary, Help of Christians,* to whom Gaspar dedicated all his missionary activity, is honored by a *feast* on May 24; and similarly the principal patron of the society, *St. Francis Xavier,* is honored by a *feast* on December 3. *Blessed Maria De Mattias* has an *obligatory memorial* on February 4. We add that the entire month of July is the month of the Precious Blood. (cf. the Precious Blood Weeks and other sources for the *Confraternity of the Precious Blood*).

A SPECIAL PRECIOUS BLOOD PRAYER

Blood of Christ, I adore you, I place my trust in you, I love you. Blood of Christ, teach me to pray, as you taught your disciples to pray; teach me to want to pray, to be a man of prayer. Teach me to recite your favors as prayerful words of praise and thanksgiving.

Blood of Christ, if I live in a godless world, may its very godlessness, the turmoil of its streets, the hum of its industry, the pride of its science and technology, its greed, its errors of mind, perversity of heart, its sanctification of sin, all conspire to manifest a deeper yearning for you, a hidden if mistaken reaching out toward you. May this inspire in me true prayer to you. Word-of-God-made-man, become man within my mind and heart.

Blood of Christ, I thank you for reconciliation with your Father in and through your Holy Spirit. In union with Mary, your Mother, who gave you to us, I embrace you and offer you to your Father through your Holy Spirit in the infinite sacrifice of your submission to God. I offer you all my joys, sorrows, trials, in union with your suffering. I accept with all my heart the total efficacy of your earthly life and its agony and death on the cross. I beg of you to share both your cross and your resurrection unto glory. Humbly I offer all your Blood, with you, for all mankind.

Heavenly Father, in deep thankfulness for the gift of your Son, who brought us the divine life which was his in union with your Spirit, I pledge with the aid of your grace a ceaseless effort to live in union with you and your Son in this same Holy Spirit. A life of love for you, heavenly Father, and for all your children on earth! Make me realize that their faults are only a mirror of my own, due perhaps to my lack of zeal in promoting your name. In union with the Eucharistic Blood I offer you all that I have and am. May I even now join this frail earthly life with the infinite bliss of the eternal Trinity. May the love which is our eternal reward even now consume me.

Compassionate High Priest, embrace us all so that we may even now begin to celebrate — with all the Church and through your constant presence in her — the eternal offering of the everlasting priesthood which is the ultimate glory of your Blood. Bless, Lord, the societies of the Precious Blood. Make the Precious Blood spirituality the true center of their lives, the source of their activities. May its prayer be their prayer, its exercise the pattern of their lives, its joys their reward. Grant the charisms of their founders and models also to the members who look to them.

Glory be to the Blood of Jesus, now and forever.

A FINAL RUBRIC

The writer recalls a remark made many years ago by Father Didacus Brackmann, professor of dogmatic theology. The scene of the agony in the garden stirred him more profoundly over the horror of mortal sin than the most fiery missionary sermon on hell. This in a day when such sermons were essential diet (a point we are far from condemning even today) in every mission and retreat. This scene of the agony has been a most common object of art and prayerful meditation throughout the Catholic world. The story of the agony is told by the synoptics, depicting the most extreme terror of the God-man in the face of his impending passion and death. And we may add, the appalling weakness of the pillars of the Church. Not only the terror of the torture appalls Jesus, he longs for the sympathy of his disciples. Obediently he accepts the Father's will, though he has begged to be spared the agony and pain. The intensity of his prayer and his utter longing for solace indicate to us of the Precious Blood spirituality how profoundly we must sympathize with Jesus in his agony. As for the Apostles, it is a warning for us that we must wrestle with temptation through prayer even though it be unto blood.

One calls to mind the dreadful labor camps and torture chambers of the totalitarian regimes in Germany and Russia, the current torture systems of dictatorships in many countries today. Some notion of the number of priests who were driven from their homes and to death toward the close of World War II may be learned from the tragic account, *Vom Sterben Schlesischer Priester* 1945-46 (*On the Death of Silesian Priests*). Tragedy still reigns in Ireland, Lebanon, Southeast Asia, and elsewhere in the world, even in the skies.

To this writer Christ faces, as we too must face, not merely evil men, but the forces of evil, the sinister Evil-In-Person, Satan (cf. Luke 22:28), malice which lies beyond all power of conversion. This evil of forces reaches its climax in high places. To describe the intensity of the anguish Luke (22:44) refers to the sweat, which like drops of blood, falls to the ground. In our litany we pray, *Blood of Christ, falling upon the earth in the agony, save us.* We need not be concerned that some ancient texts do not contain verses 43 and 44; there can be no doubt of the extreme anxiety of the Savior.

We place this rubric here in our study of the Precious Blood spirituality not merely because of the sin which caused his suffering, but because the account is a unique crisis in the suffering of Jesus, perhaps more marked than the crucifixion itself. We of the Precious Blood spirituality must face today the total aversion from God, the absolutization of man, his work, his humanization. Is it possible with the aid of the grace from the Blood and prayer of Jesus to turn even Nihilism back to God, making this one of the greatest missions of our spirituality? For this we must pray: *Blood of Christ, falling upon the earth in the agony, save us!*

In the following we lean heavily on Hubertus Mynarek: *Der Mensch Das Wesen der Zukunft (Man the Essence of the Future,* Schoeningh, Paderborn, 1968). What seems most paradoxical is the position taken by Mynarek, according to which Nihilism is the final and ultimate stage and consequence of atheism, unmasking it, exposing it in its utter barrenness. And yet it is a proof for human freedom by its very centering on man, on the "self-determined I." Fully did Nietzsche realize that his denial of God, "the murder of God in the heart," had the most direful consequence. But he hoped to supplant this by a new and tremendous will to power, by new values found in the *Uebermensch,* intensifying, activating, elevating man. But Nietzsche could not fail to realize also that his "system" corresponded to no reality, that it was eternally meaningless.

But can we not proclaim with and against Nietzsche that if we have destroyed the absolute of reason, yet assert reason in its very denial, then we assert it in full truth? Instead of Nietzsche's no truth, no absolute, no universal norm, each man his own GOD, we assert the reality of truth, of absolute, of universal norm, in the ABSOLUTE beyond all this, who is God, the Father of our Christ. Can we with the weapons of the Precious Blood spirituality reject the ABSOLUTE DENIAL for the ABSOLUTE REALITY? Then ultimately, with the grace of the Blood dripping to the earth in the agony, we may turn to the face of our Christ: the depths of the misguided heart of man now turns in love to him. Only the infinite Creative Love can so give to creature this dynamic power to turn against him, but therein lies the power and the challenge to turn back to him in love through his Son.

These thoughts, we feel, belong to the Precious Blood spirituality in their prayer and meditation. They help us understand the meaning of Gethsemani, retreat, work, prayer and, above all, entry into self in union with the Jesus of the agony facing the reality of death. Finally, as to the agony, Gaspar himself was wont to say that this shedding of Blood was unique, because it was not caused by the executioners, by instruments of torture, but solely by the love of the Christ of agony (*With A Thousand Tongues,* p. 3). Let us ponder!

THE SEVEN OFFERINGS

The *Seven Offerings* are the Precious Blood prayer *par excellence.* The writer recalls the incident (especially stressed in a retreat for seminarians by Father Boniface Russ) that Bishop Joseph Dwenger, the first of our

American province to be raised to the episcopacy, in his last illness thanked some of his visitors for pausing reverently before approaching his bedside as he was moving his lips in prayer: "I was reciting the seven offerings. I never fail to say them daily."

Theologically, the offerings are founded in our desire to share in the offering made by Christ on Calvary and in the holy Mass, for all the needs of the Church. In this sense they are our perpetual, sacrificial prayer. As to the arrangement itself, the number *seven* traditionally refers to the most painful sheddings of Blood by Jesus and aims at embracing his whole life, passion, death, and the piercing of the sacred side. Obviously the number aims primarily at pointing out the painful events, without sharply distinguishing one from the other. Thus they include the circumcision, the agony in the garden, the scourging, the crowning with thorns, the bearing of the cross to Calvary, the crucifixion, the piercing of the sacred side. The contents of the seven offerings, however, do not at all correspond to the sacred-cruel events, but to the variation in the petitions themselves directed to the efficacy of the Blood.

As members of the sacrificial-sacramental Church we join in "pouring forth" this Blood. Because its work of liberation is universal, our prayers join with the sacrificial offering for the benefit of all mankind. The Blood penetrates all areas of human activity. We think of it as touching on every need, purging the very abyss of man's wretchedness, but rising also to the heights of divine glory.

To be freed from our guilt through the Blood of Christ and accepted by Christ our Mediator, our High Priest, should make us most anxious for that unique fellowship with Christ. With him we offer the Blood in complete submission of ourselves to God the Father, because the pardon of our sins means that we have been accepted by Christ in the work of redemption. Thus accepted we bear the cross with him, join in the Christ-redemptive-action by placing the destiny of the world with the cross on our shoulders with his. In this manner we recite the seven offerings of the Precious Blood for all mankind.

By way of introduction to the recitation of the seven offerings, we present two versions: first, the author's own, and then the officially approved version.

First we explain the structural forms. As address we prefer to say *Heavenly Father* (rather than *Eternal Father* found in the official version), a term which seems to us the more biblical and endearing. In the Lord's Prayer we pray to "our Father who *art in heaven*."

In the *first offering* we unite with Christ the priest. Our purpose is to show that the oblation of the Blood is by Christ who offers his Blood in sacrifice. Thus far, none of our devotional prayers refer to *Christ the priest*. A point to stress: in each of these formulas we refer to both the sacrificial offering on Calvary and the mystical oblation in holy Mass on our altars.

Through the offerings our prayer is directed to the ends and purposes for which the Blood is offered and which we join Jesus in offering. In the *first of the seven* we state the purpose underlying all offering of the Precious Blood: the glory of God and the coming of his kingdom. In the *last of the seven* we have the final and ultimate. Here is the eschatological prayer. We have in mind death, purgatory, final union with Christ in glory. We think that thus far none of our Precious Blood prayers has directly referred to Christ resurrected and in glory, though of course Precious Blood iconography clearly extols the Lamb in eternal glory and the final invocation of the new litany calls out to the Lamb "most worthy of all glory and honor."

Between the first offering and the last, there is the following progression of ends and purposes: the *second* offering is for the whole Church, its head, its hierarchy, its religious communities, all the people of God. Next, the *third* offering is for the spread of the faith, the acceptance of the divine truth, removal of error and the enlightenment of unbelievers. The *fourth* offering is for the conversion of sinners, the flowering of Christian life and moral ideals among all men. The *fifth* offering pleads for the universal temporal order, for ecumenical love, for peace and justice and solicitude for those in misery and neglect. The *sixth* offering turns to our own needs, begs for all who are close and dear to us, for our enemies, and all in pain and suffering, and for those who look to us to pray for them. The versicle is a final part of the doxology: *Glory to the Blood of Jesus.*

I

For God's Glory Heavenly Father, in union with Christ our eternal priest, we offer you the Precious Blood, shed on Calvary and mystically offered on our altars, for the glory of your name and the spread of your Kingdom.
Glory be to the Father and to the Son and to the Holy Spirit,
As it was in the beginning is now and ever shall be, world without end. Amen.
Praise and thanksgiving be evermore to Jesus.
Who with his Blood has saved us.

II

For the Church Heavenly Father, we offer you the Precious Blood of Jesus, shed on Calvary and mystically offered on our altars, for the spread and exaltation of your holy Church, for the safety and well-being of her visible head, Pope N. N., Bishop of Rome, in union with our bishops, priests,

ministers of the sanctuary, religious communities and all the people of God.
Glory . . .

III

For the Spread of God's Word Heavenly Father, in union with all
members of the Mystical Body we offer you the Precious Blood of Jesus,
shed on Calvary and mystically offered on our altars, for the loving acceptance of the divine Word, the removal of error and the enlightenment of
unbelievers.
Glory . . .

IV

For the Conversion of Sinners Heavenly Father, in union with all the
redeemed, we offer you the Precious Blood of Jesus, shed on Calvary and
mystically offered on our altars, for the conversion of sinners, the flourishing
of Christian life and moral ideals among all men.
Glory . . .

V

For Peace and Justice Among Men Heavenly Father, we offer you
the Precious Blood of Jesus, shed on Calvary and mystically offered on our
altars, for the ecumenical love among all religious groups, for peace and justice among all nations and races, and loving care for those who suffer misery
and neglect throughout the world.
Glory . . .

VI

For Our Own Special Needs Heavenly Father, we offer you the Precious Blood of Jesus, shed on Calvary and mystically offered on our altars,
for our own sanctification, our special needs and just desires, for our relatives, friends, and enemies, and all those in pain and suffering who need
and seek our prayers.
Glory . . .

VII

To the Precious Blood in Glory Heavenly Father, reigning with Christ,
we offer you the Precious Blood of Jesus, shed on Calvary and mystically
offered on our altars, in union with all who love this infinite treasure, for
those who are to die today, for the holy souls in Purgatory and for our resurrection with Jesus in the ultimate triumph of the Precious Blood in heavenly
glory.
Glory . . .
Glory to the Blood of Jesus.
Now and forever.

Following is the officially approved text used in our common recitation.

1) Eternal Father, we offer you the Precious Blood of Jesus, poured out on the cross and offered daily on the altar, for the glory of your name, for the coming of your kingdom, and for the salvation of all men.
Glory be to the Father . . .
Praise and thanksgiving be evermore to Jesus. Who with his Blood has saved us.

2) Eternal Father, we offer you the Precious Blood of Jesus, poured out on the cross and offered daily on the altar, for the spread of the Church, for Pope . . . N . . ., for bishops, priests, and religious, and for the sanctification of all the people of God.
Glory . . .

3) Eternal Father, we offer you the Precious Blood of Jesus, poured out on the cross and offered daily on the altar, for the conversion of sinners, for the loving acceptance of your Word, and for the union of all Christians.
Glory . . .

4) Eternal Father, we offer you the Precious Blood of Jesus, poured out on the cross and offered daily on the altar, for our civil authorities, for the strengthening of public morals, and for peace and justice among all nations.
Glory . . .

5) Eternal Father, we offer you the Precious Blood of Jesus, poured out on the cross and offered daily on the altar, for the sanctification of our work and our suffering, for the poor, the sick and the afflicted, and for all who rely on our prayers.
Glory . . .

6) Eternal Father, we offer you the Precious Blood of Jesus, poured out on the cross and offered daily on the altar, for our own special needs, both spiritual and temporal, for those of our relatives and benefactors, and also for those of our enemies.
Glory . . .

7) Eternal Father, we offer you the Precious Blood of Jesus, poured out on the cross and offered daily on the altar, for those who are to die this day, for the souls in Purgatory, and for our final union with Christ in glory.
Glory . . .
Glory to the Blood of Jesus.
Now and forever.

THE LITANY OF THE PRECIOUS BLOOD

On February 24, 1960, the Sacred Congregation of Rites approved a Litany of the Most Precious Blood for public and private recitation by the following pronouncement:

> In his desire to see the cult of the Most Precious Blood of Christ, the Immaculate Lamb by whom we were redeemed, grow from day to day, His Holiness, our Pontiff, Pope John XXIII, has deigned to approve the said litany, composed and given above by the Sacred Congregation of Rites. And he has granted that it be published and placed in the Roman Ritual under the title XI, after the Litany of the Most Sacred Heart of Jesus, for both public and private use in the entire Catholic world by the faithful.

Shortly thereafter the Holy Father granted the indulgences for the recitation of the litany, as indicated in the printed pamphlets of the prayer.

The approval of this Litany of the Most Precious Blood (and the granting of the indulgences) is one of the most significant acts of the popes in the history of the devotion in our Precious Blood spirituality. In our documentation of the spirituality in its theological presentation, this papal decision ranks with the approval of the *Feast of the Precious Blood,* the approval of the *societies* of the Precious Blood (with their rules and constitutions), and the *canonization of their great Founder,* Saint Gaspar Del Bufalo, and the beatification of the *Blessed Maria De Mattias.* We are looking forward hopefully to the beatification of the Venerable *John Merlini,* the third Moderator General of the Missionaries of the Precious Blood. The first step, the official approval of the decree on the heroicity of his virtue, has already been taken.

The approval of the prayers, especially of the litany, places a solemn and authentic seal of the Church on the Precious Blood spirituality and devotion. It is now officially ranked in the prayer of the Church with the devotion to the Holy Name and the Sacred Heart. The reason is evident: *the law of prayer is the law of faith.* The litany differs in form from all others. Simple, almost lapidary in style, it is not pompous or ornate, largely the work of Pope John XXIII or at least personally supervised by him. Finally, we note that in the divine praises by the very special direction of John, the invocation was added: *Blessed be his Most Precious Blood.*

THE LITANY: APPROVED FORM

Lord, have mercy on us.
Christ, have mercy on us.
Lord, have mercy on us.
Christ, hear us.

Christ, graciously hear us.

God, the Father of heaven, *Have mercy on us.*

God, the Son, Redeemer of the world, *Have mercy on us.*

God, the Holy Spirit, *Have mercy on us.*

Holy Trinity, One God, *Have mercy on us.*

Blood of Christ, only-begotten Son of the Eternal Father, *Save us.*

Blood of Christ, Incarnate Word of God, *Save us.*

Blood of Christ, of the New and Eternal Testament, *Save us.*

Blood of Christ, falling upon the earth in the Agony, *Save us.*

Blood of Christ, shed profusely in the Scourging, *Save us.*

Blood of Christ, flowing forth in the Crowning with Thorns, *Save us.*

Blood of Christ, poured out on the Cross, *Save us.*

Blood of Christ, price of our salvation, *Save us.*

Blood of Christ, without which there is no forgiveness, *Save us.*

Blood of Christ, Eucharistic drink and refreshment of souls, *Save us.*

Blood of Christ, stream of mercy, *Save us.*

Blood of Christ, victor over demons, *Save us.*

Blood of Christ, courage of martyrs, *Save us.*

Blood of Christ, strength of confessors, *Save us.*

Blood of Christ, bringing forth virgins, *Save us.*

Blood of Christ, help of those in peril, *Save us.*

Blood of Christ, relief of the burdened, *Save us.*

Blood of Christ, solace in sorrow, *Save us.*

Blood of Christ, hope of the penitent, *Save us.*

Blood of Christ, consolation of the dying, *Save us.*

Blood of Christ, peace and tenderness of hearts, *Save us.*

Blood of Christ, pledge of Eternal Life, *Save us.*

Blood of Christ, freeing souls from Purgatory, *Save us.*

Blood of Christ, most worthy of all glory and honor, *Save us.*

Lamb of God, who take away the sins of the world, *Spare us, O Lord.*

Lamb of God, who take away the sins of the world, *Graciously hear us, O Lord.*

Lamb of God, who take away the sins of the world, *Have mercy on us.*

℣. You have redeemed us, O Lord, in your Blood.

℟. And made us, for our God, a kingdom.

Let Us Pray

Almighty and Eternal God, you have appointed your only-begotten Son the Redeemer of the world, and willed to be appeased by his Blood. Grant we beg of you, that we may worthily adore this price of our salvation, and through its power be safeguarded from the evils of this present life, so that we may rejoice in its fruits forever in heaven. Through the same Christ our Lord. Amen.

A REFLECTION

Though the Litany of the Precious Blood is not chanted with the same solemnity as some of the others, it is frequently recited and, in our opinion, should be solemnly chanted on special occasions, e.g., at retreats, missions, novenas. For both simple recitation and solemn chant, it merits reflective study in our spirituality: we offer here a few insights into the pattern for Precious Blood prayer and meditation.

THE PATTERN

The litany begins with the frequently recited appeal for mercy: there are three pleas to the *Supreme Lord*:
>Lord, have mercy on us.
>Christ, have mercy on us.
>Lord, have mercy on us.

There follows the double appeal that the Christ of mercy hear us:
>Christ, hear us.
>Christ, graciously hear us.

Next follows the fourfold invocation begging each of the divine persons for mercy, and closing with the appeal to the Holy Trinity, One God:
>God, the Father of Heaven, Have mercy on us.
>God, the Son, Redeemer of the world, Have mercy on us.
>God, the Holy Spirit, Have mercy on us.
>Holy Trinity, One God, Have mercy on us.

Then follow the invocations directed to the Blood of Jesus, to which we shall refer later. The litany closes with the impressive *Agnus Dei*, the final appeal for pardon, the versicle, response, and the closing prayer.

Within this framework, which is a humble prostration of soul before the all-merciful Christ, the most varied invocations and petitions are sent heavenward. All within the articulate unity of the Church: there is invocation, petition, with the constant chorus or response! All heaven is summoned. All needs of earth are pleaded. Supreme adoration mingles with humblest petition.

THE INVOCATIONS

There are twenty-four invocations of the Blood of Christ. The first three are basic to the whole order of redemption through Blood. Uniquely this group turns to the *Logos* or *Son of God* in the *Divine Trinity*. The Blood is addressed as the Second Divine Person in his work of redemption. We note throughout this study that *Sanguis Christi, Blood of Christ,* means the Redeemer, the God-made-man in his entire work of redemption. The invocations are basic to the divine plan in the *theologia-economia*:

> Blood of Christ, only begotten Son of the Eternal Father, *Save us.*
> Blood of Christ, Incarnate Word of God, *Save us.*
> Blood of Christ, of the New and Eternal Testament, *Save us.*

We repeat what we have explained at length elsewhere: when we call upon the Blood of the only begotten Son of the Eternal Father, we have in mind the Sonship in the life of the divine Trinity. It is this communication of God in the Trinity, which is the source of the divine life, the God-life in us, by which we too become sons of God. This comes to us through the conception and birth in time of the Son, the incarnate Word of God. We ask the Blood of the eternally begotten, the divine Word-made-man to save us, in and through his Holy Spirit. We ask the Blood of the New and Eternal Covenant or Testament, which is the Blood of Christ's priesthood, to save us.

PASSION AND DEATH

The next four invocations refer to the Blood shed in the passion and death of Christ: through this Blood our salvation will be wrought:

> Blood of Christ, falling upon the earth in the Agony, *Save us.*
> Blood of Christ, shed profusely in the Scourging, *Save us.*
> Blood of Christ, flowing forth in the Crowning with Thorns,
> > *Save us.*
> Blood of Christ, poured out on the Cross, *Save us.*

We note at once that there is no reference to the sacred circumcision nor to the piercing of the sacred side. But with the stark simplicity the whole life and death of Christ and his work of satisfaction, merit, sacrifice, liberation are summed up in the great climax of *passion and death*. There is a simplicity and finality, an avoidance of horror-emphasis, a deep sentiment of reality which is especially effective in the straightforward Latin forms: *in agonia decurrens in terram, in flagellatione profluens, in coronatione spinarum emanans, in cruce effusus.*

THE FRUITS OF THE BLOOD

The fruits and effects of the shedding of the Blood are referred to in the following invocations: the first four are the most generic effects, relating to its necessity: the Blood is the price paid for our salvation. Through the Blood alone is sin remitted. Through the Blood we have the Eucharist, food and drink for our souls. Through the Blood the abundant streams of divine mercy, particularly in the sacraments, flow to us. More specifically, these invocations call to mind the necessity of the Precious Blood: for salvation, for pardon, for the Eucharist, for the whole work of divine mercy.

> Blood of Christ, price of our salvation, *Save us.*
> Blood of Christ, without which there is no forgiveness, *Save us.*
> Blood of Christ, Eucharistic drink and refreshment of souls, *Save us.*
> Blood of Christ, stream of mercy, *Save us.*

The next invocations create an awe over the power of the Blood, victor over all the forces of sin. The very demons are crushed by the power of the Blood. The Blood gives courage to martyrs, strength to confessors. From it flows all the purity of virgins. Summarily, these three invocations include all who are saved and brought to eternal life: martyrs, confessors, virgins. The Blood is the help (how clear and forceful the Latin word, *robur*) of all who are in peril. All the inner strength which sustains man in his frailty is from the Blood.

> Blood of Christ, victor over demons, *Save us.*
> Blood of Christ, courage of martyrs, *Save us.*
> Blood of Christ, strength of confessors, *Save us.*
> Blood of Christ, bringing forth virgins, *Save us.*
> Blood of Christ, help of those in peril, *Save us.*

CONSOLING INVOCATIONS

The next six invocations refer to the efficacy of the Blood in all of life's trials. It leads men through this vale of tears to eternal life. It brings relief to the burdened, solace to those in sorrow, hope to the penitent, consolation to the dying, peace of soul and tenderness of heart to all. It is the pledge of eternal life.

> Blood of Christ, relief of the burdened, *Save us.*
> Blood of Christ, solace in sorrow, *Save us.*
> Blood of Christ, hope of the penitent, *Save us.*
> Blood of Christ, consolation of the dying, *Save us.*
> Blood of Christ, peace and tenderness of hearts, *Save us.*
> Blood of Christ, pledge of Eternal Life, *Save us.*

The final invocations relate to the ultimate triumph of the Precious Blood. The Blood not only frees souls from the *depth* of Purgatory, it gathers all the redeemed who have used its graces and finally presents them to the Father. The last of the invocations sees Christ the high priest in

eternal glory. He is most worthy of every glory and honor. This is the fulfillment of his work of redemption in the celestial priesthood through which
Christ reigns in glory evermore.

> Blood of Christ, freeing souls from Purgatory, *Save us.*
> Blood of Christ, most worthy of all glory and honor, *Save us.*

The versicle: You have redeemed us, O Lord, in your Blood; and
response: And made us, for our God, a kingdom, suggests the Apocalyptic:

> To him who loves us and freed us from our sins by his own blood,
> who has made us a royal nation of priests in the service of his God
> and Father — to him be glory and power forever and ever!
> (Rv 1:5f).

ANOTHER VERSION

Lord, have mercy.
Christ, have mercy.
Lord, have mercy.
Christ, hear us.
Christ, graciously hear us.
God, the Father of heaven, Have mercy.
God, the Son, Redeemer of the world, **Have** mercy.
God, the Holy Spirit, **Have** mercy.
Holy Trinity, One God, Have mercy.
Blood of Christ, only-begotten Son of the Eternal Father, Save us.
Blood of Christ, Incarnate Word of God, Save us.
Blood of Christ, of the New and Eternal Testament, Save us.
Blood of Christ, trickling to the earth in the Agony, Save us.
Blood of Christ, spilt in the Scourging, Save us.
Blood of Christ, bursting forth in the Crowning with thorns, Save us.
Blood of Christ, poured out on the Cross, Save us.
Blood of Christ, price of our salvation, Save us.
Blood of Christ, sole pardon for sin, Save us.
Blood of Christ, Eucharistic drink and refreshment of souls, Save us.
Blood of Christ, stream of mercy, Save us.
Blood of Christ, victor over demons, Save us.
Blood of Christ, courage of martyrs, Save us.
Blood of Christ, strength of confessors, Save us.
Blood of Christ, fountain of virginity, Save us.
Blood of Christ, help of those in peril, Save us.
Blood of Christ, relief of the burdened, Save us.
Blood of Christ, solace in sorrow, Save us.

Blood of Christ, hope of the penitent, Save us.
Blood of Christ, consolation of the dying, Save us.
Blood of Christ, peace and tenderness of hearts, Save us.
Blood of Christ, pledge of Eternal Life, Save us.
Blood of Christ, freeing souls from Purgatory, Save us.
Blood of Christ, most worthy of all glory and honor, Save us.
Lamb of God, Who take away the sins of the world, *Spare us, O Lord.*
Lamb of God, Who take away the sins of the world, *Graciously hear us, O Lord.*
Lamb of God, Who take away the sins of the world, *Have mercy on us.*

℣. You have redeemed us, O Lord, in your Blood.
℟. And made us a kingdom for our God.

Let us Pray

Almighty and Eternal God, you have appointed your only-begotten Son the Redeemer of the world, and willed to be appeased by his Blood. Grant, we beg of you, that we may worthily adore this price of our salvation, and through its power be safeguarded from the evils of this present life, so that we may rejoice in its fruits forever in heaven. Through the same Christ our Lord. Amen.

Precious Blood Meditative Prayer

Two of the Church's most popular devotional forms — the Marian Rosary and the Way of the Cross — uniquely combining prayer and meditation have marked the exercise of the Precious Blood devotion throughout the Church and the devotional life of the Precious Blood societies. The brevity of our present treatment should not be construed as a measure of their importance in the development of countless pious souls in our American religious life.

We can do no more than mention and recommend the so-called Chaplet or Rosary of the Precious Blood, which prayerfully reflects on the seven Blood sheddings (circumcision, agony in the garden, scourging, crowning with thorns, the bearing of the cross to Calvary, the crucifixion, the piercing of the Savior's side (cf. *Daily Prayers, C.PP.S.*).

The Marian Rosary: Communal Prayer, Private Prayer

The long and fascinating history of the rosary reveals that it sprang from a desire of the faithful to share the worship of the Church in holy Mass and the divine office recited by the monks and clerics in the cathedral chapters. The Lord's Prayer, of course, derived from the master himself, but the Hail Mary with its biblical basis in the words of annunciation of the incarnation by the angel, according to Luke 1:28, and the salutation of Elizabeth, "Blest are you among women and blest is the fruit of your womb" (Luke 1:42), only gradually developed with the public prayers of the Church. Only gradually the two, Our Father and Hail Mary, were structured on the pattern of the 150 psalms which "from time immemorial . . . have comprised the most important part of the canonical hours."

> Today the rosary is divided according to the three sets of mysteries — joyful, sorrowful, and glorious. Each consists of fifty Hail Marys. This division is derived from the Irish practice of dividing the Davidic Psalter. It comes to the rosary not directly, but only through this Irish custom of dividing the Psalms of the Bible (Franz Michel Willam, *The Rosary: Its History and Meaning*, tr. by Edwin G. Kaiser, C.PP.S., Benzinger, New York, p. 17).

Our concern in this study is the meaning of the rosary as the Church presents it today in its relation to our Precious Blood spirituality. The liturgical prayer in the Mass of the Feast of the Rosary points the way:

> O God, your only-begotten Son has *purchased for us* the reward of eternal life by his *life, death,* and *resurrection.* May we who *meditate* on these mysteries in the most holy rosary of the blessed Virgin Mary *imitate* the virtues they proclaim and obtain the rewards they promise.

In the second prayer (the *secret*) we ask that we may *recall to our minds* the *life, passion* and *triumph* of Mary's Son. And in the final (*postcommunion*) prayer we speak of the "mysteries we reverence." These prayers clearly indicate that the rosary is *meditation on, recalling to mind, reverencing* the great mysteries of redemption which has been wrought by the ransom of the Precious Blood (*Christ has purchased eternal life* by his *life, death, resurrection,* as we have often noted in this study). In these great mysteries we recall, we ponder, we reverence the three great groups: the joyous, the sorrowful, the glorious decades. And we beseech the divine grace through Mary so that we may imitate in our lives all the virtues we see in the mysteries, and we look forward to the triumphant Christ and the glorious rewards.

We have already spoken of the Precious Blood meditation. In the rosary we combine the recitation of the sacred prayers with a certain insistent repetition in the fifteen times we recite the Our Father and the hundred and fifty times the Hail Mary with the meditation. Mere repetition will create monotony, but the very monotony is to help us fix our gaze on the mysteries which gradually should create in our life an atmosphere or habit of Christ-mystery-meditation, so that our whole waking life becomes habitual meditation. It should be filled with Nazareth, Galilee, Jerusalem, the glory of Jesus resurrected: with the living mystery of the living Jesus, the suffering Jesus, the dying Jesus, the Jesus of the resurrection-ascension. Mary is ever at hand pointing out her Son, in tears and joy, as only a tender mother can.

The story of the rosary, as told by such writers as Franz Willam and Josef Jungmann, traces its development in the prayer life of the Church. Many hagiographers tell of its influence on holy men dedicated to the care of souls. The splendor of Lepanto and the sainted Pius V are the triumph of our Lady of Victory. Among our most noted theologians today the rosary prayer is practiced with deep devotion and dedication. Nor should we be surprised that the Rev. J. Neville Ward, a Protestant minister, has written a beautiful book on the rosary, *Five For Sorrow, Ten For Joy: Consideration of the Rosary,* Doubleday Publishing Co., Garden City, 1971. Nor is it merely incidental that the learned Leo XIII, in sixteen Apostolic pronouncements, recommended this Marian prayer (cf. *NCE* Vol. 8, Leo XIII, see also Jungmann, *op. cit.,* p. 159 and elsewhere).

In our own Precious Blood community in America the recitation of the rosary was a common daily exercise. The pioneer Fathers and Brothers combined the daily work in the fields, the shops, the kitchen, with the communal recitation of the rosary. Many saintly souls in the society, who in the author's opinion practiced the most exalted virtue, loved and practiced the rosary devotion as part of the Precious Blood spiritual heritage in the community. Perhaps they were frequently weary and distracted, perhaps the words seemed like "saying the same thing over and over again," but monotony in life is essential bearer of the purposes of life, of its deep silence, of its bond of love with those who are too close to us for many words. In this monotony of the rosary is borne the grace-will to be one with Jesus, with all his mysteries, in a love that is more deep and real precisely because it is least exciting. There is blessing in the mystery of monotony with Jesus, his Mother, and St. Joseph, that Silent Man of the Holy Family. This is part of the blessing of the rosary.

The writer wishes to add by way of caution that the *entire rosary* of *fifteen mysteries* belongs to the Precious Blood spirituality, both historically in its use in the societies of the Precious Blood, and in the doctrinal basis of spirituality as we propose it in this study. Narrowly limiting the prayer to the *sorrowful mysteries* seems to arise from a very restricted concept of the deeper meaning of the *Sanguis Christi.* On the contrary we see no reason why the present rosary should not be expanded in the public recitation, even to suit particular occasions.

We must add, for those who object that rosary and way of the cross are not strictly liturgical prayer, that both do center in the Eucharist. We may say that they conjointly point to each other, and flow from the devotion to the Presence and Sacrifice, and/or lead us to the altar of worship and adoration. Obviously the way of the cross leads to the sacrifice of Calvary, which is reenacted bloodlessly in the Eucharistic liturgy. And similarly the rosary leads us meditatively through the life, passion, death, resurrection, and glory of Christ. We must also add that all public prayer ultimately turns to the Eucharist and derives its value from the Blood of the cross (cf. Lothar Schreyer, *Das Christusbild und die Kunst des* 20 *Jahrhunderts,* Mueller, Salzburg, 1960, p. 186, 233, 235). Each of us may well say with Karl Rahner, "for me it is a very wonderful thing" (*Space in Freedom,* p. 130, H & H, 1969).

THE WAY OF THE CROSS: COMMUNAL PRAYER, PRIVATE PRAYER

With the starkest of realism the four gospels describe the *via dolorosa,* the sad and painful journey of the Savior to Calvary. Only a divinely revealed religion could link the excruciating pain, the grossest injustice to Perfect Innocence, with the deep sympathy of man's prayer to his suffering God. The *praying Church,* says Engelbert Neuhaeusler (*Der Heilige Weg,* Duesseldorf, 1959, p. 5), relates the sad story in these four gospel versions to the *praying Church* for all time. The worshipping community in its cultal assembly thanks God for her vocation fashioned through its crucifixion with Christ and resurrection with him. Though this is particularly evident in baptism and Eucharist, all is focused against the background of the great passion prophecies and the graphic descriptions in the gospel accounts of the *via dolorosa* and the bloody death. From early Christian times these have become part of her meditative prayer. Historically this is associated with the sacred pilgrimage to the holy places in what has always been the Christian Holy Land. A sacred instinct, common to all historical religions, developed into a flaming love for this *holy and sacred soil* and its shrines which mark the Savior's life and death. It is difficult for us today to grasp the concept of *profanation by infidels* or the flaming enthusiasm for wars of liberation as the Crusades were called, the mixture of fierce devotion, fanaticism, cruelty, and the sad simplicity of the incredible Children's Crusades.

Yet the mystery remains — divine, profound mystery it is — the God-made-man did live in this land, the eyes of Jesus looked upon it and its people heard his voice, received his blessing. The cruelty of those who rejected him and blasphemed him furnished the torture and the instruments of his death: instruments of their cruelty became the means of our redemption. Sad is the historic fact that the followers of the patient and suffering

Jesus, should rather imitate his persecutors in their possessive clutching of his land and his shrines. This seems the horror-paradox of the Crusades!

Love for the actual shrines and spread of the devotion to the passion and death in the 12th and 13th centuries eventually led to *pilgrimage in little,* throughout Europe. Commemorative shrines were set up to recall the sacred places and events. Here the faithful for whom the painful pilgrimage to the Holy Land was impossible were given the opportunity to pause, ponder, pray in loving sympathy with the suffering Lord. The practice soon became wide spread, though with great diversity in structure, e.g., in the number of stations, the titles, the sacred images. The term, *station,* is derived from the practice of *stopping* or *halting* before the images for prayerful reflection.

Today we find the stations in most churches and chapels. The number is now fourteen as a rule, which of course is quite arbitrary in itself. Rules have been established for setting up the images and for the pious prayer and meditation in making the *way of the cross.* The ideal placed before us, pondering the suffering and dying of Jesus, is joined with a minimum of recitative prayer. To be meaningful the way of the cross must be the thoughtful and prayerful joining the condemned Innocent One in his death, as we stand beneath the cross and in spirit abide until the glorious resurrection.

The stations begin with the condemnation of Jesus to death (I Station) and his taking up the cross (II Station), which usually was not the entire cross but the *arm beam.* They end with the death of Jesus on the cross (XII Station), his being placed in the arms of his Mother (XIII Station) and the burial (XIV Station). At each station the priest or leader pauses for prayer and meditation. Often parts of the *Stabat Mater* are sung. Where the space is ample the deep unity of faithful among themselves and with the suffering Lord is manifested by the group moving in unison with priest or leader from station to station. A representative group of the larger congregation, in other instances, serves the same objective. Massive out-of-doors stations are always deeply impressive.

The mysteries of our redemption are placed before us for our personal in-depth reflection. *Supreme humiliation* is evident above all in the *condemnation* (who was this *petty ruler* Pontius Pilate to condemn the *Lord of the universe?*), in the many falls to the earth under the weight of the cross (the three stations, Jesus falls beneath the weight of the cross, are merely symbolic of the complete exhaustion of the *strong Son of God*), and the disrobing of his beautiful and sacred body now horribly bruised. *Supreme obedience* (what notion have we of obedience today even in religious communities?) is evident in his taking up the cross, bearing this instrument of shame reserved for the vilest of felons, even beyond his waning strength, so that a certain Simon of Cyrene (V Station) is forced to help him. At least three of the stations reveal the *supreme tenderness of Mary's Son*: he meets his Mother (IV Station), accepts the cloth of Veronica to wipe his sweated brow (VI Station). Here Christian legend has left us a profound theological truth. Veronica from its Greek derivation means true image; the true image of Jesus is imprinted in our hearts when we sorrow with him in his suffering. He speaks sympathetically to the mourning women of Jerusalem (VIII Station). The strength and loyalty of the *women of the passion* compared to the fidelity of one sole Apostle is significant in the current discussion of woman's rights and duties.

The final Station, the burial of Jesus, should be completed by reflection on the *resurrection*. Some of our current texts conclude with the note: the way of suffering with Jesus leads to the glory of resurrection. Have we followed the *cross?* We shall receive the *crown.*

This writer entertains no illusions; it is to be regretted that our societies do not stress the *stations* so much as formerly. The way of the cross is being neglected. Nevertheless it ranks among our traditional exercises. It belongs to the Precious Blood spirituality. It should be associated with the gospel readings of the passion and death. It might well take up a considerable portion of the days of recollection. The *way of the cross* is a comprehensive spiritual retreat.

Christ himself on the cross asks the heavenly Father to pardon those who have nailed him to the cross, for they did not truly know what they were doing (Lk 23:34). In his discourse after Pentecost Peter tells his hearers that they acted in ignorance (Acts 3:17; cf. 1 Cor 2:8), and even went so far as to excuse their leaders. These latter could hardly have been excused for putting an *Innocent Man* to death, even though they may not fully have realized the Messianic dignity of Jesus.

The thought suggests itself that today we too readily excuse sin almost to the point of holding a subjective standard of moral right and wrong. We think too little of the obligation to seek the good, to solve our doubt, to harken to God's teachers.

At least we who meditate on the mysteries of Jesus' passion and death should not so readily excuse ourselves on the plea that we are acting out of ignorance when we commit any sin of perdition. To our mind the special stress of the meditation on the *way of the cross* is to create in us a full awareness of the malice of sin in relation to the mysteries of redemption, sorrow for sin based on grateful love, and imitation of the virtues proper to the beautiful devotion: obedience, submission to God, mortification and penance for sins committed: tender love, should we say, especially for those who have offended Christ. It is well to bear in mind that the great saints have always considered themselves great sinners. They could have had in mind only that the very abundance of the graces given to them made any sin especially evil. Their very realization of offense against God made every sin seem heinous to them.

Such indeed should be our attitude, we of the Precious Blood spirituality, who can think of sin only in relation to the offense to Infinite Innocence. A final caution: no one knows how numerous are the grave sins of men. It is folly to say there are only few such sins! Mortal sin is rare! *Is it?* We simply do not know, but even though there be few, even a few are far too many: this we must say as we follow Jesus with his cross.

In the background of the way of the cross is the great kenotic text of Philippians 2:6-11, which we repeat again as our prayer:

> Though he was in the form of God
>   he did not deem equality with God
>   something to be grasped at.
>
> Rather, he emptied himself
>   and took the form of a slave,
>   being born in the likeness of men.
>
> He was known to be of human
>   estate,
>   and it was thus that he humbled
>   himself,
>   obediently accepting even death,
>   death on a cross!
>
> Because of this,
>   God highly exalted him
>   and bestowed on him the name
>   above every other name,
>
> So that at Jesus' name
>   every knee must bend
>   in the heavens, on the earth,
>   and under the earth,
>   and every tongue proclaim
>   to the glory of God the Father:
>
> JESUS CHRIST IS LORD!

A Final Note: The Masses Cry Love to Jesus

As the fifteenth station is the resurrection with and through Jesus, so the first or the introduction to the way of the cross is the clamor of the mob: Crucify him, give him the cross of Barabbas. The political worldly power, which washed its hands of him, sent him to his death. For all mankind Jesus' way of the cross must be the *way for every man,* and the total race of men/women. Only Rahner could say it: "The street signs are changed . . . the names are tragedy, cancer, divorce, atomic warfare" (Roeper, 99, *The Fifteenth Station,* Herder, N.Y.). The safe little pre-Copernican world had its tragedies, war, plague, starvation, petty tyranny, superstition, only to yield to Enlightenment, mass destruction, mass dictatorship, mass starvation in the midst of science enlightened beyond all history's dreams. We need only recall the mass starvation in World War I, the genocide, the gas chambers, the total war and atomic horror a few decades later. The forced migrations are still with us. Our abortion mills continue to grind. The fearsome thrust of planned evolution reaches into the hidden sources of life itself awakening we know not what ghastly realities from their depths — all create an awesome insecurity.

Our only safety lies beyond the finite in the God-man, in making his way our own — his cross our own. One with him in prayer, in loving intimacy, we must follow HIS WAY. Each individual can ponder in this context his own life-way, each family form prayerfully its own *way of the cross.* All the more should each community in the Church think out its own communal way of the cross in accordance with its own spirituality. But this involves a Jesus-love for all peoples and their love in return. Especially the oppressed masses must be led to the desire to bring HIM to themselves as the way of their life. We must endeavor to enrich them with spiritual goods as we relieve their wretched and hungry bodies. Our concern must also be the *moral ghettos* with their sophisticated refinement of sin. We must bear the love of Jesus and the warning of Jesus: the cross is the bright hope of resurrection: This is our Christocentric mission to all mankind as we follow the WAY OF THE CROSS. We can read no other meaning into human life.

As the masses cried: Crucify him; so now they must cry:

Love to the Lord Jesus
Now and forever!

Way of the Cross in the Vision of Henri Matisse

Lothar Schreyer looks upon the way of the cross as significant and beloved means of prayer, most helpful in preparation for the celebration of the Eucharistic mysteries. The devotion prepares for the Eucharist and flows from it. The order of the stations, their unique sequence, their total impact are in the spirit of the liturgy, their effectiveness increasing as we draw closer to the Eucharistic sacrifice. The devotion thrives on spiritual participation in the passion and death of Jesus, which in turn cannot fail to be enriched and deepened by the exercise.

Our author singles out the chapel at Vence in France with its work by Henri Matisse for its artistic expression and the interest it aroused even outside the Church, (cf. *NCE* Vol. 14, art. "Vence, Chapelle du Rosaire," p. 594f, and art. "Way of the Cross," illustration, p. 833). He looks upon this work of Matisse as belonging to the decisive representations of Christ in our time, decisive in Christian as well as artistic renewal. The fourteen stations, painted in 1951, the Rosary Madonna, and the huge figure of St. Dominic are painted on the ceramic tiles embedded in the wall.

Produced by a nervous brush in black linear designs, the stations make no pretense at historical or ornamental significance. Rather they may be considered signs of mystical experience, signals from the Christian mystery of the passion and the cross. They have their place set apart for them in the area of monastic prayer and the liturgical service for the Dominican nuns. Dominic, the stations, the Madonna and Child turn our minds to the liturgy on the altar.

M. A. Couturier, noted authority on the new art, looks upon the Stations as the most significant and beautiful objects in the chapel, but concedes that they might well be disappointing to men of our age. The younger men accept the work as a matter of course and love it. They live in harmony with it for it speaks the language they understand. And spirits as diverse as Picasso and Bazaine feel at home with it. Couturier finds no resemblance in this work to any prior modes or forms of Matisse. Nowhere else is there such forceful impact, total renunciation of even the slightest striving for beauty: here the lust of the eyes no longer prevails. Even the ciphers seem to be brushed brutally. (This critic recalls favorably a comment of Père Festugière that the *holy* recedes in art when the conscious urge for beauty appears). In the very great epochs, he says, art is naught but a language. No ornamentation. Speech may even be expressed in signs difficult to make intelligible to all. But it is certainly the artists' duty to offer all of purity and truth in the signs through which they reveal themselves to us (cf. P. Couturier in "L'Art sacre," Juillet-Aout 1951, p. 24-26). The Arabic ciphers help prayer to follow the individual stations as they lead upward through the fourteen stations suggesting meditation with a simplicity as we find in the beads of the rosary. Shunning hyper-intellectuality, they lead to meditation and as well flow from it.

We suggest that both rosary and stations are meditation-prayer and because of their objective prayer order are always prayer of community, even should the individual recite them as personal or individual exercise. They fill the space before and after the liturgical prayers of the Mass, prepare for them and thrive on the celebration of the mysteries.

Matisse starts at the bottom and leads upwards in what we might call *three stages*: the first comprising stations from 1 to 4: Jesus is condemned to death, takes up his cross, falls the first time under the cross, meets his Mother. The *middle* stage comprises stations 5 to 9: Simon of Cyrene is forced to take up the cross, Veronica offers the veil (*sudarium*), Jesus falls the second time, Jesus speaks to the women of Jerusalem, falls the third time. The *top row*: from stations 10 to 14: Jesus is bereft of his clothing and given gall and vinegar to drink, he is nailed to the cross, he dies on the cross, his body is taken down from the cross, he is buried.

The group of figures proceeds in two turns, from 4 to 5, and from 9 to 10. We may speak of it as a wave movement to the heights, the goal being the burial of Jesus. Here we repeat the ciphers:

$$10 — 11 — 12 — 13 — 14$$
$$9 — 8 — 7 — 6 — 5$$
$$1 — 2 — 3 — 4$$

The composition of the figures is Trinitarian in structure as is self-evident for the Christian image-proclamation. Consequently we have the intermingling of the *circle* structure, the *cross* structure, and the *triangle* structure. In what we have called the wave movement the circle structure is apparent, the periphery being held together by the great *cross* structures: the *perpendicular cross structure* with the cross as the center of the way of the cross extending from the center of the middle row of figures upward and downward, and to right and left of the entire middle series. The fifth figure, Simon of Cyrene takes up the cross, points to the head of the Christ, hanging on the cross. The diagonally cross structure has its center under the feet of the crucified, over the head of the Lord fallen the second time beneath the cross. The one diagonal manifests through this fallen Savior the direction of the tenth station, which shows Jesus bereft of his garments and given gall and vinegar to drink. The other diagonal extends from the first to the fourteenth station, from the condemnation to death to the burial. These diagonals form four triangle structures over which there is laid a great triangle structure from the first to the fourth and to the twelfth station, hence the raising of Christ to the cross as the embracing center of the entire way of the cross. From this center only the final goal, the fourteenth station, the burial becomes clear: the certainty of the resurrection from the grave.

Thus externally the way of the cross is a succession of fourteen stations but viewed inwardly the way of the cross is an intermingling of the stations in the order which is given them through the Trinitarian image structure. It leads through the *circle-structure, cross-structure,* and *triangle-structure* to the *focal point* of the picture, which is designated as the *cipher 12,* next to the hanging Christ, the divine sacrifice, the divine triumph of the God-man. The twelfth, which points to the crucified, points also to the *Veil of Veronica* which likewise emerges from the great triangle. Here on this, near the earthy form of the quadrangle of the veil, appears the *cipher 6* and the countenance of Christ. The *6* is not next to the figure but is drawn within the veil in the mystical signal of the mystery. It says in conjunction with the countenance of Christ: God had become man, and in the soul of man the image of the God-man as the image of Christ should be impressed. Jesus himself impresses it into our souls on his way to the cross, on those who pray and prayerfully ponder his cross. We must impress this image firmly within us, as Veronica impressed it indelibly on the veil.

Henri Matisse has written down the Christian truth of his age in the runic writing of the way of the cross, not death runes but victory runes celebrating the splendor of the triune God. Before that splendor every created appearance vanishes, also man himself into an *empty* transparent sign, from which only the face of the God-man peers at us, and that only in contours: for the glory of God is too transcendently great for us to grasp. The artist knows the truth: not human salvation is the actual center of Christian life, but God's glory. The center of divine service, of Christian prayer, of our religion is not man, but transcendently the great glory of God. Such is the utterance of these runes of the way of the cross in the atomic age. Only in the beginning of this age can the way of the cross be written down as Henri Matisse has done (*op. cit.,* p. 233-238).

CHAPTER NINE

PRECIOUS BLOOD SPIRITUALITY SONG AND HYMN

In the Second Vatican Council the Church Assigned to Sacred Music a Ministerial Function in the Liturgy. It Is Her Wish That the Faithful Participate in the Worship Through Song. She Encourages What Is Most Splendid in Her Traditions and Most Profoundly Embedded in Man's Heart When He Turns to His God.

Cf. *NCE*, Vol. 10, p. 97, Art. Sacred Music.

OUR SPIRITUALITY IN SONG AND HYMN

Music, song and hymn, according to both Old and New Testaments, belong to man's prayer and worship. Musical instruments such as lyre, harp, tambourine, and sacred dance expressed the joy of man's praise of God in the Old Testament. The opening psalm of our breviary, *Come, let us sing joyfully to the Lord,* is psalm 95. Glorious are the canticles of Moses and the Israelites over the delivery from Egypt (Exodus 15:1-18), David's elegy for Saul and Jonathan (2 Sam 1:19-27), Judith's song of thanksgiving (Judith, chapter 16), and the beautiful canticle of the three youths in the fiery furnace (Dan 3). Most significant is the Old Testament book of Psalms, which has become a great part of the Church's book of prayer, the sacred office, our holy hours, which contain also the triumphant *Benedictus,* the jubilant proclamation of the herald of the Savior, John the Baptist, by Zachary, his father, the *Magnificat,* the glorious praise of the God-to-come by his maiden Mother, and finally the *Nunc Dimittis* from the lips of the venerable Simeon. All these proclaim the official salvation history.

The early Christians, according to such writers as Balthasar Fischer and H. Leclercq, proclaimed their faith through hymns in their liturgical worship. Some of these hymns glow like jewels in the inspired scriptures. The most splendid, we think, is the kenotic hymn of Philippians 2:6-11, which we repeat several times in this study and recommend for meditation, prayer and song in our Precious Blood exercise. For us, too, these hymns must be "community cultic hymns." Their purpose was praise of God and instruction for the faithful in the revealed truth. Paul, who takes over some of the hymns, admonishes the Colossians, (3:16) to "sing gratefully to God . . . in psalms, hymns, and inspired songs." Similar is his thought in Ephesians (5:19). James advises that we in "good spirits" sing hymns of praise (5:13).

David Stanley, S.J., cites two fragments of early Christian song which are significant in salvation history and in our Precious Blood spirituality.

> Wake up, you sleeper,
> and arise from death,
> and Christ will light you up . . . (Eph 5:14).
> Who was revealed through his humanity,
> was justified by the Spirit,
> was beheld by angels,
> was proclaimed amongst nations,
> was believed in throughout the world,
> was taken up in glory (1 Tm 3:16).

Father Stanley, whose paper, "The Divinity of Christ in the New Testament," appears in *Proceedings SCCTSD*, Vol. 4, 1958, p. 12ff, cites the opinion of the above-mentioned writers in evidence that the early Christians turned to the Old Testament book of Psalms, and away from their own hymns when the latter were "seriously compromised by Gnostic abuses." But from the earliest times Christian writers in East and West also composed magnificent hymns for the liturgy and for sacred use, to combat error and give glory to God. Some of these hymns rank among the world's great religious poetry. Their purpose was to instruct men in the divine truth, defend it, in praise and worship of God.

The hymn is a literary, usually poetic, religious form used in Christian worship. A fine study of the history of the hymn is given in considerable detail as to texts and authorship in the *NCE* under the titles *Hymnology, Hymns and Hymnals*. In the first of the two articles we have a few columns dealing with the early Christian period, and then the more specific discussion: the Greek hymnody is said to have emerged in reaction to the powerful Gnostic propaganda. Similarly, the Syriac hymnody arose in defense against heresy, producing the great work of St. Ephrem (died in 373), whose hymns "lent luster to the Christian assemblies," according to the writer cited in Vol. 5, p. 464 (art. "Ephrem"). Among the Greeks the *Akathistos,* probably from the sixth century, is the most celebrated hymn of the Byzantine Church. Among the Armenians there was also a very active hymnody, according to the first of the articles cited (*Hymnology,* p. 288).

In Western or Latin hymnody St. Ambrose (died 397), the great archbishop of Milan, Father and Doctor of the Church, has been called the *Father of Liturgical Hymnody.* His influence through his hymns, their imitation in style and structure has been tremendous. The texts were originally most probably directed against the Arian heresy. The doxologies give ample evidence of their apologetic intent. We note, but with considerable doubt, that even the jubilant paschal hymn, the *Exsultet* has been attributed to Ambrose. We rank it among the great Precious Blood hymns.

From the sixth century throughout the Middle Ages until Renaissance and Reformation Latin hymns with marvellous variation in their poetic structure celebrated the mysteries of faith. Unfortunately the attempt to return to classic forms in the Renaissance proved a failure, for the spirit of deep Christian piety could not mingle well with concepts of Olympian gods and godesses. The medieval hymns and sequences shared in the creation of the religious atmosphere which we have in mind when we speak of the ages of the faith.

Heading the list is what we may call the most popular and magnificent of them all, the *Te Deum Laudamus* which probably dates from the fifth century. It is the hymn of the Trinity, the incarnation, the redemption through the Precious Blood, the hymn of total creation jubilantly giving glory to God and hoping through his mercy to be united with him in glory forever. In a very true sense the *Te Deum* is a great doxology of the Precious Blood spirituality.

Significant in this early period is the pope who may be called the founder of the Middle Ages, Gregory the Great (died in 604). Many of his hymns and their popular melodies have found their way into the Roman breviary. At about this time *Venantius Fortunatus* composed the hymns which celebrate the triumph of the cross and the mystery of redemption. They rank among the masterpieces of Latin poetry. We like to call them processional and associate them with the palms of Christian victory won by the cross: *Pange Lingua Gloriosi Lauream Certaminis* and *Vexilla Regis Prodeunt.* For a thousand years religious song and hymn sanctified the day, the feast, the whole Christian life. Especially vivid are the sequences in the liturgical prayer, and we feel that many of the faithful were sufficiently versed in Latin to join in them and understand them unto their spiritual profit.

Only the splendor of the medieval cathedral could match the beauty of medieval Latin religious poetry. We cannot so much as picture the cathedrals without also calling to mind the synthesis of architecture and sculpture with the gorgeous, rich beauty of the stained-glass windows. We call to mind the beauty of the books of hours. And finally, the flow of sacred prayer in choral recitation by the cathedral chapters or the monks. The Gregorian chant is the most perfect symmetry of rhythmic words of chanted prayer and the liturgical acts of the sacred sacrifice ever wrought in two thousand years of Christian worship — here is the very center of worship.

Before the high Middle Ages the invocation of the Holy Spirit, the *Veni Creator Spiritus*, was written. From the 10th century, it rivals even the majestic *Te Deum Laudamus* in its warmth of appeal to the human heart begging the Spirit who is the Love of Father and Son to enrich us with his grace. The *Jesu Dulcis Memoria* is probably the most fervent expression of the Jesus-love in all Christian prayer and song; attributed to Saint Bernard of Clairvaux (died in 1153), it is probably the work of an anonymous English Cistercian of the 12th century. From the 12th century or earlier the *Dies Irae* ranks with the *Stabat Mater* as the greatest hymn of the Middle Ages. The *Stabat Mater*, probably from the 13th century, seems to us today an essential part of the way of the cross. Both hymn and sequence, it has had over two hundred translations into vernaculars. Among the great composers who set the poem to music, the work of Palestrina is especially noted. Usually attributed to Thomas of Aquin are the Eucharistic hymns, *Verbum Supernum Prodiens* and *Lauda Sion Salvatorem*, which are probably the most perfect synthesis of word and rhythm in medieval poetry. The *Adoro Te Devote Latens Deitas* is even more deeply touching, though according to the *NCE* (art. "Hymnology", Vol. 7, p. 294) it is not the work of Thomas. Much later, in the very period of decline, we have the popular non-liturgical Christmas hymn *Adeste Fideles* attributed to John Francis Wade (cf. *NCE,* art. "Adeste Fideles", Vol. 1, p. 128).

Hymn and Song in Vernacular

If Renaissance signified an impossible turn to classic models and decline in the Church's hymnody, the Reformation on very broad lines turned to sacred hymns of great popular appeal and religious beauty. In German language areas because of the success of German song throughout the religious worship (though Luther himself moved cautiously in Germanizing the Mass), the Catholics also accepted the vernacular in the liturgy. From 1605 there developed the so-called *Singmesse* and the use of hymns in German. The writer recalls sharing in such worship in which the people in a vast congregation joyfully participated through worship-in-song. The Catholics also produced their German books of hymns, even antedating Luther's death with publications from 1537, 1567, and 1584. In England the Protestant groups were, with few exceptions, singing worshippers. Perhaps the most influential were the Methodists whose founders, Charles and John Wesley, contributed to religious revival through translations from the German and also through original compositions, which are truly an inspiring heritage of *worship through song*.

The Oxford Movement and its spiritual renewal meant a liturgical renewal in the Church of England. One of the results was the translation of many ancient hymns from Latin and Greek. The spiritual treasures of the ancient Church were made available to millions in English-speaking countries.

From the beginning in our country the Catholic attempts to produce hymnody reflect the missionary efforts to reach the people in Spanish, Aztec, Huron, English, German and the native languages of the immigrants. For a more complete account we call attention to the article in the *NCE* on Hymns and Hymnals (Vol. 7, p. 302 ff), which includes the history of the 20th century hymnals, and a proposal for the hymnody of the future. The conclusion is that we should work toward a "variety of hymnals" with basic common elements. Thus our great and varied Catholic people could "sing with one voice the praise of their God and Creator" (*ibid.*, p. 304).

We have presented this extended historic profile of song and music in worship as clear evidence that the Christian worship and prayer life must be in the context of music and song. Even though today we have the vernacular in the liturgy throughout, each spirituality must endeavor to express itself and its exercise in this context. If indeed we have Precious Blood spirituality in its prayer, we must also have it in its song.

Accordingly there are three cogent reasons to place in our study of the Precious Blood spirituality an historic background that embraces almost the entire area of the Church's worship:

1) The great hymns of the past are largely redemptive: e.g., the *Te Deum Laudamus*, the *Exsultet*, the *Pange Lingua Gloriosi*, the *Stabat Mater*, etc.

2) By the very nature of man and our divine worship, music and song form a context in which every spirituality must find its place, though preserving its distinctive characteristics. Thus the Precious Blood spirituality with its distinctive prayer, exercise, etc. as we show in this study, must also have its distinctive hymnody. It would other-

wise be impoverished, deprived of one of the beautiful essentials of all worshipful and meaningful spirituality.

3) As in the past we must use this means for the instruction and formation in our own societies of the Precious Blood. We must use it also in this our age to confront the present world in its isolation from God, its confrontation with the masses of men, to draw them to Christ. The lesson of history is clear: almost invariably the Catholics reacted to the errors and needs of their age with music and song. Such is the lesson from the days of the Gnostics and Arians who spread their error through popular song.

In our own community, progress has been made by our own writers and composers. Now the communities and societies of the Precious Blood cry out to us to continue their work, create and expand the Precious Blood hymnody. They seem to cry out to us:

Pange Lingua Gloriosi Sanguinis Mysterium.

A Word on the Hymnody of the Eastern Churches

Elsewhere we refer to the splendor of the Eastern Churches and their liturgies. Amid this splendor the sacred hymns mingle with the consecratory and processional prayer, in deep faith and love for God, Christ, God-man, High Priest, Mary, Theotokos, Christ bound up with the Church, and Mary too, whom we might call the Mother of the Church. In prayer the liturgies extol the spiritual beginning which is the very incarnation, for the Church was born in the *Epiphania* of the *Logos*. In the East Syrian Christmas hymn Christ is sung as gathering all peoples as *ecclesia* which he sanctified through the glory of his divinity, for he was truly and fully man. The Church is Christ, living from him and constantly renewing his salvific life in her sacramental mysteries. The Ethiopian liturgy links Church and Mary, for both are God-receiving, God-embracing. In the Church is the Bridal Chamber, the Immortal Bridegroom, whence the rebirth of us children, through baptism. Here too is the table, the altar at which the priest stands, empowered by the great High Priest reigning in glory, bidding us to share the table, the Eucharist.

We shall refer specifically to only one hymn, the *Akathistos Hymn* which commemorates the deliverance of Constantinople from the barbarians in 626. Probably the most splendid Marian hymn of all times, it glorifies Mary as the *Theotokos*. It has been translated into all languages of the Byzantine rite, and many times into Latin. There are a number of English versions. We give here only two stanzas, which make clear that it is a noble *Precious Blood Hymn*:

Being minded to save the world, the Maker of all came willingly into it and, shepherd because God, to us and for us did he appear a man; and having called like unto like, as God he hears: Alleluia.

When he who payeth all men's debts was minded the ancient debts to pay, self-exiled he came to them who were exiled from his grace and, tearing up the bond, he heard from all: Alleluia.

(From the Akathistos Hymn, Blackfriars Publications Oxford, 1947, by Vincent McNabb. For the references to the Hymnody of the Eastern Churches, cf. "Heilige Theophanie," *op. cit.*).

CHAPTER TEN

PRECIOUS BLOOD SPIRITUALITY
THE KERYGMA

If We Are Filled With the Spirit of Jesus We Shall Proclaim in Word and Deed the Sanguis Christi Unto All Men. Countless Are the Themes Suited to Every Phase of Human Life and Need. The Spirit Who Is the Love of the Father and the Son Shall Teach Us How to Speak On the Wonders of Redemption-Through-Jesus-Blood. If We Live and Experience the Precious Blood Spirituality, If Its Three Great Mysteries Basic to Revelation Are the Context of Our Spiritual Life and Love, Then We Can Proclaim to This Post-Christian, Anti-Christian World the Whole Theology of Salvation History.

How shall we preach, how proclaim the Precious Blood spirituality? The *Sanguis Christi* as the person of Christ in the entire work of redemption is the source and object of our *kerygma,* but in relation to all the needs of mankind. As the Word Incarnate communicates the divine, the God-life to us, so by our word we communicate it to all mankind. The whole Christ was communicated to us in the *Apostolic Preaching.* Christ is the whole of revelation, *tota revelatio Christus est.*

Paul is the model in our *kerygma.* He preached Christ, Christ crucified — the cross — the Blood — the death. We accept the message from his lips, embrace and repeat it. Our model and justification for our *kerygma* is the Apostolic *kerygma,* the basis for the Church's whole teaching. Christ has always been proclaimed as crucified — died and buried — and risen from the dead.

In the light of the *Sanguis Christi* the preacher and every Christian teacher explains the whole Christian truth and the whole Christian law. With the rich resources of Scripture and tradition at their disposal, they explain the truth of Christ and law of Christ. A profound penetration of the biblical concepts with their redemptive significance is imperative: *covenant, blood, reconciliation; mediation, priesthood, sacrifice; cross, death, Eucharist, Church; Christ, merit, grace, vision.* Throughout they must hold fast to the one Christ, the one priesthood, the one redemption through blood, one action-presence.

The preacher has his task set for him: to study the theological data and apply them to this age and his audience. First he must fashion his mind *and* heart in the Precious Blood spirituality for this age with its *EPOCHAL TURN* from traditional thought and life. Like all the great crises of the Church in the past — the turn from the small Jewish community converts clinging to the Jewish ritual, the dietary strictures, to the Pauline concept of the message for the whole Gentile world; the Constantinian conversion with the gradual enmeshing of powers of temporal and spiritual; the feudalization of the Church; the Gregorian Reform; the Renaissance-Reformation, etc. — the present crisis negatively threatens ruin for the Church, and positively offers a *KAIROS*, the providential call of grace in her life, her theology and her mission. *THE NOW* faces modern evolutionary man in an evolving universe. Science, technology, the evolutionary outlook are concerned with a reality that extends from atom to cosmos. The total structure of man in his bio-psychic reality — his origins, his genetic structure, and even his future as a race — are studied and explored. We are now facing the making of man and his world, his traditions, his social and economic structures from which sacred and sacral have been exorcised.

According to Walter Kasper (whose thought we reflect in the above) we are now witnessing the culmination of the Enlightenment, in which finally *man has become the measure of man, the center of all reality.* Sharp is his German term: *Bezugspunkt,* the *target-point* to which all is referred, from which all is perceived, judged, and fashioned. This we call the *ANTHROPOLOGICAL TURN.* The result is transformation in every order, social-cultural-religious-political. Man in freedom and equality challenges authority in family, the Church, society. We repeat: no structure is immune, not even the genetic heritage which fashions man's future on our planet, and this, the most bold thrust of the crisis, involves the gravest moral problems, which the theologians have scarcely dared to face — much less solve.

The Precious Blood theology in its *kerygma* must confront these problems involving the doctrine of the origins of man, the natural and supernatural order, original sin, planned evolution (the thorniest of all), man's task in the world. All theology must be concerned that our Christology shed light on our anthropology. A new Precious Blood Christocentrism must place the CROSS AND THE RESURRECTION in the heart of the *brave new world.* Evolutionary science points to man as the goal of this evolving universe. Our theology holds that man representing this vast universe — in a real sense making it his own — must turn to Christ the Redeemer as the center and goal. According to Chenu, man "leads the world to its fulfillment and destiny by leading it to God, in his understanding and love . . . man can bring about this return through and in Christ."

The same writer says that all the works of man, whose summit is the building of the world through the centuries, are recapitulated by Christ. "Assimilated into his Body they thus center into his work and his mystery as total creation. So the believer can read and live Christ's death and resurrection there."

> All the current morality of work, all the roots of professional life, in man, in the universe and in the community, are thus elevated to the divine quality of praise, offering, and liberation which are the three characteristics accomplished in the paschal act of Jesus Christ (Chenu, *DOC*, no. 124).

A NOTE SUGGESTED BY SCHNACKENBURG

Rudolph Schnackenburg in *The Truth Will Make You Free* (H. & H., New York, 1966) contrasts tiny man with the expanse of worlds in the universe; yet it is man who has reached out to distant orbs to *scoop up their sand.* In a very true sense we may apply the words of the philosopher, *"esse est percepi."* Man is indeed master of this universe and the psalmist rightly proclaims that God has given man dominion over all the works of his hands. He has put "all things under his feet" (Ps 8:7). But the unity of all the universe, says the distinguished exegete, is only because it is apprehended by man (*op. cit.*, p. 86ff). The message of divine revelation is directed not merely to each man, but to the whole of mankind. He cites the pertinent warning of R. Eucken in *Der Wahrheitsgehalt der Religion* (p. 43) that "we have won a world and lost the soul."

Indeed, before us is the tremendous task of saving the soul through winning the world, bringing the Christ-loving soul to the universe. If God's revelation is to all the universe, and his holy law and will rule it, then it can only be through Christ that this revelation and this law shall prevail. The Lord of history directing all of salvation history centers it in his Christ whom we of the Precious Blood spirituality proclaim as *Sanguis Christi.* The great events proclaimed by Yahweh in the Old Testament are re-echoed in the new, especially in the Book of Revelation. The final triumph shall be Christ's, on whose thigh is written *King of kings and Lord of lords* (Rv 19:15f). This we shall never cease to proclaim in our Precious Blood *kerygma.* (For the above cf. Walter Kasper, *Einfuehrung in den Glauben*, Gruenewald, Mainz 1972; Hubertus Mynarek, *Der Mensch, Sinnziel der Weltent-wicklung*, Schoeningh, Muenchen, 1967; Rudolph Schnackenburg, *The Truth Will Make You Free*, H. & H., New York, 1966. Cf. also the writer's paper in the *CTSA, Proceedings*: Cosmic Evolution: The Contemporary Setting of Theology, p. 31ff, Manhattan College, 1973).

A RUBRIC ON THEILHARD DE CHARDIN

In a very perceptive review of a recent book by Wolfgang Klein on Theilhard de Chardin and the Second Vatican Council, Alois Guggenberger calls our attention to this new view of the world set before us in *Gaudium et Spes* — a new task of cosmic proportions for the Church. It would be a great disservice to the divine revelation to sever what has constantly been united in it: God and the world. Rather sarcastically, he cautions against the attitude: We do not want to defile our hands with the world. We must view our great task in the tremendous mainstream of the evolving universe with Christ as its center. The writer confronts us with the parallel: Kant said *Without God the world is blind,* and completes the thought: According to Theilhard, for us God without the world is empty (*TR*, no. 3, 1976, cols. 230ff).

A SPECIAL URGENCY

Highest priority in the *kerygma* is the explanation of our spirituality to the members of our societies of the Precious Blood. Such urgency arises from the nature of the societies, their place in the Church, their relation to a diversity of tasks, opportunities, graces — their relation to all mankind in this age. Surely those entrusted with formation programs would be grossly derelict in duty should they fail to present the Precious Blood spirituality to all those who are to cultivate it, lead and guide others in accordance with it.

If the Church herself beatifies and canonizes chosen souls on the basis of their spirituality and in many instances holds up their life and work as special patterns in distinctive areas of doctrine and practice, then surely the Precious Blood societies have the duty to fashion and form their members in the spirituality which distinctly marks them as chosen societies and communities in the Church.

Throughout the societies there must be the constant concern for enrichment of our spirituality. The persistent inquiry, the unrelaxed attention, the deepening hunger — and correspondingly the response from the scriptures, the hagiography, the biographical models from their own midst. This opportunity offers itself in the formation programs, in the explication of the Precious Blood vocation. As underlying *vocation* the appeal must first be directed to the truly essential rather than to the merely existential, though the latter will always have its place in the providential call to religious or priestly state. Our Christian spirituality, our true devotion should be focused on the *Sanguis Christi* and the Precious Blood spirituality. Here too a certain priority belongs to those characteristics most suitable for our current needs and the life of the Church in our day.

THE KERYGMA: A NOTE ON THE EXERCISE

This writer deems it imperative that we never cease to point out that each spirituality in the Church cultivates its own genius, which marks its communal prayer, its work, even its silence, its variety and flexibility, allowing for diversity of groups, religious, priests, students, laity, etc. Going a step further, one might encourage and urge the practice of every form of shared prayer in the most varied groups, suited to need, occasion, devout desire. The center, of course, is the Eucharist, sacrifice and sacrament. Never to be excluded is the Eucharistic presence, the public and private adoration, all of which relate to the Eucharist. In our covenant with the Father, sealed with the Blood of the Son, we have the sacrificial-meal (the German is beautiful, *Opfermahl*), the meal-sacrifice, (the German says *Mahlopfer*) and permanent sacrament. Such is the object of our *kerygma* as it is of our whole prayer life.

Basic, of course, is the sacrificial liturgy — the holy Mass itself — but essentially flowing from it is the *Sacrament of the Presence*. The empty churches in the Northern lands and in Britain (and some of the magnificent churches in our country, e.g., St. John the Divine in New York) when the liturgy is not being conducted, despite the unsurpassable rhythm and cadence of the biblical and liturgical idiom of the official prayer, may well be due to the absence of the *sacrament of the Presence*. This calls attention to the necessity of a well balanced Eucharistic doctrine and explanation also in our time. Occasionally we note today the lack of stress of the Mass as a sacrifice, a tendency to disregard the Presence in the tabernacle and the Eucharistic blessing called the Benediction of the Blessed Sacrament, the silent visits, and the Eucharistic processions. Our Eucharistic and Precious Blood *kerygma* must correct any imbalance of this kind, as departure from sound doctrine and our tradition.

The Precious Blood spirituality must be open to every spiritual form, to every Christian who turns in love to Christ the Savior. And utterly shun all zealotry and partisan propaganda! Positively drawn to the Christ-presence-and-action in the Mystical Body, we look forward to the Second Coming. We hallow the name of God in the most intimate union with Jesus' love for men and in the most intimate bond with Jesus' love for God his Father. We share in the merit, atonement, satisfaction, sacrifice, spiritually shedding our blood with his. Loving adoration of God through his Son and in his Holy Spirit embraces the everlasting covenant and seals us in the divine life of the Trinity. Sealed in the Blood of the cross, we are pledged to eternal resurrection.

If we wrestle with new forms, we see the old in a new and richer light shed by the Spirit of Jesus, who is infinitely rich and diverse in his gifts. The *kerygma* must include preparation for sharing these exercises and promoting them by an ever deepening appreciation of the basic Precious Blood spirituality.

N. B. The instruction summarized in the above pages is concerned with the Precious Blood spirituality as such. We imply no neglect of the usual catechetical *indoctrination* (we do not apologize for the word) and the comprehensive theological disciplines, though not according to the ancient handbooks. It is beyond our purpose to present an organized curriculum, though we do refer to the matter in our notes. (cf. note 3).

CHAPTER ELEVEN

THE PRECIOUS BLOOD SPIRITUALITY
THE VOCATION

*If God Calls Every Christian by Name to His Service,
He Himself Will Guide And Direct Him Through His
Holy Spirit. The Call to the Spirituality of the Precious
Blood Is the Vocation With Its Special Grace, Its Challenges, Its Opportunities, Its Loving Providence. If the
Great Book of Ignatius of Loyola Is the Book of Destiny
Still Unrivalled in Its Power to Transform Men Who Embrace It in the Spirit of Its Author, Then Our Precious
Blood Spirituality Must Also Transform Us Totally in
the Love of the Sanguis Christi (cf. Ertraege der Fors-
chung, by Jedin and Baeumer, p. 129, and the reference
of Karl Holl, Evangelical Theologian, to the Ignatian Exercises).*

Vocation is divine invitation, divine call, divine summons to special
service in salvation history. The response, we may say, is the grace of
vocation in its fulfillment. Vocation is far more than initial call and response, it is continuous summons and faithful response unto final perseverance opening to eternal glory. We must learn with docility from salvation
history written large in the inspired pages what the divine call means for
the individual and for God's people. God's call was announced through
the patriarchs and the prophets of Yahweh in the Old Testament. Abraham was to be the father of a great people, Moses saved the Chosen People
from the serfdom of Egypt, sealed a covenant with God in blood of sacrifice
for them. And the great prophets reminded them of God's love which made
them his children. The vocation, the call from Yahweh went out to the
leaders and all the Chosen People. Such was the divine vocation to all the

Chosen People and their leaders. Thus official salvation history draws men to Christ in all ages.

In our study of the Precious Blood spirituality we speak of a Precious Blood Vocation: going beyond the vocation to all Christians, it is a call to membership in the Precious Blood societies throughout the world. It is a unique call to those who are to lead the way, the founders, the models, some of whose names are scattered throughout this study — and to many more. Here we single out one who was most dramatically called by a conversion-vocation, the account of which is emblazoned in the inspired pages of the Acts of the Apostles. In the very violence of his stride to persecute the followers of Christ comes the summons to be the great Apostle of the Redemptive Blood through which the world is to be won for Christ, called to be the New Redeemed, the New Chosen People, sealed with the Blood of the Eternal Covenant, — the *Sanguis Christi*. Stricken, fallen, blinded, as by a fierce light of divine grace, he hears the call: "Saul, Saul, why do you persecute me?"

His unique vocation as Apostle of the Redemptive Blood is told in the inspired accounts, in his apostolic journeys, his preaching, in his followers of the first ages and all ages to come in the Church. It is Paul who issues the challenge to the early Church to become truly catholic, universal. It is Paul who responds with total commitment, total renunciatory love, tremendous *kerygma,* in spoken and written word which is by God's own inspiration. Even in his chains he proclaimed the word, for the word of God was never fettered (cf. 2 Tm 2:9).

Our study of the other great spiritualities, the call to great saints in their historic backgrounds, and to the holy men and women who sought salvation for themselves and others through them should awaken in us a desire to penetrate more deeply into our own spirituality of the Precious Blood. But we must at least mention the very noted ones and suggest their study. The *NCE* has three long articles on the *Benedictine Spirituality,* the *Dominican Spirituality, the Franciscan Spirituality.* In the third volume of Karl Rahner's "Theological Investigations," the great theologian gives us his reflections on the Sacred Heart devotion and on Ignatian mysticism. Special value attaches to the encyclopedic articles because of their extensive background study and the historic influences.

We repeat there is the Precious Blood vocation to all our Precious Blood societies as such. They are summoned not only to offer and adore the Precious Blood in the liturgy, but also to ponder and meditate on the Blood of the Redeemer, to join together in the Precious Blood prayer, to form their membership in the Precious Blood spirituality, in a word to honor and imitate their great founders and leaders. One of the special duties of the societies is to cultivate the Precious Blood exercise in their spirituality, and finally their supreme duty, the unique duty of their Precious Blood vocation is to lovingly and fervently accept and practice the Precious Blood *kerygma* for all mankind. In this they share in the charisms of their leaders and founders and providentially in their graces.

The individual members of the Precious Blood societies, those attracted to membership may indeed be called to priesthood, brotherhood, to a community of sisters of the Precious Blood (with their great variation in rule and way of life) by many providential forms of external grace. Almost invariably vocation to priesthood or religious life involves many concrete, even social, cultural, and educational realities which extend far beyond the spirituality of the religious society they may enter. Practical opportunity suited to one's backgrounds, gifts, reasonable desires, cannot be ignored. The entire *Dasein* of the community itself taken concretely — not the mere ideal or abstract reality — is the object of the vocation.

We hold that the vocation to a Precious Blood religious society may never fail in true love for the Precious Blood spirituality in the sense in which we have explained it. If this is not present in the very beginnings of the entry into the society, it must be formed and developed. And once it is present, it must be nurtured into the fruition of the vocation which demands loving growth by the very exercise of the spirituality. This involves the *Precious Blood Dialogue* between member and member, member and superior. One of the great tasks of every superior and spiritual director — all who are dedicated to the tasks of formation in the *Sanguis Christi* — is precisely the cultivation of in-depth Precious Blood spirituality.

Obviously the old rigidity, with the tyrannical stress of command and obey, has already largely faded from our scene. At present there is rather need for caution: we may never permit the more familial and gentle life style to open the doors to a fallacious fluidity leading to an undermining of essential structures and forms. If, indeed, some shudder at the very word *obedience,* they must humbly recall the Christ, who was *obedient unto death,* the death of the cross. It was placed on his shoulders to atone for our *disobedience,* — by his own loving Father.

The uniqueness of the structures established by Christ, — involving the relations between shepherd and flock, between official-Sacramental priesthood and priesthood of all Christians, between hierarchy and laity, — is rooted in the very constitutive will of Christ. It would be a fatal error to ground all forms and structures of the Church in a mere social order which essentially fluctuates and varies in time and place. The Church rests on the mandate from Christ, not from the ecclesial community. To seek analogies between the One-and-Holy and the political structures, between the universal

call to the Mystical Body and the will of men to form social and political de-
mocracies, is fraught with peril precisely because such endeavor rests on a
false concept of the Church. In the spirit of Newman and of the Second
Council of the Vatican, we indeed accept a development in the doctrine and
the life of the Church, but not the destructive evolutionary changes involving
her essential structure and form. Pointedly in reference to our own Precious
Blood communities, in the distinction between ordained priest and brother/
sister member, we stress the difference in the service to the work of priesthood
itself, though we never denigrate the reality of the sacred order.

All, but all, must keep ever in mind the great dignity of the evangelical
counsels of poverty, chastity and obedience. Especially exalted is the vow
taken by some of the societies. But where there is no vow, all the greater
must be the will to attain to the spirit of the vow, a point we think that
is too often overlooked in the actual concrete way of our life.

The founding will of Christ is basic to the Church. Through his incarnation, his life, teaching, passion and death, the sending of his Holy
Spirit, he called her into being. In an infinitely rich idiom of image, word,
deed, whose meanings are inexhaustible, he founded and fashioned the
Church and her entire spirituality. Into this our vocation must be fitted
as we shape and mold it amidst many concrete realities. Through the grace
of his Blood we respond to that call which is our vocation to the spirituality
of the Precious Blood.

In deep gratitude for our membership in the Church, for our vocation
to the Precious Blood spirituality in the societies of the Precious Blood —
which she embraces, approves, and urges to great and holy action — we
hold fast to the *Sanguis Christi*. We are asked: Who is the Church of
Christ, Christian and Catholic? We respond: We who are the societies of
the Precious Blood. We respond: We, all of us. We! It is our duty to
make the command of John XXIII that we spread the devotion to the *Sanguis Christi,* his greatest achievement. Can we measure up to this ideal?
Or should we continue in the backwater of history? — the challenging term
of Karl Rahner (*Grace in Freedom,* H. & H. 1969, p. 13).

THE COROLLARY: THE VOCATIONAL TASKS

From the above pages on the vocation, it is evident that both the societies of the Precious Blood and their individual members bear the deep
responsibility of the exercise of the spirituality of the Precious Blood. This
obviously implies an involvement in all that relates to the spirituality as
presented in our study. But unique tasks flow from the vocation (and the
kerygma): these vocational tasks confront and challenge the societies of
the Precious Blood in their call and the individual as well. Obviously the

two are distinct, but to the mind of this writer they are not separable. The individual's vocational task must be set in the context of the larger vocational task of the societies of which he or she is a member. Particularly today this calls for much study upon the membership of the societies themselves. However, it cannot be made the object of an extensive study in this work. We can do little more than lay down a few principles or guidelines.

1) A Proximate Immediate Guide in the practical order: the societies should follow the rule and norm laid down by their constitutions as approved by the Church. To this we add the guidelines of their traditions. They should not seek to limit themselves to these lines of action, but go far beyond, always with the proper approval and under the guidance of the Holy Spirit. We speak of this as the proximate norm for ordinary procedure. However, the deep spirituality of the Precious Blood must be the motivating force in all action. The special gifts and charisms must be deeply cherished by individuals and groups.

2) The Ultimate Norm: the Precious Blood vocation extends to every spiritual activity in the Church, every field of activity, within the limits of the capacity of the members — in matter of numbers, talent, opportunity, physical, moral, intellectual means — and the superiors. The profoundest study in research, the greatest diversity in teaching, the active care and pastoral ministry — all are included.

3) The Ideal to be Striven For: concern for the poor, the needy, the imprisoned, the disadvantaged, the most desperate. It is imperative not to show too great a concern *for our own parishes, our own institutions, our income financially.* Here we stress the concern for the charismatic, the unusual, individual vocation under the special guidance of the Holy Spirit.

4) To be Shunned: the activity that disregards the guidelines of the Church and obedience to superiors, while presuming to follow one's own choice as the will of God.

> *The Precious Blood Vocational Task: Supreme Effort*
> *To Be Guided by the Holy Spirit In the Redemptive*
> *Work in Union with the Sanguis Christi.*

OUR SPIRITUALITY: SUPREMELY ECUMENICAL

Though Gaspar's followers have the great *charism of zeal for souls,* as should be apparent from this study, I do not think we have set forth ecumenism as one of our most basic tasks. It would not be an unfair appraisal to say that we have rather neglected the deeper study and the far-reaching implications of the great *Decree on Ecumenism.* This decree and the mandate of our own Pope of the Precious Blood must again call to mind our ecumenical concern. The Precious Blood spirituality must find true leaders in the ecumenical movement on every level. With all the warmth of the

loving Heart of Jesus, we must reach out to all who profess the Sacred
Name of Jesus and "accept them with respect and affection as brothers"
(*DOV*, "Decree on Ecumenism," no. 3).

The basic attitude of the Church is obvious to anyone familiar with
the documents of Vatican II. The Catholic Church holds that in her the
Church of Christ *subsists,* and that she possesses the total revelation of Jesus
Christ. This she will not concede to any other Christian church or community. But rather than condemn or anathematize them, she sees in them
in varying degrees much of the divine revelation. And with a stress that
is most truly Catholic, calculated to deepen and enrich our own deep faith.
This holds for what we might call the Orthodox groups, and for the Evangelical and Anglican churches. And it is true that even before Vatican II
our Catholic theologians had opened up the rich treasures of biblical
thought in the Protestant research unto the vast enrichment of our Catholic
theology.

Ecumenism is not to be understood as indifference to the truths and
practices of our faith. Rather the truly ecumenical Catholic must be deeply
informed on the Catholic truth, and practice his religion with deep piety
and concern. If he is to engage in ecumenical discussion with other Christian groups, he must be thoroughly grounded both in his own Catholic theology and in the teachings of the partners in the ecumenical discussion. It
has been stressed that true ecumenical discussion bears the triangular mark:
it combines the Catholic, the Protestant including the Anglican communities,
and the Orthodox churches. Only in this way can the deep riches of the
entire Catholic heritage preserved beyond the confines of the Catholic Roman Church be grasped. Often the fully Catholic has been more profoundly stressed in these so-called separated groups.

As to this latter point we may single out Martin Luther. His stress of
the written word inspired by God makes him for us a "prophetic force unto
the Gospel." Thus we speak of him, not as a canonized saint or doctor of
the Universal Church, but in all sincerity as a *Catholic prophet.*

For an understanding of the divisions among Christians and the effort
to work ecumenically toward unity, it is first of all essential to study the
origins of these divisions and their development. Here, above all, it is necessary to dismiss the polemical attitude that often deepened the divisions and
made unity impossible. The sharp and bitter attitude toward Martin Luther
has almost completely disappeared in the last decades as we strove for historical truth. This we must also hope for in the other partners in our dialogue. Very closely allied to this is the rejection of patterns of thought with
the insistence that they be applied to the thought of all the partners. How
often have we heard that Friar Martin was not adequately trained in the

High Scholastic, and therefore repudiated the ancient doctrine which we cling to with a scholastic and traditional mind-set. Here we must rather search into the theology of a totally different type of thinker. For an honest appraisal of Luther we must study him in the life and context of the explosive reformer, the violent preacher, wherein we might well find many contradictions if we study him with Thomistic guidelines. Only recently Otto Hermann Pesch, O.P., has given us a massive study of the doctrine of justification in Luther by comparison with that of Aquinas, and found that they do not differ substantially (cf. *Die Theologie der Rechtfertigung bei Martin Luther und Thomas von Aquin*, Matthias-Gruenewald-Verlag, Mainz, 1967). The second chapter of the *Decree on Ecumenism*, no. 6, warns us to make a careful distinction between the deposit of faith and the formulation of the doctrine. The same chapter admonishes us to present our doctrine in terms that the separated brethren can understand, an admonition which is essential for the entire presentation of the Catholic truth to the present generation.

Very significant is the teaching of Vatican II regarding the "hierarchy" of truths on the basis of the relationship to that which is the very foundation of the faith. Obviously the Catholic ecumenist will be able to discern and fashion a closer bond between certain non-Catholic Christian bodies than with others, without disrupting the common bond which unites all in the profession of our faith in Christ.

The student of our Precious Blood spirituality must welcome the engagement in ecumenical discussion, the joining in common prayer through Christ our Lord Redeemer. He seeks light in the great Precious Blood texts: Colossians (entire first chapter); Ephesians 1:7ff, chapter two; 1 Tm 2: 3-6, and the 17th chapter of John.

The SANGUIS CHRISTI, source of all life, all meaning, must be the basis of our prayer and study for unity of all Christians.

THE ANONYMOUS CHRISTIAN

We conclude with that brilliant insight of Karl Rahner regarding the *anonymous Christian*. On the basis of the noted text (1 Tm 2:4) that God wills all men to be saved, Rahner finds the anonymous Christian in the underlying yearning of many who are *explicitly atheists*, in those who seek after truth or the absolute good. Scarcely different is the teaching of Hubertus Mynarek in his work, *Der Mensch Das Wesen Der Zukunft*, to which we refer in our *Final Rubric* following the pages on our Precious Blood Prayer. Uniquely the Precious Blood spirituality, the vocation, the *kerygma*, relate to this insight of Rahner and Mynarek.

Only the redemptive Blood gives these concepts their deeper meaning. Wherefore the Precious Blood spirituality must be borne up by the universal salvific will of God: the redemptive grace offered to all men must be most effectively offered to those whose vocation and *kerygma* rest in the Precious Blood spirituality. Tremendous must be our task in the light of our universal vocation to make the anonymous Christians *explicit* Christians. As we seek to make all men better Christians, we cannot conceive of the Precious Blood spirituality with its vocation, its tasks, its *kerygma* without this ideal ever before us. One of the prime aims of this study is precisely the proclamation of the deeper and broader meaning of the "salvific will" of Christ in the light of his redemptive Blood. We of the Precious Blood spirituality may never be *anonymous* members in this spiritual fellowship.

DAH   2 TM. 2:9

CHAPTER TWELVE

THE PRECIOUS BLOOD SPIRITUALITY
OUR MODELS

*Those Granted the Grace of the Precious Blood Vocation
Have Set Before Them the Great Exemplars of the Precious Blood Spirituality: Our Models. In Life and Death
They Bore Witness to Jesus, Living, Dying, and Risen
to Glory. They Call Out to Us to Follow Them in Love
for the* Sanguis Christi, *Each with Unique Charism.*

We have already referred briefly to the pioneers who helped to
fashion the doctrine and history of the spirituality of the Precious Blood.
Here we study the models close to our members in their history and organic
formation. The writer can himself bear witness that many to his own
knowledge practiced what he would call heroic devotion to the Precious
Blood — and its virtues of self-renunciation, sacrifice for others, zeal for
souls, stark love for the crucified, and pure joy in the resurrection — heroic-
ally without clamor. Tranquil was their service. We may hope that some
will become subject of selective biographies in due time. But of all, we
know that God will bear witness to them in the eternal years with his Son
in glory.

First we shall speak of one *model* whom we may call the source or
chalice of the *Sanguis Christi,* (suggested by a beautiful poem by John Kostik) whose Precious Blood spirituality was exemplary, perfect and necessary
for our imitation: *Mary* the Mother of Jesus and the *Mother of his Church.*
And all too briefly we add a page on our second model — who next to Jesus
was closest to Mary, her beloved, virginal spouse, St. Joseph. His union with
Jesus and Mary places him in the hypostatic order, we repeat, with unique
sanctity in the whole work of redemption.

OUR LADY OF THE PRECIOUS BLOOD

With the sure insight of sanctity, Gaspar Del Bufalo discerned the intimate bond between the Precious Blood, which he proclaimed with exalted fervor, and the Mother of the Redeemer. His followers cherish the image of Gaspar, missionary in Italy, holding aloft a huge crucifix or a portrait of the Madonna of the Chalice. In this picture, copies of which are preserved in the Precious Blood houses today, Mary bears in her arms the Infant offering men the chalice of the Precious Blood, inviting them to the *chalice of salvation*. Not only does this affectionate relation of Gaspar to the heavenly Mother awaken community spirit and pride, but the position of Mary in the redemptive plan is pointedly indicated by her many titles, *Our Lady of the Chalice, Our Queen of the Precious Blood,* and perhaps more pointedly, *Mary Mother of the Precious Blood.* This latter title most aptly relates to our biblical explanation of the *Sanguis Christi* as the person of the Redeemer in the total work of redemption.

Our doctrine placing Mary in the hypostatic order (explained in *A Note on Mary*) through which the divine plan of incarnation-redemption was carried out clearly implies that as Mother of the God-man in a truly maternal or physical sense — this is our revealed truth — she is Mother in the whole plan of creation-incarnation-redemption *ab initio.* For all mankind she accepted him who is our salvation. With a love which she alone could encompass she said *YES* to God the Father who sent his Son into the world. As Mother she nestled him in her womb giving all that mothers can give — a body with flesh and blood — tender care for the sacrificial victim of Calvary. God spoke the Eternal Word in the incarnation offering mercy to man. Mary consented to be his Mother, speaking in the name of all men, accepting salvation for all men. By this very bond with the Christ-center-of-the-world she became also our Mother.

This role of Mary in redemption is revealed and proclaimed — not created — by Christ's own word on Calvary. On the wind-swept hill of the skull the Savior nailed to the cross whispered the words to Mary and John. Decades later the gospel of John gave this report of one of the great scenes of the world's history:

> Near the cross of Jesus there stood his mother, his mother's sister, Mary the wife of Clopas, and Mary Magdalene. Seeing his mother there with the disciple whom he loved, Jesus said to his mother, "Woman, there is your son." In turn he said to the disciple, "There is your Mother." From that hour onward, the disciple took her into his care (Jn 19: 25-27).

With this stark and loving scene in the background, Alphonse Spilly,

C.PP.S., explains the role of Mary as indicated in this text. In his paper in *Precious Blood Study Week III* he writes:

> These very words are reminiscent of other Johannine formulas: "This is the Lamb of God" (Jn 1:29-36). "Here is the man" (19:5) and "Here is your king" (19:14). All these are proclamations under various images of the role of Jesus in God's plan of salvation. The simple but solemn words of Jesus to Mary and John seem to announce to all their new role in this saving mystery. A study of the over-all context as well as the style of the passage itself reveals that these words are not only of human concern but Messianic as well. This seemingly insignificant interchange is at the very summit of Jesus' work. By waiting until the last moment, Jesus made it clear that this motherhood of Mary was intimately connected with his very death and that there is a question here of an entirely new relationship between mother and son. The use of the title *Woman* is a key to the deeper meaning of this event. Mary is called *Woman* here as at Cana to signify her spiritual maternal role.

> After many years of reflection on this scene in the light of the resurrection-faith, John must have recognized the relationship between the woman of Genesis 3:15 and the woman standing with him beneath the cross. Perhaps an earlier description of this is to be found in Revelation 12, where the *Woman* is identified as the Mother of the Messiah *and* of all Christians. What is Mary's role on Calvary on this theological level of the narrative?

> First of all Mary is the *Daughter Sion*. She realizes in her presence on Calvary the metaphorical maternity of Sion as announced by the prophets. Through her pain-filled maternal role beneath the cross, the wonderful promises of consolation are finally accomplished. The Hour of the Woman who must give birth to the Messianic people coincides with the Hour of Jesus. The New People of God is born through the passion.

> Secondly, Mary is the *New Eve*. John presents Jesus as the New Adam in the passion narrative. For example, John alone notes that the passion begins and ends in a garden (18:1; 19:41) reminiscent of the garden of Genesis 2-3. John sees the salvation activity of Jesus as a new Creation. Mary is not only the associate of this New Adam in his saving work, but the "Mother of all the living." As such she represents the Church through whom men come to believe in Jesus and receive the new life of the new creation through her sacraments. Mary's presence on Calvary, for John, is not simply an indication of her motherly concern for her Son. She is present as the companion of Jesus, as his associate in this work of the New Creation. But the full meaning of the scene strikes home only when we recognize her universal, spiritual, maternal role with regard to all believers.

That Mary is our Model in Precious Blood spirituality is apparent in the conclusion of this perceptive biblical study:

In reflecting upon her role in salvation, we are led to ponder on the Church. By reflecting on her role, we are led to a deeper appreciation of her Son, Jesus. Our devotion and preaching about Mary should not end with her but must go beyond her to her Son just as he himself leads us on to the Father. In this way, we can demonstrate what we mean when we call her the "Mother of all the living."[15]

We conclude these few pages with a poem on our *Lady of the Precious Blood*. It has deeply impressed the writer these many years of his interest in the Precious Blood spirituality. Written by a classmate, John Kostik, C.PP.S., in seminary days, it is taken from the *Nuntius Aulae* of July 1919. We place it here in loving memory of the ordination class of 1921.

CALIX BENEDICTIONIS

Fadeless, inviolate, calm and serene,
    Balm-breathing Lily, snow-vested Queen;
Lifted on high o'er sin's murky flood —
    Filled to the brim with Precious Blood!

Lily of snow, incline thy sweet cup,
    Pour from thy dew but one ruby drop.
Lo, 'tis enough our sins to efface
    And flood the whole world with God-giving grace!
                      J. K. '21

In our study we place the two Madonnas, that of Gaspar for its historical and inspirational significance, alongside the great bronze of Epstein. She who is uniquely our Mother is presented to all the world. Our Precious Blood vocation and *kerygma* today must ponder our unique world mission as suggested by the bronze of Epstein. It most eminently suits the Precious Blood in our spirituality and our current redemptive reflection.

THE EPSTEIN MADONNA

From the darkness of the unhappy world the Mother of Mercy emerges, offering to mankind the Lord of Mercy, the Child of the heavenly Father, the Son of God. Thus she stands before us at Cavendish Square in the West End of London. Over the archway of a convent of nuns is this great bronze statue of the Mother and her Son, consecrated by Cardinal Griffin in 1953.

It is the work of Jacob Epstein, son of a Jewish emigrant family from Russian Poland. It is a great call to the homeless produced by a humble artist who knew what homelessness meant and recognized the true homeland of mankind.

The figure is over the archway of a convent of nuns facing the turmoil of the modern city, but with the silence and reverence of the cloister near at hand. The Mother is tall, leans slightly forward. Tightly wrapped in a long garment, her shoulders and head are almost completely covered. Her arms are lowered and somewhat extended as though to release the Child. Close to the Mother he spreads out his hands in the form of a cross with submissive gesture ready to embrace the world. The small and vigorous figure, enfolded in narrow clothes from feet to throat, suggesting a shroud, radiates a fullness of vitality, ready to draw all the world to himself with his bare firm arms, to embrace it, to go out into the stony streets. He looks out to mankind with all the earnestness of the merciful Redeemer. Profoundly moving is the solitariness of these two, the God-man and the Mother of God, as though the two were all alone in the world. Unhappy shall the world remain which passes them by without harkening to the inner call (Schreyer, *op. cit.,* p. 183).

Joseph, Head of the Redemptive Family

Joseph is significant in our study because of his essential role in the divine plan through which the *Logos* became man and wrought our redemption. Through the most human of ties, an earthly family, Jesus became one of us. Joseph occupied a unique position in relation to that family, to Mary as her true, virginal husband and to Jesus to whom he was the virginal father. (The term derives from Augustine: cf. *NCE,* art. Joseph, St., Devotion to Vol. 7, p. 1110).

The hypostatic order to which Joseph belongs ranks above all apostolic and sacred ministry — precisely because in the infinite councils of God, the *Logos* was to become incarnate, enfleshed in Mary virginally through the Holy Spirit — as all the ancient creeds solemnly attest. Mary in turn was bound to Joseph with the most sacred of bonds: here were the three *values* of marriage: *proles, fides, sacramentum.* We cannot call him *adoptive father,* for Jesus was not adopted into this family, nor was he *foster father* (a vulnerable term often used), but true, though *virginal father* of Jesus Christ. To none on earth did Mary and Jesus owe such unique love, fidelity, obedience as to Joseph! Mary's love finds holiness in Joseph and makes him holy through her Son — as she makes all men holy though in a far lesser degree. Her presence — through many years — sanctifies, her tenderness exalts and raises her own to God. Unlike human love the divine love *effects* the worth in the object loved. Jesus' love, divine-human, is *creative-efficacious.* Jesus' love for Joseph as his virginal father made Joseph holy and worthy of that love — and of ours. The familial love of Jesus, Mary, Joseph, mutual and indivisible, hallowed the name of the Father in heaven and partook of the great work of man's redemption. Next to Mary, Joseph was the object of the Redeemer's supreme redemptive love.

As head of the tiny family in which Jesus was born and reared, Joseph was provider, guide, instructor. As such he reflects his position in the Church as Universal Patron, of the total family of Christ. In consequence there is also a unique Joseph-spirituality, practiced by many saints. We give only the instance of Teresa of Avila, now Doctor of the Church. This spirituality reflects his meekness and patience in suffering and anxiety (note the biblical reference to his fearsomeness when finding that Mary was to be THE MOTHER having conceived of the Holy Spirit, until God quieted his fears, cf. Mt 1:18ff). The first agony over the Redeemer seems to have been that of Joseph over Mary's Son not yet born. Striking is the simple obedience of the *just man* (Mt 1:19) indicated by the account of the *flight to Egypt*: no complaint, *that night* Joseph leaves (Mt 2:13ff).

Next to Mary he is the greatest of saints precisely because of his bond with Jesus and Mary. We see in him the dignity and sanctification of work, fidelity to duty, prudence and loyalty in God's service centering in love and peace with and through Christ. He is patron of the dying — linking us all redemptively to the presence of Jesus at our dying, linking us with Jesus dying. In this way he is most of all our model of Precious Blood spirituality.

Of the many beautiful prayers and pronouncements of the Church relating to Joseph we have space only for the following from the solemn preface in the Liturgy. We recommend also the Litany of St. Joseph for private and public recitation, as especially suited for vocational prayer for students for the priesthood and all priests. He is patronal guide of all priests, patronal model for the virginal chastity which is the most sublime adornment of priestly life. The beautiful liturgy of Joseph the Worker has lost nothing of its depth and significance in our social apostolate especially among the working men, though the feast has lost much of its stress in the recent liturgical alterations. (cf. Edwin G. Kaiser, C.PP.S., *Theology of Work*, index under *Joseph*, Newman Press, 1966).

> He is that just man, that wise and loyal servant, whom you placed at the head of your family. With a husband's love he cherished Mary, the virgin Mother of God. With fatherly care he watched over Jesus Christ, your Son, conceived by the power of the Holy Spirit (Liturgical preface: St. Joseph).

PRECIOUS BLOOD SPIRITUALITY IN THE FOUNDING OF THE SOCIETIES

Uniquely the Precious Blood societies contribute to the Precious Blood spirituality through their founders and foundresses. A study of these sainted men and women enriches our reflective doctrine through a profound and most diverse spiritual exercise. Only in this sense do we speak of them as our models. Here we begin with a special trio closely bound together in their life and work: Gaspar, Merlini, De Mattias, as our first group:

St. Gaspar Del Bufalo is the founder of the *Congregation of the Missionaries of the Most Precious Blood,* the first religious community in the Church to be dedicated to the Blood of Christ and the only community of men dedicated to this divine mystery. Rightly we place him first in our list. (C.PP.S.)

Venerable Giovanni Merlini may be called co-founder of Gaspar's society. By his close bond with the founder and as third Director General he contributed much to the rule, the structure, the tradition of the work of Gaspar. Both these sainted men are also founders of the institute of Blessed Maria De Mattias. But most specifically Merlini guided and directed her and her great work.

Blessed Maria De Mattias is the foundress of the *Congregation of the Sisters Adorers of the Most Precious Blood.* (Ad. PP.S. or A.S.C.)

Francis de Sales Brunner is the founder of the society of Gaspar and Merlini in the United States of America. With the aid and under the inspiration of his saintly mother, he founded the *Congregation of the Sisters of the Precious Blood* (C.PP.S. Dayton, Ohio).

There is also a small parent group which was originally united with the American sisters. They are now independent, with their Motherhouse at Schellenberg, Liechtenstein. They are the *Sisters of the Precious Blood.*

Mother Catherine Aurelia of the Precious Blood founded the *Institute of the Sisters Adorers of the Most Precious Blood of our Lord Jesus Christ* (A.P.B.)

We have selected Mother Catherine because of the widespread influence of her sisters both in the United States and Canada, and likewise because we consider her life unique in the Precious Blood spirituality.

(For the above we are largely indebted to Father John Behen: *Religious of the Precious Blood.* We likewise note that we have not at all attempted to follow a standard pattern in our pages on the models, nor consistently repeated the official titles. Finally, the pages on the models are only a small portion of our study.

PRECIOUS BLOOD SPIRITUALITY: A MODERN PARABLE

In the Society of the Missionaries of the Precious Blood we think our Lady of the Precious Blood has chosen Gaspar Del Bufalo as her favorite

son. Special patron of the Precious Blood spirituality and the Precious Blood
vocation, Gaspar was a Roman priest born on January 6, 1786 in the Holy
City itself (he is considered the only native Roman to found a religious order
or society).

Only gradually is the literature dealing with our Precious Blood history
and backgrounds being researched and made available in English. Occasionally we call attention to this work even though the writer cannot at all
do it justice in the few pages available. We can do little more than deal
with those essentials which are especially appropriate for our broader theme
in this study. And with their application to our vocation.

It is clear from his life that Gaspar was an activist from his teens. He
was most effective in catechetical instruction of youth, in spiritual concern
for those in correctional institutions (a bequest which his followers have
honored more in the breach than in the observance), and for those most
destitute and abandoned in the Papal City and Papal States. His work
among the *banditti* transformed what we would today call the *ghetto areas*
by means of the GRAND STYLE MISSION, so common in his time. This
involvement is the most spectacular tradition and lesson of Gasparian kerygmatic spirituality. One wonders why such a fascinating theme has not been
taken up even in anecdotal or fictional literature.

To apply to our own times all that lies at the heart of Gaspar's love
of this *neglected ghetto* should be the hallmark of current Precious Blood
spirituality and demand many specific vocational tasks for our members.
Of course such undertakings are not at all possible, without special thera-
peutic training, a degree of brashness in pastoral psychology and psychiatry.
Required above all is patient and knowledgeable direction of those in the
physical, mental and moral ghettos, a rare spiritual empathy. The discipline
of patience required today in dealing with new concepts of obedience and
authority, with violence, drug abuse, (including alcoholism), self-assertion
even in opposition to divine revelation and law is perhaps the contemporary
equivalent to the physical mortification which was so prominent in Gaspar's life. (The writer still shudders at the memory of Gaspar's penitential
instruments, the scourge, the chain occasionally displayed among his relics
at the little church and religious house at Santa Maria in Trivio in Rome.
With or without the *scourge* and *chain* we all must suffer and embrace the
passion of Jesus).

Despite the harshness of personal discipline, Gaspar founded a community bound by no vows, no promise, but only by a bond of love (cf. the
deeply sympathetic booklet, *The Spirituality of Our Society According to the
Charism of Our Founder,* by Luigi Contegiacomo, C.PP.S., translated by
Andrew Pollack, C.PP.S. and William Volk, C.PP.S.). Though his rule was

a model of moderation and restraint, keyed to the conditions of his times, the current revision seeks to reflect the spirit of present-day needs. To this writer the most welcome change in the whole community structure is that which stresses the greater variety of apostolic tasks and the total removal of the aristocratic attitude toward our brothers as *fratres inservientes* (serving brothers). Criticism of such aristocratic bias (in America we did not have even the excuse of an aristocratic society or background, but it is only honest to concede a considerable degree of bias toward the *fratres inservientes* concept up to the present time) is the sheerest hypocrisy unless all members become *fratres inservientes* serving not the priest, but the priesthood and the total priestly ministry, each according to what God has given him. And indeed with the generous activism in the spirit of Gaspar!

Surely we cannot, dare not, shun the contemporary need for involvement, GASPARIAN activism in the *bond of love*. Maturity, responsibility, enlightened obedience must crowd out any mere *self-apostolate*, which always looks for the self-creative, and occasionally lapses into identification with the grotesque, like gargoyles on God's temple. How theologically false, untrue to Gaspar is the notion that we may accept the mission, offer the prayer, share in the liturgy, only if we feel that we *get something out of it*, which is to make the divine call a *do-it-yourself*, and divine worship and service a kind of glamorous *ex opere operantis*. (We have already touched upon the point in the above pages. Cf. also Contegiacomo, cited above).

Such exercise neglects the inner reality which is the grace of Christ working within us, perhaps most effectively in the dark night of the soul, neglects the significance of the public witness to the suffering Christ who gave and gives all his Blood, a public witness drained of all glamor. This is especially pertinent in the sacrificial-sacramental life where the *opus operatum* is God's mighty hand, his work far more than our own. How can the dedication to the poor and neglected, the retarded, the underprivileged be constantly exhilarating? But it must be vital, personal, real, far more than a metaphysical category.[16]

A SPECIAL TRIBUTE TO GASPAR

Probably the most beautiful official tribute to Gaspar is the following:

In the Decree of Canonization (June 13, 1954), Gaspar is specifically associated with the Apostles Peter and Paul in emphasis upon the importance of the Blood of Christ in the economy of Redemption and, as their modern counterpart, is given the glory of being the *greatest apostle today of the devotion to the exalted price of our Redemption*: *Unus omnium nitet Beatissimus Gaspar del Bufalo.*

The lines are taken from the little book, *With a Thousand Tongues* (p. 2) by Luigi Contegiacomo, C.PP.S., *Precious Blood Institute,* St. Joseph College, Rensselaer, Ind., translated by Father Andrew Pollack, C.PP.S. and Sister Delphine, C.PP.S. The work of Father Luigi Contegiacomo has now appeared in a revised version: *Il Sangue di Cristo in S. Gaspare Del Bufalo* (Rome, 1968).

A PAINTING OF GASPAR: COMMENT OF LEO XIII

The *Nuntius Aulae* of July 1919 (Vol. 2, no. 2) has for its frontispiece a remarkable painting of Gaspar, as he is often portrayed — the Missionary. He holds in his hand the huge mission cross. The work was done by the Italian artist, Domenico Gagliardi. "The characteristic pose, the choice of the color, red for the table and blue for the sash, renders the effect very striking. . . . This picture which was at first hung in the community library, was exquisitely mounted and presented to the Vatican Exhibit for Pope Leo's Golden Sacerdotal Jubilee. As the central tablet indicates, the pope's ordination and the death of Gaspar (*coelo receptus*) occured in the same year. On the occasion of the presentation of the gift . . . the Pontiff referred to his personal acquaintance with our Apostle. He frequently attended Gaspar's sermons" (*ibid.,* 189).

GASPAR: OUR SAINT

We assume in the above pages about Gaspar that our readers are somewhat familiar with the life of the founder available in English for many years despite its obvious inadequacies (the adaptation was done by the writer himself). We add these final lines largely because they reflect solemnly the final and, according to many theologians, the infallible judgment of the Church on his sanctity, and therefore her special approval of the Precious Blood spirituality.

Almost to the moment of his death Gaspar was engaged in preaching. In the intolerable heat of August amidst an outbreak of cholera he preached in the principal churches of Rome. Pale, worn, totally weakened he continued preaching to immense crowds. After returning to Albano, he soon came back to Rome because some of his own penitents among the Sisters of St. Cecilia had been stricken. As the masses were fleeing the city, the heroic dying saint was returning to the very section where many had died of cholera. When he was asked, "What are we doing? Everybody is fleeing and we go to Rome?" The answer bears the great mark of Gasparian spirituality: "We are doing God's will." He exhorted a priest: "You should admonish, you should preach, you should exhort men to practice the devotion to the Precious Blood of Jesus Christ" (*Herald of the Precious Blood,* p. 120). That utterness which is characteristic of his spirituality he expressed in such words as these:

Iesu et Maria, amores mei dulcissimi, pro vobis patiar,
pro vobis moriar, sim totus vester, sim nihil meus.

(Jesus and Mary, sweetest objects of my love, let me suffer for you, let me die for you, let me be entirely yours and not at all my own). His death was totally heroic: for Gaspar it was the Great Will of God. His last words, when Merlini exhorted him to accept death from the hand of God, conforming his will to the divine will, were: "Si, si." Yes, yes. Gaspar's whole life was saying *YES to the will of God.*

He died on December 28, 1837, in the presence of Merlini and Pallotti, as only saints can die. He exemplified an exhortation he often repeated:

Let us repeat always with Francis de Sales: 'If I knew that one thought of my mind, one affection of my heart, one work of my hands would not be entirely for God, I should not choose to possess mind or heart or hand' (*ibid.,* p. 129).

Here is exemplified that *total giving,* the Precious Blood spirituality on the heroic level.

Gaspar was beatified on December 18, 1904 amidst all the splendor of the Church's ritual. Crowds had been massing in the great piazza of St. Peter's as only Roman crowds can. When the bells ring out, the picture of the Servant of God is unveiled high above the altar of the Cathedra in the main apse and the *Te Deum* is intoned. The solemn Mass is celebrated at the beautiful altar (not the high altar) of the Cathedra. (The account is given in greater detail in *The Herald of the Precious Blood* on p. 131f).

The solemn act of canonization was fifty years later. It took place in the piazza of St. Peter's. The beloved Pius XII proclaimed to the whole Christian world that Gaspar was a saint to be honored by the Universal Church. We add these few pages on Gaspar our founder and patron of Precious Blood spirituality, again suggesting to the reader to follow all the new studies on our great saint and, to the societies of the Precious Blood that with special intensity of effort they spread the spirituality of the Precious Blood.

In the honor of the Holy and Indivisible Trinity, for the exaltation of the Catholic Faith and the increase of the Catholic religion, by the authority of our Lord Jesus Christ, of the Holy Apostles Peter and Paul, and by our Own, after mature deliberation, ever imploring the divine assistance, by the advice of our venerable brethren, the cardinals of the

Holy Roman Church, the patriarchs, archbishops and bishops present
in the Eternal City, We decree and define as Saints the blessed Peter
Chanel, martyr, *Gaspar del Bufalo,* Joseph Pignatelli, Dominic Savio,
confessors, and Maria Crocifissa Di Rosa, virgin, and We inscribe their
names in the catalogue of the Saints, ordering that their memory be
celebrated . . . with devotion every year in the Universal Church
(*ibid.,* 134f).

Giorgio Papasogli
Vita e Tempi di San Gaspare del Bufalo

Papasogli's work (1977) has raised our hopes regarding a meaningful
life of the founder, suggesting as it does vast vistas of further Gasparian
studies revealing the saint in his own tempestuous times. Presenting the deep
personal development of Gaspar the saint in the face of the persecution of
the Church he loved ever more dearly, Papasogli underscores the uniqueness
of the Blood-grace-power to convert even the scofflaws, the cutthroats, and
brigands to Christ. In Gaspar there is patently the Precious Blood spirituality
in heroic dimensions, in mystic heights of which John of the Cross is the
model and teacher.

Actually startling, confirming the thesis of Lortz that sanctity is the
highest genius, is the Papasogli account of the power of the Blood-love
with its mysterious, persuasive redemptive-socio-politico-psychological influence spreading through cities and towns of papal Italy. We do not find its
like in the whole history of missionary conversion, search as we might among
the great servants of God. Nor have we — *culpa nostra* — explained it effectively in our Precious Blood literature. But do we not have here the blessed
evidence that the shedding of the *Sanguis Christi* lies at the very heart of
human destiny, that it is the motive of creation itself, the deeper meaning of
the *Cur Deus Homo?*

If man's history is his shame, how shameful the revolutionary explosion
through all of Europe! How shameful the expulsion of priests as felons to
Devil's Island in French Guiana, the exaltation of an actress, sex symbol, as
goddess of reason in Mary's Notre Dame in Paris, or the obscene cheering
and jeering at the chopping of the guillotine! And the dizzy turn of the
mobs from the tumultuous choreography of *reason and democracy* to First
Consul, Emperor, dominating a church in which he never believed. And
how absurd the new catechism with a mock *Saint Napoleon, Martyr* on its
cover!

In this age Gaspar was born of Antonio and Annunziata Quartierone
Del Bufalo at Rome on January 6, 1786. We are deeply indebted to Papasogli for the account of Gaspar's early education which was far more

thorough than we had been wont to believe. We may say simply: he was
an exceptionally talented student at the Gregorian University, with an excellent academic record. By nature ardent and fiery, he was religiously modest,
controlled, methodic. In difficult studies he would turn to the Crucified
and to the Madonna for help. And in free time to deep meditative prayer
before the *Sedes Sapientiae* in the Gesu or at St. Mark's, till Mamma would
rouse him and take him home.

As Gaspar grew to adolescence — very rapidly — life with his gentle,
sainted mother at home (usually Antonio was at work), his study, his prayer,
soon opened to the way of spiritual vocation to priesthood, missionary zeal,
and unique spiritual greatness. But note: throughout was sharing, sharing
with all mankind. Long before we made a fetish of the word, the reality
was a vital part of his life-style, expanding ceaselessly.

Here a word from Papasogli about the *Two Parallels* which we must
pursue to understand Gaspar adequately. One was the development of his
ecclesiastical life, the other the line of fire and blood traced out in revolutionary Italy. The latter sustained his constancy in the path of the first,
the great, unique levitical call. From his First Communion (1797) and his
assumption of the ecclesiastical garb (1798), he followed the path to priesthood, mingling unusual activity in preaching and catechizing to the very
day preceding his First Holy Mass, August 2, 1808. Hoping ardently to
begin his life work — his guide and spiritual director was the saintly Fran-
cesco Albertini — Gaspar began at Maria in Vincis and San Nicola in
Carcere at Rome. At this future center of the Precious Blood devotion in
Rome, at Albertini's request, he preached on what was to be his life's theme:
the Most Precious Blood.

Less than two years in the priesthod Gaspar was forced into exile. He
rejected the oath of allegiance to Napoleon: *Non posso, non debbo, non vog-
lio.* We still treasure this *I cannot, I may not, I will not.* In exile under the
most dreadful conditions from Piacenza to Bologna, to Imola, and finally to
Lugo, he endured the most horrible conditions and, saddest of all, the news
of his mother's death, October 20, 1811. Four times he rejected the sacri-
legious oath. (Parallel to all this, Pius VI, sick and enfeebled, was forced
to leave Rome (1799) never to return. It had been the year after Gaspar
began to wear the sacred garb). Finally February, 1814, Gaspar was able
to return to Rome and to take up his life work under Pius VII. He too had
long been in exile, harrassed by the French, suffering with the martyred
Church. His final return to Rome was on June 7, 1815.

The love of the Blood of Christ, substance and symbol of the fidelity
of all firmness and grandeur of martyrs, of all holocausts offered by

man to God, this love followed Gaspar from prison to prison. It was the force and power of his resistence. It built up in him the structure and the stature of a saint (p. 212).

THE MISSION AMONG THE DEPRIVED AND DEPRAVED

Great was the task of Pius VII in the re-Christianization of the papal domain. We may say it was Gaspar, aided by priests, bishops and cardinals, who could face every group with the Blood-pardon of the crucified. The lowly of the slums huddled amid the great ruins of the ancient splendor, the proud curialists who dealt with law and order, the bandits who formed an entire network of violence in the pope's own heritage.

Let us note Benevento. The missionaries were men of doctrine and zeal under Epiphanio Mazio, Basilian monk of Grottaferrata. Here was a city of 15,000 souls. More than a thousand were to be classed as nobility, "togati," citizens, politicians, the rest as rabble without birth, education, dignity. The sixth commandment suggested only public concubinage. Religion was distorted by superstition and enmeshed with the texture of blasphemy. Feast days had no meaning. Cafes, streets, public centers were the scene for quarrels with clubs and firearms. Well could the missionaries say, we were sent to untamed beasts, not to rational men and women (p. 258). And yet the missionaries were accepted with enthusiasm. They were the first to be seen in the city for over two decades. The confessors were kept busy for several weeks.

At Ancona, before his carriage could enter the city, Gaspar was begged to turn back. The "sectaries" were strong, the Masons, the Carbonari were a threat of violent attack. But Gaspar, asked to turn around and go back, gave the order: on to the Cathedral. All went well, the crowd was extraordinary. The estimate was: 20,000 souls, 30,000 Holy Communions.

GASPAR'S SPEECH

Gaspar directed his language to the character of the fault which dominated these souls clutching hatred. In simple words he placed before them the King of Love, wounded, crucified, dying, risen, infinitely merciful (p. 227). To these masses impoverished, in depressed conditions! Many were far from any church, with little contact with priestly care. Gaspar, who lived in his own great debt to the passion of Jesus, faced them with the burning desire to press them, his own, dear in the Blood of their Christ, into his own loving heart. Of Mary he could ask: Grant this, O Mother who loved Jesus as did no other: *Sancta Mater, istud agas!* (p. 271). He places before them the love of Jesus, the Blood-love, his agony, the mercy of the Father, love among the brethren. They must permit him to be their Redeemer, pay the price of his Blood. The ugly, deformed women must be freed of what is ugliest of all, sin. But only through his love. Who can fail to love such love. All else is damnation, forever (p. 272).

ALWAYS THE PARDON OF JESUS

Even in opposition to civil authority, to his friends, to those who had suffered from the cruelty of the brigands, Gaspar insisted on seeking papal pardon for the brigands. The great magnanimity of his heart extended to the most diverse of men with the one language of Jesus-love, Jesus-blood, Jesus-pardon. All have souls to redeem, the rich, the poor, the aristocrat. Most striking is Gaspar's insistence that he place before the pope the crude letter of the bandits asking for clemency. Small wonder that not hundreds, but thousands, sought to hear him. The following instance should not be considered unusual:

> There were 20,000 listeners. The voice of Gaspar rang out over the air waves. So closely did the people hang on his words that at one of his missions, the people locked the city gates, and hid the keys, so that the missionary could not slip away (p. 289).

A FEW POINTS FROM PAPASOGLI

Gaspar in the providence of God has a singular destiny. He does not speak of God without making one love him. Such is the overflowing of his love (p. 288). Above all, he does not wish to have the police force on hand when he deals with the bandits. Only the redemptive-pardon, the Precious Blood-love. And the Precious Blood-love is the Precious Blood-love-pardon.

A FINAL EXAMPLE: GASPAR SPEAKS TO THE MEN OF LAW

Gaspar had moved thousands of consciences among the rude and simple folk, as he dominated his own flesh according to the theme of the Passion. How face *curialists?* (We may ask the question regarding the many other diverse people he addressed). He begins with the moderate-incisive-reasoned. Strangely they are overcome. The preacher descends to the canonical-forensic dialectic, but then gives free rein to his love for Christ the Redeemer and speaks out about what he most loves: immolation of Jesus for us. Now the "dialectic of the Blood enters the area," substituting itself for that of the laws, and the alchemists of the codes suddenly recognize a new language. None of them, not even the most impetuous penalists in prosecution or defense, had ever spoken as Gaspar spoke of human sin and divine pardon. And suddenly they realized that the controversies and conflicts between man

and man, all seemed petty in the light of the infinite drama between earth
and heaven (p. 285).

In faceless men Gaspar sees the Sacred Face of Jesus, to faceless men
he shows the face of Jesus. We hope that many will read the impressive
text of Vita E Tempi Di San Gaspare Del Bufalo by Giorgio Papasogli.

GASPAR'S CHOSEN PATRON AND OURS: ST. FRANCIS XAVIER

As we note elsewhere in this study the Society of the Missionaries of
the Precious Blood celebrates the liturgy of St. Francis Xavier as a *Feast*:
Francis Xavier, Priest, Principal Patron of the Society.

Beautiful is the opening prayer:

> Lord,
> merciful and compassionate God,
> you opened the door of the Orient
> to Francis, the missionary.
> Send us to the ends of the earth
> so that we may complete the joy of Mother Church.

The biography of Gaspar projects the providential relationship between
Gaspar and Xavier. In his very infancy he was cured of measles and impending blindness by the intercession of Xavier. As a mere lad Gaspar
served Mass at the beautiful altar of the saint in the Church of the Gesu
in Rome. Here the saint would later recount how deeply he was moved during the sacred liturgy as he gazed at the picture of Xavier's death, a splendid
painting by Maratta above the altar. Here too was the most precious relic
of Xavier, the right arm of the missionary to the Orient who had baptized
thousands brought to Christ by his word and work. This writer still recalls
a most solemn procession in which he and other members of the Society of
the Precious Blood joined as this relic was borne triumphantly through the
streets of an Alban city outside Rome, many years ago.

We extend this account on St. Gaspar with another word from John
XXIII, whose pronouncements on the Precious Blood are so significant.
Very striking is Pope John's statement on Gaspar made on the last day of the
Roman Synod, Sunday, January 31, 1960: "One of the shining glories of
the Roman clergy . . . (was) St. Gaspar Del Bufalo . . . the true and the
world's greatest apostle of the devotion to the Most Precious Blood of Jesus"
(cf. *Gasparian*, March 16, 1960, p. 1). Pray for us, St. Gaspar!

Gaspar chose Xavier as the patron of our society. We join with the
founder in begging our patron to promote in us the fulness of the Precious
Blood spirituality. Perhaps our failures, and such there surely are, arise from

our lack of loving cultivation of veneration for one whom Gaspar loved so deeply. The life of Xavier, probably the most extensively researched of any modern saint, is too well known for us to attempt even a concise summary in this limited space. A few points, however, do suggest themselves:

1) Xavier's influence on Gaspar and the community he founded can be effective in us through our turning to him to plead our cause before the throne of the Lamb in glory.

2) Preeminently the Precious Blood *kerygma* was exercised by Xavier as the greatest missionary apostle since the time of St. Paul. In our own time, in our own circumstances — no matter what they may be — we must fulfill the same vocation, exercise the same Precious Blood *kerygma*. His charisms will be imparted to us.

3) Our Precious Blood prayer, particularly the seven offerings should reach up to him in a great love for the crucified and for all men redeemed by the *Sanguis Christi.*

St. Gaspar, lead us to Francis our patron.

APPENDIX: THE GASPAR LETTERS

At present the letters of Gaspar are being assembled for publication. From Father Raymond Cera who is actively engaged in the work of translation the writer has gleaned the following as our Precious Blood study goes to press. This little appendix leans heavily on Father Raymond's eulogy of Gaspar on the feast day of Oct. 21, 1976, at St. Joseph's College. A thumb nail sketch of Gaspar's missionary activity precedes the account of the Gaspar correspondence. Father refers to the 150 missions (a week or two in length), more than 75 retreats, Lenten and Advent series, novenas, months, of the Precious Blood and of Mary, special talks to particular groups, such as artists, nuns, prisoners, catechetical instruction to children and the poor. Then Father refers to the almost unbelievable correspondence. At present he has completed three volumes, each of about 400 pages.

This work of collection of the correspondence goes back to Merlini and was continued throughout the process in preparation for the beatification and canonization of the founder. At first the collection consisted of fourteen huge volumes to which four small volumes were later added. Other letters continued to flow in to the collectors. At present the body of the "Writings of the Founder" embraces twenty-three volumes. We must note that these are all handwritten letters from the pen of the founder himself, not of secretaries or helpers. The original handwritten letters are estimated to be about 3000, which of course do not include many that may have been destroyed. We can imagine the pain, the torture this work caused the saint.

The letters deal with every occasion and are addressed to the most varied of correspondent. Gaspar dealt in these letters with cardinals, bishops, prelates, with missionaries, priests, pastors, brothers, with relatives and friends. Though some of the matter or content may seem trivial, the sum total conveys to us, Gaspar's sons and daughters, a picture of the man, of his inner self, that could scarcely be portrayed in the mere biographical recitation of his life and activity. As Father Cera, quoting Father Luigi Contegiacomo, remarks, they are the "relics" of his "living soul." They are fragments of our Father Gaspar, vibrant testimony of his complex personality.

We insert this note as an appendix, not because of its unimportance, but because we hope that it will create many "second thoughts" in the mind of those who have read our few pages, and the biographies of Gaspar: a new and in-depth reflection on the saint, who is in the most diverse human activity our beloved Father.

GASPAR'S NOBLEST SON: GIOVANNI MERLINI

As this little chapter is being prepared for publication the cause of the Venerable Giovanni Merlini's beatification is progressing and the studies of his life and work are expanding. The special issue of *Vita Nostra,* official publication of the Italian province of missionaries, gives us the official decree affirming the heroicity of his holiness (May 1973). A second decree must establish the fact of miracles or signs of divine favor — we might call them God's message announcing the divine will that we pay this chosen soul special honor and call attention to the holiness which we should imitate in Christ's Church. The solemn proclamation will be the beatification of this chosen servant of God, to be followed by the definitive declaration of sainthood in the great act of canonization. All this is clear from the above pages on Saint Gaspar.

Meanwhile the special Merlini studies are calculated to awaken in the societies of the Precious Blood a better understanding of this model of our spirituality. Available and recent is: *Giovanni Merlini and His Message,* published in English in 1975. Though we draw from it in our present study, we suggest that it be carefully read and prayerfully pondered by all the members of our societies, particularly those concerned more intensively with the Precious Blood spirituality. Our readers, we humbly hope, will supplement our few pages with this varied work of research.

The political and social background of the life and labors of both Gaspar and Merlini is graphically depicted by Sister Nicla Spezzati, A.S.C., in the paper on Historical Background (pp. 12-29). After the Congress of Vienna, the Papal States with Rome as their capital, were restored to papal dominion. In the year 1870 all Italy was united under Victor Emmanuel of the House of Savoy, with the pope a "prisoner" in the Vatican and Catholics excluded from political activity.

Throughout this period economic unrest, extreme poverty, to the point of starvation, outrageous disparity between masses and nobility created bitter opposition to the papal government. Brigandage reached alarming proportions by the year 1820. The spiritual life of the people had sunk to an abysmally low level. With the religious orders dispersed, the secular clergy demoralized, the clergy in control of the major posts in government administration, creating ugly clericalism and bitter anticlericalism, Luigi Bottiglia, delegate of Benevento, could report:

> I have been sent into a forest of wild animals rather than to save men. The sixth commandment is very little known here and, much to my displeasure, I must say that unfortunately the ecclesiastical rank is also stained with this tar, to the scandal of the public both in the city and as well in the dukedom (*ibid.*, p. 19).

Gaspar speaks even more sharply.

As to the society founded by Gaspar, according to Merlini's own testimony, many thought it consisted of a "crowd of fools discarded by the dioceses, desperate and starving." Conversely, they were held to be "proud, ambitious" and looking for "honors and pensions" (*ibid.*, p. 20). Gaspar's very "intention to reform the clergy and the Church" aroused bitterness. Even Pope Leo XII was influenced by the slander and indulged in unfavorable criticism, much to Gaspar's sorrow. With all this in view we must ask: Why did Merlini join this society? Why did he become so close to Gaspar? But first a few facts about Giovanni and his upbringing.

Giovanni Merlini was born at Spoleto, a *quiet papal town,* August 28, 1795, of Luigi and Antonia Arcangeli Merlini, the third of thirteen children. The father was of Sicilian origin, very jealous of his wife who was rarely permitted to go out. The Merlini house was called by the town folk the Merlini Convent, and one of the daughters attested that the family lived as in a monastery. He accompanied his father to church, was a serious punctual altar boy. Perhaps even going to church was an escape. From his earliest thoughts, priesthood was uppermost in his mind, which he was permitted to follow against the will of his father only by the birth of a brother.

> He was tall, with red hair, blue eyes, solid bones and a very masculine appearance. . . . He was an interesting type. . . . Giovanni wore the cassock in a period when the ecclesiastical career was not the most enviable. The boy's will knew no obstacles and he did not give in easily. Inclined as he was to order, he went about carrying it out in

his life through diligent and careful work. In his studies he succeeded especially in those disciplines which concern man's behavior, law and ethics. This is a most significant factor. He always sought the will of God in order to conform his own will most closely to that of God, (adapted *ibid.*, p. 32ff).

Merlini was ordained to the priesthood in 1818. Shortly thereafter he came from Spoleto to San Felice to make a retreat under the founder of the new society, Gaspar Del Bufalo. . . . Here we see the great first crisis and its providential grace, (the personal *kairos*). He found in Gaspar, a new spiritual father. Providentially they read the signs of the times, and found in the new institute the great means of reform, the mission as Gaspar had planned and practiced and which Merlini now also took up. Later it was said of him on one occasion:

> He undertook mission work in the valley of Loreto, and he worked for 82 days without a single break, and later on, as long as his health and strength permitted, he always took up the work of the missions. By doing so the Servant of God was an example for every member of the Congregation to love this ministry; after the example given by the Servant of God nobody ever, without grave necessity, refused to undertake the work at any time (*ibid.*, p. 22).

If Merlini was son to Gaspar and carried to realization the ideas of the saint, he may also be called the father of Blessed Maria De Mattias. Beautifully Michele Colagiovanni speaks of the three as "an inseverable nucleus of sanctity and spirituality" (*ibid.*, p. 7).

Ten years after Gaspar's holy death Merlini was chosen to be the Director General of the Society of the Missionaries of the Precious Blood. Under him the society spread rapidly in Italy and beyond the Alps. But a persecution, which can only be duplicated by the Nazi regime many decades later, wrought havoc in many of the houses of the society, the missionaries were driven out, the churches were desecrated. Such was the tragic year of 1860.

We must also make a reference to Merlini's influence on Pius IX in the extension of the Feast of the Precious Blood to the entire Church. We shall again refer to him in our pages on the Sisters Adorers and the Blessed Maria De Mattias. Finally the brutal story of his holy death. Though technically his cause is being presented as that of a Confessor, we feel that he really died the death of a martyr for the cause of Christ. He was struck down in the streets of Rome by a fanatical anticlerical cab driver according to the following account:

> His death was occasioned by the hate of a cab driver, not for the victim personally whom the driver did not at all know, but for the priestly

garb and what it stood for. The venerable missionary cherished the image of the Blessed Virgin Mary in Sant' Andrea delle Fratte.

The Madonna honored there is connected with the marvellous conversion of Marie Alphonse Ratisbonne (*NCE,* Vol. 12, p. 93). On one occasion, returning from such a visit, he was spied by the venomous cabbie, who whipped his horse to a gallop and struck down the pious pilgrim, thus verifying the prediction of Blessed (now Saint) Gaspar, that Merlini would die of a severe fall. He died on January 12, 1873 (*Souvenir: Centenary Celebration,* p. 74).

A Final Word on the Spirituality of Merlini

Michele Colagiovanni singles out in Merlini the special capacity to harmonize by means of the exercise of a very strong will all his resources, even those which seem at first sight to be incompatible (*ibid.,* p. 37). To this writer, Merlini seems to have attained a great personal control and harmony largely because of the influence of Gaspar and Maria De Mattias. He reaped abundant fruit from his association with Gaspar, the spiritual father reforming him in the image of Christ, by contradistinction to his father Luigi, who may well have been responsible for an inflexibility and almost Jansenistic rigidity.

Indeed, he attained a greater freedom of spirit and was able to reflect on man and things more moderately and justly, though he was rather inclined to severity. In fact, he found the means of overcoming an impediment which was the greatest obstacle for him on the way to perfection — the spirit of anger, to which by nature he was prone. Striving to imitate the life of the master, therefore, he progressed so far that he seemed gentleness itself and was pointed out by the founder to the Congregation as an example for imitation (*Vita Nostra,* p. 24, Maggio, 1973, *Speciale*). As to this point the writer himself recalls, after many years, the striking remark of Father Joseph Schaeper, Procurator General of the society, who was well aware of the traditions at Rome: Father Giovanni is said never to have lost his temper.

The Church has officially authenticated the heroic virtue of Merlini. The testimony of many who knew him well reveals his avoidance of even the shadow of sin, of all defect, his constant union with God in the midst of manifold activities. Should we not now join in humble prayer that the divine message of the signs of holiness, or miracles, lead to his beatification and canonization? So that all the Church will pray to him as we now may well do in our hearts: Beloved, Giovanni Merlini, pray for us now and evermore. Deepen our Precious Blood spirituality by your prayers before the Blood of Christ in his glory.

BLESSED MARIA DE MATTIAS

If we speak of Gaspar as the founder of the societies of the Precious Blood, we think of him as the source of the Master Plan and the Grand Outline of both communities: that of the Missionaries and of the Sisters Adorers. And we think of Merlini as the providential agent, the builder who carried out the plan. This is particularly evident in the instance of Maria De Mattias, whose spiritual director and immediate guide he was until her death. The copious correspondence of Merlini and the sainted Maria bears witness to a great and holy friendship in the most profound spirituality of the Precious Blood.

> It was during the year 1824 when . . . del Bufalo sent the missionary Don Giovanni to preach the lenten sermons. Maria who was then a fervent young girl (she was born at Vallecorsa, Feb. 4, 1805) took part with great fervor in this lenten practice; in fact she must have been fascinated by the sermons and the person of the missionary. She suddenly felt the urge to present herself to him, to speak about the things of her soul, but she waited about twenty days, fearing that she was being pushed by human motives and also being herself very sensitive, reserved and very jealous of her own heart. Grace, however, had arranged everything: Maria was very much at her ease and she opened her heart to the one who from that moment was to be her only spiritual director and whom she obeyed as she did the will of God.
>
> Thus began the story of a soul which had blossomed forth before the striking image of the crucifix, with which St. Gaspar preached in 1822 at Vallecorsa, and which burst out through torments, 'thorns, nails and crosses,' as Merlini said, and would be consumed for two great loves:
>
> Christ crucified
> the good of souls which were the price of the Blood of Jesus.
>
> The human instrument used by Providence to be responsible for this simple and wonderful story was Giovanni Merlini (*op. cit.,* Sister Maria Cifelli, A.S.C., p. 72ff).

The social, economic, political and religious conditions in Italy at this time made the beginnings of Maria's new institute very difficult. The sisters and their schools were rather despised. This in part was due to the fact that they drew their membership in great part from poor families. They were forced to live a very frugal life, to earn their bread by teaching. Grave difficulties arose from the fact that in the beginning none of them were licensed to teach.

But encouraged by Merlini, Maria and her institute did not falter. She never did anything without his advice. The sisters consider March 4, 1834 as the date of their founding, the date of the opening of the school in Acuto, which is sixty miles southwest of Rome. From Acuto where Maria had judiciously formed her first group, the community spread to other towns in Italy, at the rate of one a year for the first ten years. In 1847 the first convent was opened in Rome.

Sister Maria Cifelli (*op. cit.*, p. 72-86) gives in documented detail the account of the letters of Merlini to Maria ("about 320 letters written in small and even handwriting"), which reveal much of the personal relationship on its noble spiritual level and as well the thoroughness of the guidance of the institute of the sisters by Merlini himself. As Director General of the Missionaries he also dealt directly with individual sisters. The sisters were a continuation of the society of missionaries. We note the two points of the personal relationship and the societal bond of the two communities:

> For forty-two years (Maria died at Rome, August 20, 1866) the two saints were to walk together along the way of the cross, having in common only one Master, the crucified (*ibid.*, p. 76). It was said, and rightly so, that Maria De Mattias was the masterpiece of Giovanni Merlini's spiritual direction (*ibid.*, p. 77).
> As founder, Giovanni Merlini arranged everything in the institute for the Sisters of the Precious Blood like that of the missionaries; he reshaped and systemized the Rule already outlined by De Mattias (*ibid.*, p. 80). After his election as Director General he approved the following at the first congressus of the missionaries: . . . "that . . . the Rule of the Sisters Adorers be reorganized and determined in all its parts . . . subject first to the examination and the assent of the congressus . . . that in order to maintain the spirit with which the institute originated and to keep up the close relationship with our Congregation, when doubts arise regarding the Rule, the Superior of the Adorers must consult our Director General, who on his own or after consulting the congressus, will give the appropriate replies or explanations" (*ibid.*, p. 79).

It is important to note that Maria and her schools were concerned with poor and needy children, and that her work was not merely educational. It was a great social concern for the needy and depressed. But this social and cultural concern flowed from the realization of the great need of religious and moral instruction. The basic foundation was the Precious Blood spirituality which she shared with Gaspar and Merlini.

The little volume *Beata Maria De Mattias* published on the centenary of her death, 1966, contains a fairly extensive life written by Merlini himself. Gradually we hope that more of the Mattias literature will be made available in English, for the enrichment of our Precious Blood spirituality.

In his preface to the *Vita* Merlini cites two reasons for his work: first, to satisfy the spiritual desire of those who knew Maria and wished to learn more of her life. And secondly, to present to the Sisters Adorers for their instruction the mother and foundress in seeking zealously their own sanctification and that of others.

If we should seek to express briefly what characterized the spirituality of Maria it would be expressed in these words of hers:

> When I feel tired throughout all my body, I am encouraged by the thought: How great is the honor to be fatigued for God and if God accepts my fatigue this is a great good fortune. With this thought my desire grows stronger: I wish to do much more if I can with the grace of God. I intend to do all I must do according to his most loveable will, willing neither more nor less than this. I look upon my misery and at the same time I fix my eyes on the goodness of God, on his mercy, on the merits of his Blood and on his word. My heart feels moved by the most ardent desire to love Jesus with a love totally unsullied, totally pure . . . This desire does not disquiet me or rob me of my peace, which increases from day to day.

FRANCIS DE SALES BRUNNER

Of all the founders of Precious Blood societies probably the most restless in searching for God's will in his own apostolate was Francis de Sales Brunner, who brought the missionaries to America about six years after Gaspar's death. This restlessness is due not merely to "searching for the divine will" or to a personal sense of incompleteness in his work, but also to the revolutionary times in which he lived, and from which he suffered. It is beyond our allotted space and purpose to give even the essential details of his life. We are concerned only with three special points, his vocation to the Society, his singular Eucharistic work in carrying out the great will of the founder, and his bond with the Sisters of the Precious Blood. For his life we direct the reader to the *History of the American Province* by Paul J. Knapke, C.PP.S. (Messenger Press, Carthagena, Ohio, 1958) and to the *Centenary Souvenir* (1815-1915, p. 82ff).

The Vocation. On his way to Rome he (Father Brunner) passed through Cesena where he met a Precious Blood missionary in the sacristy of the old Servite church (later in charge of the Precious Blood missionaries) bearing the huge mission cross on his breast. In his diary he says:

> On the 13th of November we arrived at Cesena and accepted the hospitality of the Sanguinist missionaries. This spot I look upon as my birthplace, for here in the sacristy of the church, I first beheld a missionary of the Society with the crucifix on his breast. At once there awoke within me a great longing to devote myself to the Most Precious

Blood and to become a member of that Congregation (Knapke, *op. cit.*, p. 151; *Centenary Souvenir*, p. 83f).

Father Brunner brought his first missionary group — the first of a vast number of priests, brothers, sisters who were to follow to the new land — in 1843-44. The ship sailed from Havre, France, in mid-October, 1843. After a long voyage across the ocean and up the Mississippi, the immigrants arrived in Cincinnati on New Year's Day, 1844. Thus began the unparalleled career in which many Precious Blood convents and churches were founded, all dedicated to the Blessed Mother of God, and a vast territory was missionized. The zeal of founder and followers, the intense devotion to work and prayer was heroic. We today are given an example which we can admire rather than imitate.

Singular Eucharistic Zeal: perhaps we may say it begins with the dramatic trip up the Father of Waters on the first Christmas in the New World. He writes:

> On Christmas eve the priests and brothers erected three temporary altars. After the regular night prayers, we snatched a bit of rest. At midnight we all arose. Then after reciting the Matins of the holy office, we celebrated the first Mass of Christmas; at dawn after the recitation of the office of Lauds we celebrated the second Mass; at sunrise the third Mass, the Mass of Christmas Day. (*Souvenir*, p. 85, 88). Each of the eight priests offered holy Mass on that Christmas feast.

Not only did Father Brunner dedicate all his convents to the Blessed Mother in her various mysteries, but he also began the beautiful practice of *perpetual adoration in ten of the convent chapels.* We should not fail to note that this was the ideal of the founder himself. Of all the followers of Gaspar, this honor uniquely belongs to Father Brunner. In the little book already referred to, *With A Thousand Tongues,* there is a reference to the common exercises for the members of the community: the Chaplet of the Precious Blood, the Seven Offerings, the Precious Blood Month, the Holy Hour and finally *Perpetual Adoration* "in order to *offer continuous reparation to the Divine Redeemer for man's ingratitude*" (p. 21). This is Father Brunner's most inspiring link to Gaspar.

The Bond with the Sisters of the Precious Blood. Long before the memorable trip to the New World, Father Brunner had established a school at the old castle of Loewenberg in Canton Grisons, in Switzerland, for the education of Catholic youth. Though the attempt was not successful, something more glorious had its origin in the failure. The castle was turned over to Father Brunner's mother and a band of women whose object was to adore the Precious Blood and seek perfection in community life. "Thus was founded," says our souvenir booklet, "one of the several communities known by the title of the Most Precious Blood; the one, we may add, which followed him to America and aided so effectively in accomplishing the great work yet to be recorded" (p. 83).

God works in mysterious ways, but though Mother Brunner died in 1836 and never saw the new world, "her deep devotion to the Precious Blood was the seed of the new community of sisters." Shortly after Father Brunner began his mission activity in the United States, "three of the sisters followed them (the priests and the brothers) to northern Ohio. Here the priests began their apostolate among the German immigrants . . . within twelve years (1844-1856) nine convents were built in northern and western Ohio" (*Religious of the Precious Blood*, John M. Behen, C.PP.S., Messenger Press, Carthagena, Ohio, 1957). The Sisters of the Precious Blood (Dayton, Ohio) still look to Mother Brunner as their foundress. They find in her that unique synthesis of mother guiding her zealous son to extraordinary virtue, and herself in later years taking up the sacred garb of yet another motherhood in the love of the Eucharistic Blood which has been so tenderly nurtured in thousands of daughters in the new distant land she was never to see.

With our own translation we append the names of the convents of perpetual adoration: Mary at the Manger, New Riegel, Ohio, 1844; Mary of Angels, near Maria Steig, 1845; Mary, Help of Christians, Maria Stein, 1846; Mary at the Sepulchre, Glandorf, Ohio, 1849; Mother of Good Counsel, Mary of the Fields, 1850; Mary, Mother of God, Gruenenwald, 1850; Visitation of Mary, Minster, Ohio, 1852; Mary, Mother of Mercy, Himmelgarten, 1852; Mary of Nazareth, Jay County, Indiana, 1854; Mary's Flight with Jesus into Egypt, Egypt, Ohio, 1856.

We place special stress on the perpetual adoration precisely because we feel that our stress of the liturgical, Eucharistic sacrifice has created a species of imbalance in our concern for the Sacramental Presence, Eucharistic visits, processions, whereas theologically they all relate to the sacrifice, draw all their meaning and power from it.

Briefly we note that the sisters who consider Father Brunner and his Mother their founder and foundress (with Saint Gaspar) are now divided into two groups, the American, the Congregation of the Sisters of the Precious Blood (C.PP.S.) with its Motherhouse at Dayton, Ohio, and the European Sisters of the Precious Blood (*Schwestern vom Kostbaren Blut*) with their Motherhouse at Schellenberg in Liechtenstein. For further details, see *Religious of the Precious Blood*, John M. Behen, Messenger Press, 1957.

John XXIII, Pope of the Precious Blood
Inde a Primis (cf. page 48).

Our Lady of the Precious Blood
(cf. page 172).

St. Joseph
(cf. page 175).

Epstein Madonna

Society of the Holy Child Jesus, London; Sr. Pamela
Hussey (cf. page 174).

St. Gaspar Del Bufalo: Giano, Italy
(cf. page 177)

St. Francis Xavier

Our Patron

(cf. page 186)

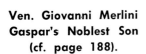

Ven. Giovanni Merlini
Gaspar's Noblest Son
(cf. page 188).

Father
Francis De Sales
Brunner (cf. page 194)

Mother
Anna Maria Brunner
(cf. page 196).

Blessed Maria De Mattias
(cf. page 192)

Mother Catherine Aurelia
(cf. page 197)

MOTHER CATHERINE AURELIA OF THE PRECIOUS BLOOD

Among our models in Precious Blood spirituality we find unique in Catherine not only her foundation of the contemplatives known as the Institute of the Sisters Adorers of the Most Precious Blood of Our Lord Jesus Christ (A. P. B.), their rapid spread and multiplication of monasteries, their practice of adoration and reparation. But Catherine herself, as providential mystic-lover of the sacred Blood and her sharing the very blood-shedding of the passion, seems to us a *sign-symbol* of our Precious Blood spirituality, its great and loving challenge to our time. She seemed providentially chosen with this Precious Blood vocation from her very childhood. Here we can give only a few lines on her life and the unique supernatural direction under the impulse of extraordinary grace.

Aurelie Caouette was born in St. Hyacinth, Canada, on July 11, 1833, and was baptized the same day. She was the eighth child in a family of nine, a devout and hardworking family. The spiritual attitude of the mother is suggested by the simple statement that she often made the way of the cross and meditated on the passion in the months preceding the birth of Aurelie (cf. *A Canadian Mystic,* by a Religious of the Precious Blood, Three Rivers, Canada, translated by a Religious of the Precious Blood, Brooklyn, N. Y., under the title, *With Dyed Garments,* cf. p. 4).

At the age of twelve, after the short period of elementary school and Sunday catechetical instruction, she was enrolled at the boarding school of the Sisters of the Congregation of Notre Dame. Intellectually and spiritually, her progress was exceptional. The girl who at the age of three seriously pondered the cross and wished to share it with Jesus, now had the grace of an exceptional confessor, Father J. Sabin Raymond. At his request she kept a spiritual diary which reveals beyond love of the Eucharist, of the cross, bodily mortification, the very desire to *suffer* by sharing the passion. With the great Teresa she could say, "either to die or to suffer" (*op. cit.,* p. 16).

It was after ten months of suffering that she could tell her director that she was cured by the great Saint of the Precious Blood, who was later to be the first patroness of her institute. Not long after, on August 30, 1854 she entered the Third Order of St. Dominic, taking the name of *Catherine* after the Saint of Siena, a spiritual act which the vow of obedience to her confessor, taken shortly before (August 15), had presaged. Not only did her sufferings, physical and mental, continue, but she actually cherished them, because Christ has "left us the Cross for our heritage . . . and also his Blood and his Love" (*op. cit.,* p. 23). When asked about her vocation by Father Raymond, the following words in her reply clearly express the *stern mystical basis* of her Precious Blood spirituality:

My principal attraction is to anoint the Wounds of Jesus Crucified with the balm of love and to sprinkle upon souls the Blood which flows from them, because Jesus still thirsts, not to receive but to give (*op. cit.,* p. 28).

The great joy created by the erection of the Confraternity of the Most Precious Blood in Canada, in the chapel of the Congregation of Notre Dame (in 1858) was followed by the agony and pain she suffered in and with the passion of her Lord. It was on the Feast of the Precious Blood in 1859, and the account is by Father Raymond:

Aurelie, the *virgin of the Precious Blood,* saw Jesus appear to her during the night, enduring the various sufferings of his Passion; she took part in them. Her heart, rent at the sight of the sins of men, opened and shed a great deal of blood; she felt the flagellation; her shoulders were all bruised; her head, feet, and hands shed more blood than ever (*op. cit.,* p. 31).

Visiting her later, Father Raymond found that

her head was all covered with blood and so were her sheets. The left hand which I was able to examine leisurely, had the very evident mark of a fresh wound, filled with blood and which was beginning to heal. The hand seemed to have been *pierced* . . . We prayed together . . . Soon she was able to rise. As she knelt at the altar rail, blood trickled down from her head. I saw it. During her thanksgiving, Jesus covered entirely with Blood, appeared to her and she heard him say: 'I accept you as a victim, I imprint upon you the seal of my Blood . . . Sprinkle it upon sinners by prayer, penance and mortification. Hasten to fulfill the orders which I give you' . . . After Holy Communion, her sufferings returned, she went back to bed and again a great deal of blood flowed from her head and heart. I went to see her towards evening and told her she had suffered enough. 'There are perhaps still more sinners who are in need of my sufferings; permit me to give more blood for them' . . . (*op. cit.,* p. 32).

Only gradually did it become clear that Catherine was to found her institute, though she never weakened in her conviction that it was God's will that she promote the devotion to the Blood of Jesus. The message came to her from "the holy Bishop Bourget" of Montreal. Space demands we omit the preliminary details, the obstacles and difficulties:

He (the bishop) received her with great kindness, submitted her to another serious examination and having made her enter his private oratory, prayed a long time with her. Finally, in the presence of the Blessed Sacrament, he uttered these words which were as the *consecration of the vocation* of Aurelie: "My child, if I were the bishop of St.

Hyacinth, I would say to you: 'Go to a very small solitary cottage and found a community of Adorers of the Precious Blood, Daughters of Mary Immaculate' " (*op. cit.*, p. 36).

Later the Bishop wrote:

Her marked attraction is for a community consecrated to the Precious Blood, and it did not occur to her that she could be called upon to found it. She ardently desired that others would be inspired to establish an institute which, in her opinion, must greatly contribute to the sanctification of souls (p. 37).

Finally the institute was founded: three young girls united with the foundress, assembled in the humble Caouette home on the Feast of the Exaltation of the Holy Cross. Shortly thereafter Bishop LaRocque arrived with his Vicar General and Chancellor. He blessed the chapel. Then the four aspirants knelt before him and expressed their desire

to be victims of the adorable will of Jesus Crucified, to immolate themselves for the salvation of souls by penance and expiation, and to spend their days for the greater glory of the Most Precious Blood and the honor of Mary Immaculate (*op. cit.*, p. 55).

After Mass Bishop LaRocque gave the group its first rule. The following Sunday he officially selected Sister Catherine superior, Sister Elizabeth Hamilton, assistant, and Sister Sophie Raymond, secretary. The institute was founded . . . Catherine died during the octave of the Feast of the Precious Blood, July 6, 1905.

The great ideal of Catherine and her followers is expressed in the thought: *I thirst.* As Jesus on the cross, they thirst with deep redemptive love to suffer for sinners. Their contemplation is supreme action for souls.

A PERSONAL NOTE

So much remains to be studied in the life and influence of Mother Catherine and the many monasteries that look to her. This we feel will be done by their own membership as the cause for her beatification continues until the Church officially places her upon our altars as Blessed Catherine, Saint Catherine, Virgin and Foundress of the Sisters Adorers of the Precious Blood. The writer sees first of all the deep synthesis of cruel suffering with the sweetness of beatifying love — the agony-joy which we find in Francis of Assisi most of all. In art it has probably been best expressed by the crosses: the *horrifying cross of Assy* by Germaine Richier and the *beatifying cross at Cologne* by Lioba Munz, O.S.B. (cf. previous pages). In Catherine

the sense of victimhood is expressed with what seems today a terrifying realism largely because we think too much of the material suffering, and far less
of the sadness, the loneliness, the mental anguish which often afflicts those
who suffer nothing of physical ache or pain.

We must, indeed, broaden our concept of sharing the suffering of Jesus.
We must apply to our age the contemplative life as *in itself* active in the
one tremendous redemptive mission of the Blood (to which we refer elsewhere in the instance of the Little Flower). We find in Catherine among
all the Precious Blood founders a unique providential-predestined model of
the Precious Blood spirituality which itself imposes on all of us, and most of
all on the members of her monasteries, the special Precious Blood spirituality
with her unique stamp. Even at the risk of boring monotony we use the
word UNIVERSALITY in joining the *Christocentric redemptive*-presence-
and-action. We must link Catherine with this Christocentric presence-and-
action in all the world. We add a special concern for the mentally ill, the
desolate — who may well possess an abundance of material bread with a
spiritual and mental hunger unto starvation and perdition, and an abundance of material wine, without the joyful cup of salvation which is the
Blood of eternal life. We include satisfactory merit for all sinners and the
Holy Souls in the spirit of Father Brunner.

Meanwhile we must pray for the beatification (and canonization) of
Mother Catherine, and from our hearts inwardly pray to her: Bless us, dear
Mother, with the Blood of salvation.

THE PRECIOUS BLOOD SPIRITUALITY: THE ESCHATOLOGY

As our study develops, this problem which has haunted us from the
inception of the *reflection on contemporary redemptive thought* clamors
for attention. Here we have a case in point where caution regarding the
dismissal of the handbooks or manuals of theology must be suggested for
a twofold reason. *First,* the stress laid on the *four last things,* death, judgment, heaven, hell (a constant in all our preaching of retreats, missions, the
entire pastoral *kerygma* and care) may by no means be disregarded. Obviously the concern was for the individual, his personal decision, destiny.
But this concern still remains. *Second,* the *cosmic theology,* though now
given the first place, must be developed precisely in a significant dialectic
with the individual and personal. Throughout we recognize that both theology and *kerygma* were groping for a true cosmic eschatology in the very
distrust and condemnation of an *apocalyptic* which was really a false eschatology. Always present, however, from the very inception of the Apostolic
Preaching was the great hope in the *Second Coming.*

Despite the constant reference to eschatology in theological writings, Rahner looks upon the scientific study of eschatology as barely in its beginnings. It is far from a well-thought-out or well-rounded theological reflection. The challenge arises especially today from man in his situation evolving, developing, shaping his world-destiny — beyond the tiny toy-world of Aristotle-Thomas to what we might consider going beyond infinite spacetime with man-unlimited, universe-unlimited. We must first caution that eschatology is not a prediction of future events. It is rather based on the continuous here-and-now: the Christ-event which places us in salvation history. We do indeed look forward but in the sense of the *supreme fulfillment* of that which is determined by the God of salvation history proclaimed in his Christ. Dismissing all apocalyptic predictions of the end of the world, with which the history of religious-enthusiasms is strewn, the Christian makes firm his decision for the ultimate only because it is present-already-on-the-way-to-fulfillment. Indeed, precisely because it is not-yet there is the obscurity, but in faith and hope there is struggle — and, saddest of all, freedom which includes the lowest form of freedom, to sin, to suffer perdition. But the Christ-event, the Christ-grace, the Christ-promise upholds the Christian decision which must always be a loving sharing of the cross with all its Blood.

The present is the future in hope and promise: the blissful end which buds even now in the Christ-grace. We can say: Our end is our beginning. Theologians stress that eschatology is turned to the end-time of glory and bliss rather than hell. But sin is still possible, the fall yawns ever before us; but hell is on a totally diverse plane than the end-glory which is eternal bliss.

We must note also the stress on man, not merely on the soul, man as a whole and as member of the community. Hence we speak even of death not as liberation from this "mortal coil" but as the *transitus,* the passing to a totally new world. The Christian takes on Christ at baptism and in the Christian existence, especially sacramentally, he shares the sufferings and joys of Christ until in death he embraces the Savior. In a sense we may speak of this as the First and Second Coming of the Lord. Similarly the total congregation of Christ, his Church exists with and through him until the final *Second Coming* or *parousia.*

In our Precious Blood spirituality we underscore the redemptive work of Christ in the pilgrim Church whose center of unity and power is the Christ-presence and Christ-action in the sacraments, centering in the Eucharist. In her solemn litanies, as we note elsewhere, she cries to him and his angels and saints, the total congregation of the blessed. Our *kerygma,* our total vocation shares in this greatness and splendor of the pilgrim Church (cf.

NCE, "Eschatology," Vol. 5, especially p. 536ff. Cf. also Rahner, E. T. art.
"Eschatology," p. 434ff, and *TD,* art. "Eschatology," p. 149f).

In the little work, to which we refer elsewhere, on Christian Prayer,
Jungmann points out (Mt 24:30) that the cross was for the early Christians
a great symbol of eschatological thought. They turned to the East frequently in prayer and uniquely to the Land of the Rising Sun in the great
expectation of the Second Coming. So too, we of the Precious Blood spirituality must turn to the cross in prayer and in constant expectation of that Second
Coming which is uniquely our own final call as it is for all men (cf. Jungmann, *op. cit.,* p. 22).

DEPTH PSYCHOLOGY AND THEOLOGY

Only in recent years have theologians, Catholic and Evangelical, come
to recognize the significance of psychology and especially of depth psychology
in theology. In a recent lead article in *Theologische Revue* (1977, no. 1,
col. 1 ff), Josef Goldbrunner insists on the need of further study of depth
psychology applied to the whole area of the theological disciplines. He boldly asks, has Western theology really come into deep contact with the Man
Jesus, or was it "almost totally covered" (C. G. Jung) by projection of the
worldly surroundings, with the result of a depreciation of the feminine?

Specifically to our purpose is Goldbrunner's comment on Hanna Wolff's
recent work: *Jesus der Mensch, die Gestalt Jesus in tiefen-psychologische
Sicht (Jesus the Man: Figure of Jesus Under the Aspect of Depth Psychology;* Stuttgart 1975). This author, both theologian, (Evangelical) and
therapeutist, looks upon Jesus as truly integrated man by contrast with the
patriarchal men of his age. "He is the prototype of renewed and redeemed
mankind." According to Jung depth psychology sees in man outwardly the
masculine which he calls the *animus,* in woman outwardly the *anima.* In
the depth, the unknown, there corresponds the *anima* in man, and the *animus* in woman. According to Hanna Wolff, Christ possessed the complimen-
tary mode of existence, the feminine in his psyche in perfect harmony and
balance. (If the *animus* is dominant and the *anima* suppressed in man,
we have the typical patriarchal figure of the Old Testament. The purely
feminine, the *anima* with the suppressed *animus* leaves blind naturalness).

According to Wolff there is in Jesus such integration of *anima* and
animus that he first of all men possessed the perfect fulness of the human.
Accordingly he was a scandal to the haughty, legalistic world of his surrounding. Depth psychology, in the mind of Hanna Wolff, sees in Jesus a
"new creative level of antithetical relationship, new psychical-spiritual understanding of the totality of man, and new and total and deepened world

understanding" (col. 5). In accord with this thought Goldbrunner suggests that the figure of Jesus corresponds to contemporary trends toward a new humanity in which the matriarchal is projected over the patriarchal, a dominance of the feminine.

Not to be outdone by C. G. Jung's statement that Jesus is the *model integral man,* Hanna Wolff proclaims that "Jesus is the first *anima* integrated man of world history, the first man who has broken through the androcentric of the ancient world" (col. 5). But we cannot agree to find in him the *Shadow* in the unknown depths, the suppressed evil, though he is indeed truly man. Rather so unique is the Man Jesus that we must agree with Guardini that we cannot write a psychology of Jesus (col. 5). More profoundly — such is the revelation grasped firmly by faith — would Jesus discern the evil in man and the forces of evil going beyond man, the forces of evil in person (cf. *DOV, Gaudium et Spes,* nos. 13 and 37, The Church in the Modern World).

It is faith which places within our reach the Jesus who is center of the universe, of the total *cosmos* with its light and darkness. His integral manhood, the *Perfect Humanum* is the very source of unity of total creation, Jesus the Christocentric, who is the motive of creation-incarnation-redemption. There looms up before us the depth of the *Cur Deus Homo* as central to all theology (as we noted in the above pages). We see him with the contemptuous and sarcastic Pontius Pilate, who with legalistic sterile masculine *animus* could ask: "What is Truth?" and the horrendous: "Behold the Man!" We respond in faith, we grasp the *Truth,* we behold the *Perfect Man* who must satisfy our every need. How great the truth: before us is the Perfect Man — the created, close to the Divine Truth and Light is indeed the Perfect Creature who gives all meaning to creation:

> Behold the Man
> The Integral Man
> Man without Shadow
> The Truth
> The Way to Truth
> The Life
> The Way to Life
> The Light
> The Way to Life and Light
> Behold the Man!
> With Deep Insight
> Psychology Yields to Theology!

CHAPTER THIRTEEN

THE PRECIOUS BLOOD SPIRITUALITY
ITS SPLENDOR

Where Men Without Faith See Only the Drab, the Ugly,
the Shameful, the Hideous, the Christian with Eyes of
Faith and Heart of Love Beholds the Hidden Splendor:
Such Is the Sanguis Christi In Our Spirituality.

THE PRECIOUS BLOOD SPIRITUALITY IN ITS SPLENDOR

So distinctive is the theology of Hans Urs von Balthasar that we feel it must be singled out as unique in the whole field of theological reflection. To shed light on the theme of Precious Blood spirituality we must view it in the vital relationship to theology as such, more specifically in its splendor. In such a context we can do no better than to follow the basic principle of *theology in its splendor* as enunciated very clearly in the classic work entitled *Herrlichkeit*, a massive *opus theologicum* which still awaits a translation into English. We call it *Splendor*.

We must repeat emphatically that the formal object of our investigation is the *splendor* of the *divine revelation* ITSELF in its manifold manifestations and conceptualizations. Herein lies *theological beauty* as such — a beauty which transcends all structures of inner worldly beauty (*Herrlichkeit*, Vol. II, p. 20).

Our author is keenly aware of the significance of beauty of concept and word in the presentation of truth, particularly of the divine truth. Prose and poetry, music and song, art and drama should be at the service of the theological reflection on the divine revelation and its worthy presentation. He cautions, nonetheless, that the choice of worldly aesthetic *idiom and media* of communication — though skillfully employed by individual theologians (and this should include the theological schools) in the presentation of their insights and visions — does not fall directly under the *formal object* of theology in its splendor. He offers this basic illustration of his position: If the *direct* or *formal object* of the theology is *God in himself,* then all else has value and meaning only insofar as God expresses himself therein. Here God-revealed is the splendor, the beauty.

With this basic clarification in mind we turn to our Precious Blood spirituality. We hold that the formal or direct object is Christ-Redeemer-Sent-by-the-Father, Sent-in-the-Holy-Spirit. This means not so much God-in-himself as a synthesis of God-in-the-world-in-and-through-Christ! Included is the tremendous human drama of sin-suffering-death-resurrection, sharing in the *formal object* (cf. *ibid.,* p. 20ff).

In the direct object we behold man, fallen man abject in his mis-identity, in state of loss and utter desolation, caught up and brought to divine-self-identity-in-Christ-God-man. We behold God not indeed in *isolation* but in supreme *condescension,* not only into the nothingness marvellously filled by creative-loving-incarnation, but in descent into ignominy of suffering, compassionate, brotherly love. (Note what von Balthasar says elsewhere in the reflection on Bonaventure). Herein lies the splendid paradox of divine-human splendor transcending the transfiguration of Thabor itself.

> The experience of the divine glory has taken on the *kenotic-mystique* in a love of compassion in which the Mighty Heart of the World broke and ceased to beat — on an ugly cross — as nature shuddered at the death of its God — all drained of his Life-Blood (cf. *ibid.,* p. 21).

It is typical that von Balthasar cautions against any Christocentric shift — or shall we say conversion — into the merely anthropological, when faith in Christ threatens to become a "characteristic" of man (Schleiermacher, Kierkegaard, and Bultmann).

Our Precious Blood spirituality rests safely on an anthropology which is truly and inexorably Christological. The Christ of Calvary is raised from the dead through the Spirit of the Father who is also the Spirit of Jesus. Through his Spirit the kingdom he preached is concretized in the Church which treasures all his mysteries, for they constitute her very reality. In her he abides forever. In some way she lives his life. Through her and in her he becomes the *totus Christus,* sharing his suffering, revealing his splendor in her dreadful human frailty as well as in her exaltation. Throughout the "bond of God's Spirit and the spirit of man in and through the Spirit of Jesus is ultimate, finalizing, form-giving" (*ibid.,* p. 21).

The unique splendor of Precious Blood spirituality rests in the grandeur of the eternal, divine decree to create a *world-to-be-redeemed.* This involves also a divine-human response in the God-man: the divine-human dialog — the covenant sealed with divine-human blood. As in all distinctive

theologies, the splendor of the Precious Blood theology must be explained —
and here we follow von Balthasar's arduous process of thought — in the
light of a free communication with the total theology in *its* splendor. We
cannot fail to see that the particular theologies are subject to the laws of
free human structuring, the movements of the Holy Spirit, the providential
meeting of human needs and desires.

> When these two, the human and the divine-human free manifestations
> of relationship are established, we have the basis for the transition be-
> tween all theology (conceived in the breadth of view of its formal ob-
> ject) and the manifestational forms of the individual theology. The
> content (of this total theology) is already divinely manifested, a divine
> splendor proclaimed throughout the world. The expression, however,
> (the expressional forms both of individual theologies and of theology as
> a whole) is subject to the laws of free human structuring. Centrally
> viewed, finished forms are not lying before us, "styles" we may say.
> Rather there is the creative process of structure-becoming of this unique
> content's emerging style. Insofar as the content itself is already ex-
> pression of God, theology is expression of manifestation. On the one
> hand there is obedient fulfillment of the manifestation of revelation
> impressing itself on the believer, on the other hand there is the action
> of the Holy Spirit, as the Spirit of the Church and her Christ, uniquely
> moving the believer, in this free acceptance of the mystery as it were
> emerging in its own self-manifestation (freely adapted, *ibid.*, p. 25f).

Hans Urs sharply scores the point that we are not dealing with matter
of the happenstance and the arbitrary. Two fixed points (poles?) guide us:
a) The *revealed truth* itself which is unique *content* of Christian theology
and its firm, abiding structure; b) doctrine of the Church which all right-
thinking theologians must follow: she possesses the *Holy-Interpretive-Spirit*,
to whom the theologians must submit in service and commitment to her. En-
couragingly, however, he adds a note on the charisms in the Church:

> These theological charisms impart to individual theologians the power
> of insight into the total theological structure of revelation or one of its
> essential parts, the power to perceive and present this theology under
> a unique aspect. An aspect, indeed, which may have been slighted or
> little noted heretofore! Such missions or charisms may be considered
> a kind of *inner form* of a great theology flowing from living revelation,
> infused into the heart in generous grace. Here *form* brings into focus
> the aesthetic slant of a personal call from God in his manifestation of
> aspect in the Church, God opening the heart of the individual and
> speaking lovingly to his spirit (adapted, *ibid.*, p. 26).

Profoundly this applies to the grand spiritualities in the Church. The
most careful study — one does not proceed hastily in the reflection of Hans

Urs — will reveal how it applies to our Precious Blood spirituality in its outstanding models, to some of whom we have already given brief attention. No less profoundly should it apply to all who study the Precious Blood theology in its depth, practice its spirituality as the basis of their Precious Blood vocation.

Precious Blood Spirituality in Its Splendor: Gerard Manley Hopkins

For our course von Balthasar has pointed the way. In the second volume of the *Herrlichkeit*, he lists among the *Faecher der Stile* (we translate: Models of Form, somewhat inadequately) Gerard Manley Hopkins. We turn to Hopkins in our present study 1) because as the only English poet-theologian in the list, he is very accessible to our readers, though one does not grasp him on the wing and 2) because his Christocentrism appears to us a unique complement to contemporary Christo-centric theology. He seems to grow taller as the decades pass. We look upon him especially as a poet of splendor in his *Inscape*: His is a Precious Blood theology and spirituality in its splendor. Only von Balthasar (shall we say in the German idiom) could have chosen him. Rightly he maintains that

> Christianity is really an *inspiration* which of its nature proceeds with the most unimpeded and spontaneous endeavor as well in the ethical (above all as love of neighbor) as in the aesthetical (as exact experience of world figures). Precisely one transcending in faith, hope, and love in Christ has the obligation to read all the revealed representations of God in Christ in the universe; and this work Hopkins the poet accomplishes. For what is to be read is not indeed concepts (of *universal* abstract truths) but images (of the unique personal, divine-human truth). Herein is theological language absolutely suited to the imaginative diction, and Hopkins can bring home to the Church the great English *tradition* in his own creative achievement.
>
> Hence his endeavor and practice in reading the figures of nature is neither in the usual sense aesthetic nor mystical nor one-sidedly, *exact-scientific*. Rather it embraces and unites all under the higher Christian Law. We may say it is really learning to read (*ibid.*, 758f).

With the sharpest insight Hans Urs concludes that the Christian is possessed of a loftier unity than the poetic, creative bond the Romantic might have with the spirit of nature:

> For the Christian the final design of unity is higher. In faith he must rise to it in the *Great Sacrifice*. His enthusiasm may have no other source than his faith. From such exaltation as thrust and strain of the whole man the poetic form utters something. The unheard-of in Hopkins' idiom is a theological phenomenon: only in this context is he comprehensible (Vol. II, p. 758).

HOPKINS' THEOLOGY: A NEGATIVE NOTE

In his comprehensive study of Hopkins' *Inscape*, James Finn Cotter presents the poet's Christology in the following interpretation of the noted kenotic text of Philippians, to which we have often referred:

> The hymn of Philippians describes the process of redemption by dramatizing the event of salvation history from eternity to time. The center is the person of Christ himself, not as the lifeless puppet of an eternal plan, but as a hero and *dramatis persona* in his decisions and actions. In a second analysis of the text which he made in his commentary on the *Exercises*, Hopkins divides the drama into scenes: "This process took place in its own fashion 1) in the procession of the Godhead; 2) in his entrance into creation, his incarnation proper; 3) on earth, in the *enanthropeusin*, the becoming man" (S, 181) . . . The point is an essential one in Hopkins' Christology for it allowed him to determine a *human existence* of Christ before he historically pitched his tent among us (Jn 1:14) and made visible a presence previously hidden from men's sight. Like Samuel Coleridge, Hopkins also concluded that before being man in Judaea "when he was now actually man and born in poverty" (S, 181) the Word took on the *forma servi* in the genesis of the cosmos. Christ is engaged from the beginning with the world of time; his *kenosis* is the first act of creation (p. 36f).

This writer — if he has grasped Hopkins' meaning — regrets that he cannot accept the poet's position: a *created nature* of Christ at the very beginning of creation. His created nature was formed by the Holy Spirit in the virginal womb of Mary of Nazareth. Such, we think is the unanimous teaching of our tradition as expressed in all the great professions of faith from the beginning. Here we also state our position (in agreement with neither Thomas nor Scotus) as to the motive of incarnation. As already stated, we place in the very center of our incarnational doctrine the *Cur Deus Homo*: By one supreme act God decreed creation-redemption. God created this evolving universe permitting its sin, in order to redeem it through his Son in the shedding of blood. We have amply explained the point before.

POSITIVELY

Despite the negative critique given above, we find in Hopkins' Christocentrism a unique quality which current theology — such is our view — has not concretely exploited. Theologians seem to have limited themselves to the Christ-presence-and-action in the Church, or to the universal dispensation of grace throughout the world. Today as never before we need to explain Christ in all the tremendous events of the world, to explain Christ passionately as Hopkins did in his great poem *The Wreck of the Deutschland* and the *Windhover*. Perhaps only a poet-theologian-genius could so sacramentalize all human events and relate them to the *Great Sacrifice,* to the Eucharist, to the Blood. Only Hopkins could see "the whole world inclosed . . . in a drop of Christ's blood" (*Inscape,* p. 45, quoting S 194). Only Hopkins could say "the whole world appears suffused in Christ's luminous Blood" (*Inscape,* p. 123, S 194). Or, "Mounted in a drop of Christ's blood, new heaven hymns the new earth, 'an ark for the listener' under a rainbow of concord" (*Inscape,* p. 81).

> Hopkins, who remained a student and teacher of the Greek thinkers all his life, found in them, as the Church Fathers had before him, a prophetic delineation of the Word-to-be-made-flesh. What reason could not comprehend came to pass: the rounded sphere was opened, uncreated Being became a creature, the All made himself nothing, the One was lost in the midst of the many. "Ground of being, and granite of it: past all/Grasp God," he glided "lower than death and the dark" (Ps 28: 32-33). "World's strand" became "sway of the sea." God, "an intelligible sphere whose center is everywhere and the circumference nowhere," had been nailed to the tree of the cross, the permanent axis on which the world turns: STAT CRUX DUM VOLVITUR ORBIS (*Inscape,* p. 21).

Most gently human is the following:

> It is one adorable point of the incredible condescension of the Incarnation (the greatness of which no saint can have ever hoped to realize) that our Lord submitted not only to the pains of life, the fasting, scourging, crucifixion, etc. or the insults, as the mocking, blindfolding, spitting, etc., but also to the mean and trivial accidents of humanity. It leads one naturally to rhetorical antithesis to think for the instance that after making the world, he should consent to be taught carpentering, and, being the Eternal Reason, to be catechized in the theology of the Rabbins" (L 3, 19-20, *Inscape,* 3f).

Beautifully Cotter reflects Hopkins' ideal:

> Nature is panchristic in its millionfold cycles and motions; material things act out their being-in-Christ. All the more are the actions of human nature, united to the All in grace, Christocentric in going out and reaching back in endless movement. In Sonship, in the place of the carpenter who fashioned the cosmos, man's strenuous day labor of rock-lifting and wood-splitting lays bare the inner zone or inscape where lies the solar heart of Being. The glory of God is a living man stooped with a dungfork or a woman bowed over a slop pail. The Kingdom of Heaven was meant, as Hopkins saw, for the ill-used workers of Liverpool and Glasgow, "without dignity, knowledge, comforts, de-

light, or hopes in the midst of plenty" (L 1, 28). Christ came and comes again for the likes of these (*Inscape*, p. 67).

This panchristic world has Christ present in all things: "Christ being me and me being Christ." One of the sonnets, *As Kingfishers Catch Fire,* strikingly brings out this thought:

> I say more; the just man justices;
> Keeps grace; that keeps all his goings graces;
> Acts in God's eyes what in God's eye he is —
> Christ. For Christ plays in ten thousand places,
> Lovely in limbs, and lovely in eyes not his
> To the Father through the features in men's faces.
>   (Quoted in *Inscape,* p. 81)

Cf. also Paul L. Mariani, *A Commentary on the Complete Poems of Gerard Manley Hopkins,* Cornell U. Press 1970, p. 178).

THE WRECK OF THE DEUTSCHLAND

This poem is the most personal and theologically the most splendidly Christocentric. We have space for only a few references. This North German vessel was wrecked in a fearful storm in the mouth of the Thames on the night of December 7-8 in 1875. It is dedicated to the five Franciscan nuns expelled from Germany in accordance with the Falk laws. The nuns with about a fourth of the two hundred or more passengers perished in the storm. The high point of the poem, dominating it entirely, is the cry to Christ by a gaunt Teutonic sister: "O Christ, Christ, come quickly."

Not the Christ of the past or the future, but the Lord of the present, now within the heart and in the universe he made, rises from the ruin of the storm to ride here "in his triumph" (*ibid.,* 147). The nun re-makes the physical disaster into a cause for celebration: "to bathe in his fall-gold mercies, to breathe in his all-fire glances." The storm becomes what Christ intended it to be: a glorious return through an innocent act of nature, since "in thy sight storm flakes were scroll-leaved flowers, lily showers — sweet heaven was astrew in them." The "martyr-master" is always ready to welcome his creature home, but some one must "fetch" him to creation's door for it to open and reveal him there. Death is meant to be a homecoming not an upheaval (*ibid.,* 149f).

The "stress" of divine presence (is) experienced by man in "stars and storms," in joy and sorrow, in the calm of contemplation and in sudden calamity. What is the nature of this presence? Christic being, energizing and filling man through his Spirit. What is its source and how is it known and acknowledged? From and through the heart. First of all, Christ's heart "is out with it" when it "was pierced and spent its contents by the opening in his side" (S 103) . . . "The piercing of Christ's side. The sacred body and the sacred heart seemed waiting for an opportunity of discharging themselves and testifying their total devotion of themselves to the cause of man," (S 255) . . . The only way to the Father is this passageway . . . opened in Christ's side . . . "Heart" is repeated 18 times in the poem . . . For Hopkins, the act of faith is a recognition of the heart and mind, revealing the presence of Christ and his "double natured name" (*ibid.*, 151).

The *Wreck of the Deutschland* is indeed

> a hymn of praise to Christ, the God-man, shaper and rescuer of the world. The Deutschland is a Pindaric song of triumph in Christ's victory over chaos and death. The historic Jesus is now the Lord of glory, reigning in the universe and in the hearts of men (*ibid.*, 152).

> The ode ends with a crescendo of seven epithets of Christ . . . the *Loss of the Eurydice* also opens with an invocation to the "Lord" and ends with a closing prayer to "Christ lord of thunder" (*ibid.*, 153).

We must note that when Hopkins refers to the *Great Sacrifice* he had in mind more than the redemptive death on the cross: rather it is the entire incarnational redemption *kenosis.*

We conclude our reflection on *Splendor in Hopkins* with the final lines of von Balthasar:

> Ultimate in Hopkins, however, are the shipwreck poems, for here the wrecking and shattering of all innerworldly images and symbols becomes an ultimate image for the sacrament of the world: collapse and resurrection in God, death as resurrection, resurrection not beyond but in death. The nun on the wave-swept deck who cries out into the raging elements, "Christ, come quickly," calls the Savior in the elements and through them christens her Wild-Worst Best. She christens (baptizes) her Wild-Worst unto the Best. The Wreck is the harvest, the shoal the goal. . . . Wrecked in God — this is the acme of the poem — man finds nothing to cling to, not even his yearnings, also no reward or heaven or any kind of characteristics of God's, for on the other Side of all that is *He alone*: *Ipse, the only one*: the Self beyond nature. Here the poet becomes jubilant because the *cor rectum*, the *simple eye* of the parable has attained the most exalted heights possible: to discern the featureless unfeatured chaos of night as *Form* (*Gestalt*) and in the meaningless to point out the pure question of who and why *loc. cit.*, p. 766 adapted.

> Ah! there was a heart right!
> There was single eye!
> Read the unshapeable shock night
> And knew the who and the why.

THE MYSTICAL HEIGHTS

We continue our study on the spirituality of the Precious Blood with a stress of three comprehensive points: the *victory over sin* and *spiritual bondage,* the *abundance of grace; the mystical heights* or the Precious Blood in its heroic dimensions.

First, the *Sanguis Christi* has triumphed over sin, uniting a redeemed world to God through union with the God-man as we have explained throughout these pages. *Secondly,* the *Sanguis Christi* has been the source of all grace, all virtue, from resistance to temptation, to act and practice of every virtue. *Thirdly,* the *Sanguis Christi* is the source of virtue in its heroic or thaumaturgic dimension.

With this we now deal under the title: *The Mystical Heights.* It is our contention that the *Precious Blood spirituality* is *uniquely completed in the Mystical Heights.* The study of the spirituality demands this final insight for a grasp of its true and deeper meaning. Our use of the term *mystical* should be clear from the context of our explanation. We begin with the question:

WHAT IS MYSTICISM?

It is Jean Gerson who thinks of mysticism as knowledge of God by experience, arrived at through the embrace of unitive love (*NCE* Vol. 10, p. 175). We consider mysticism "the perfection of supernatural prayer" open to all men. Extraordinary indeed in the sense of rarely attained! The marvellous phenomena associated with some of the great mystics are rare and, we hold, not of the essence and substance of mystical prayer. Divinely bestowed, they call attention to God's marvels and to that which is essential to true mysticism, the most intimate union of the loving soul with God. There is surely a great diversity among the mystics, suited to the varied conditions of life, official duties and positions. Bernard is not Thomas, Teresa is not Catherine of Siena, nor is Francis of Assisi John of the Cross. None of these is at all like Henry of Susa, nor the Little Flower. Teresa of Avila herself critically underscored differences between her approach, if we may use the term, and that of Juan himself.

Basically, however, the aim and goal of all mystics is the most intimate union with God as we noted above, union direct, immediate, medium-less, not discursive, and certainly not to be confused with the beatific vision. This involves two things primarily: the gradual purging of the heart of earthly desires; and mind and imagination of sense images as manifestation of divine things and as center of our prayer-thought.

Gradually the grace-moved soul experiences God directly and immediately with unifying love. Surely Christian mysticism is deeply founded in the incarnational faith-love rather than in the absolute-ground-of-all-being. God comes to us in Christ, the countenance of the Father shines forth in the face of Jesus, his Son. Hence in the Jesus-bond and the Jesus-love we come to the Father united with him in the love-bond between Father and Son which is the Holy Spirit.

The union with God is often expressed in the symbol of mystical espousal, the marriage, the exchange of hearts. Often a certain frankness in terms of human love is exalted to infinite chasteness and purity in the soul's embrace of its God. But always it is God who reaches out to embrace his creature, creating in him the depths and heights of love. If Augustine spoke directly to God unveiling his most intimate thought and feeling, it was in the *I - Thou* relationship to which we have already alluded in our first pages.

Francis of Assisi: Saint of the Stigmata

Almost beyond human conception is the *mystical height* of Francis of Assisi. In him and in the entire Franciscan spirituality Christ is the center. We dare assert that not even Saint Paul himself so identified himself with Christ as did the Poverello of Umbria, for with Paul he could say that through the cross the world was crucified to him and he to the world (cf. Gal 6:14). For Francis in his ecstacies, "the whole man was a prayer, not only a praying man." "He seemed to be consumed like a fiery coal in a flame of heavenly love." Walter Nigg says of him: "Francis is the personification of Christian mysticism: in him it has become a human being" (*Great Saints*, p. 58, Regnery). Men who saw Francis saw Christ in him as though he had incorporated Jesus into his own body. We can understand Francis, all his work, his poverty, his utter renunciation of all worldly, even family ties, only in the light of this identification with Christ.

His was the *utterly renunciatory love* which is the high mark of the Precious Blood spirituality. It is expressed, still faintly, in his marriage to Lady Poverty in the bond of the Jesus-love. But the summit, the extreme was the joy-in-pain which linked him visibly in his very body with the crucified. None other than Bonaventure vividly tells the story in his commentary, formerly recited for the feast of the Imprinting of the Sacred Stigmata of Saint Francis, Sept. 17.

According to the commentary of Bonaventure, on the morning of the Feast of the Exaltation of the Holy Cross, Francis was praying on the mountain of Alvernia when there appeared to him a flaming Seraph, or Christ in the form of a Seraph. Radiant and aflame the heavenly Visitor approached

Francis. He was both winged and crucified: of the six wings two were above his head, two extended in flight, two wrapped about him covering his body. His hands and feet, marvellous to behold, were extended and affixed to a cross. Though vehemently shaken by the apparition, Francis was filled with a mingling of deep joy and pain. Marvellous, familiar, the "Seraph" created excess of joy amidst the dread of the cross, piercing the soul as with a sword. He who appeared outwardly enlightened Francis inwardly. It was evident that the Seraph was spiritual and immortal and could not suffer; nevertheless the apparition made known that he was the friend of Francis and transformed him not by the searing martyrdom of the flesh, but by the ray of fire that united his heart totally to the likeness of Christ crucified.

This vision, therefore, after intimate and familiar colloquy inflamed the mind and heart of Francis with an interior seraphic fervor. His flesh was made like to that of the Crucified as though they were welded together by fire. And suddenly there appeared on his feet and hands the signs of the nails. And his side was pierced as though by a lance. And often blood flowed forth from these wounds. No saint has ever been so intimately bound up with Jesus crucified. Francis had only a short time to live on earth. But blind, desolate, he continued to afflict his body, turned away from any tasty food and totally to Jesus crucified. He died on October 3, 1226, with the song on his lips: "Welcome, my Brother death!" Elias of Cortona saw the wounds on the corpse of Francis. We treasure the *mystic heights* of Precious Blood spirituality in Francis of Assisi: the awe, the admiration we view from afar. Only in some small measure can we imitate him.

Very different is John of the Cross to whom we must devote a few paragraphs not merely because he too reached the *mystical heights* which we associate with our Precious Blood spirituality, but also because the Church herself has pronounced him our guide as Doctor of the Church and special patron of mystical theology.

JOHN OF THE CROSS: A REFLECTION AND AN IMAGE

God the absolute presents himself to the soul through utter withdrawal and deprivation. In consequence the soul is in agony, dereliction, captive, as though in the depths of hell. But on God's part it is a purging. Juan hurls his challenges to the world: *God alone suffices,* hence forsake all things as Christ enjoins. He indeed left all. He had no place to lay his head. He was crushed and in his desolation cried out: *My God, my God, why hast thou forsaken me.* This forsakenness, the greatest in his life, wrought a greater effect than all the wonders and deeds on earth or in heaven: namely reconciliation of our race through grace . . . at the very point when he was most crushed . . . he reconciled men who scoffed . . . with God who left him desolate. "God forsook him so that he could pay the most untainted price of guilt."

For Juan union with God consists not in joy, delights, sentiments, but in unique vital death on the cross. His citations from the Old Testament, e.g., Job, Jeremiah, are all dictated by the experience of the love-death on the cross. His whole concern with the inspired pages turns to the cross of Christ. All is directed to the cross or proceeds from it. To go to the Father we must follow Christ, leave all. The absolute, the preponderant must also be preponderant in the-relative-creature. God who is pure love wills that we participate in his being . . . this is possible only by making the God-love the love-act of the creature, though creature and God are always distinct. Thus the creature is immersed into the depths, even into hell, to distinguish all else from the all-pure-God. Only in the dereliction, as in the fire of hell, is the soul purged, purified, blackened with smoke, till it is set aglow and inwardly shaped as purged with love-flame for future heaven-love, become more divine than human. Faith is dark night for the soul, and in this manner God enlightens her and the more he merges the soul in darkness, the more does he bestow on her something of his light. The night illumines in that it blinds. The more the things of God in themselves are high and bright, the more are they unknown to us and obscured.

The only authentic image of God is the crucified. Juan sketched his vision: the cross is horizontal, beam and bar with the body hanging from them, hands and feet in the darkness of the night, hurtling down, down, toward the world and hell . . . Christ appeared to Juan as dashed down in vehement vertical falling movement. The head down, down, draws after it the breast with the throat vertical, neck arched, arms taut, stretched, the hair fallen over the face, the skull, the upper back hips visible. Tense gripping light strikes from above. What seems brutal force produces the effect, though the lines are flexible and tender . . . Imposed on the artist is the hovering vision, the falling apparition in dizzy light, the divine body flickered with shadows, with nerves rather than bones, arms coiled with painfully swollen fibers. The pliant, narrow chest seems to shrink from the rigid wood seeking to wrestle itself free and to plunge to earth. Sheer weight has torn the left wrist and the nail is newly driven into the swollen soft hand. The heart bleeds in a long and painful flow on the stiffened breast. The artist himself contributes the sovereign dignity to this convulsive sketch, all tension and yet almost weightless, so tenderly and impulsively did he undertake his task. The reality is entirely at the service of the EVENT.

The above was drawn freely from *Herrlichkeit*, Vol. II, "Juan de la Cruz." The reflection on the image of the Crucified is specifically taken from

p. 524ff of the same work. It is cited from Michael Florisoone, a noted authority whose work, *Esthétique et Mystique d'après St. Thérèse d'Avila et St.
Jean de la Croix* (Seuil 1956), is referred to as one of the principal sources
by the author of *Herrlichkeit, ibid.,* p. 467.

In *The Collected Works of St. John of the Cross,* translated by Kieran
Kavanaugh and Otilio Rodriguez, the frontispiece is *Christ Crucified, A
Drawing by St. John of the Cross.* On page 39 there is a *Note on Drawing
of Christ on the Cross*:

> One day St. John of the Cross handed Ana Maria de Jesus, a holy nun
> at the Incarnation, a small piece of paper on which he had drawn in
> pen and ink a picture of Christ on the Cross. It represented a vision
> he had recently had. Fortunately the small drawing has not been lost,
> but is still preserved in a reliquary at the Convent of the Incarnation in
> Avila. This is an enlarged photo of the original.

(The *Drawing of the Crucified* and the above *Note on Drawing of Christ on
the Cross* are from *The Collected Works of St. John of the Cross* translated
by Kieran Kavanaugh and Otilio Rodriguez, Copyright (c) 1964 by Washington Province of Discalced Carmelites, Inc. Paperback edition published
by ICS Publications, Washington, D.C., U.S.A.).

We limit this study to the two great exemplars of the *mystical heights* —
there are obviously many more — because these two are sufficient to point
the way, the mystic way for our further study of Precious Blood spirituality
and Precious Blood mysticism in our own societies, its models, founders,
leaders. We shall add but one more point, let us call it the final ecumenical
stress to this study. We have already indicated that the Precious Blood
spirituality is profoundly at home with the spirit of ecumenism. We who
practice this spirituality must evince a most profound love for all other
religious societies, all other spiritualities, cooperating without envy, in the
work of all. And learning from all. Shall not we in our workshops, our
guidance of youth, our total *kerygma* see the guidance of the Holy Spirit
in the formation of vocations also to other societies and to the diocesan priesthood, as well as to our own? This is especially practical in the matter of
vocations among youth in our schools and colleges, in our priestly assistance
to diocesan pastors in charge of God's people in the various dioceses. We
are confident that God will bless our own work the more zealously we share
our spiritual efforts and our spirituality with others. As we give spiritual
goods to others, the more we bestow, the more we retain and enrich our own.
Only matter divides, the Spirit unites.

Per Christum Hominem ad Christum Deum

(Hilda Graef: *The Way of the Mystics,* p. 59)

Crucified Christ

Drawing by St. Juan
(cf. page 216)

The Liturgical Conclusion

St. Andrae, Salzburg, Austria
(cf. page 218)

CHAPTER FOURTEEN

EPILOGUE

(*Suggested by Romano Guardini:
Das Bild Von Jesus Dem Christus*)

Our inquiry into the structure and meaning of the sacred reality which is the work of redemption through Blood is not solely theological investigation. It goes beyond the reflection on the *Sanguis Christi* as found in the sacred page and traditional document. Far less is it an effort to exhaust the conceptual theological content which expands before our eyes as we reflect and ponder. We aim rather at guiding the reader toward a more profound entry into the foundations of the life in redemptive faith and deep reflection into the mystery of redemption. In this light — we prayerfully hope — *they will grasp fully the breadth and length and height and depth of Christ's love, and experience this love which surpasses all knowledge . . . so they might attain to the fulness of God himself* (Eph 3:18-19). The short span of the earthly redemptive event between the birth at Bethlehem and the death on Calvary extends through the eternal ages beyond earthly existence, for our Redeemer is the Word who was with and in God in the eternal birth. And through him all things were made. In union with the Father and their Holy Spirit he continues his redemptive love in grace-laden history unto eternal glory with an everlasting priesthood which we hope to share forever.

JESUS CHRIST TODAY
JESUS CHRIST YESTERDAY
JESUS CHRIST FOREVER
PRAISED FOREVER BE THE BLOOD OF JESUS

St. Andrae in Salzburg: Liturgical Conclusion

The brilliant windows in the church shall serve as a liturgical conclusion, even though our illustration is in black and white.

> The windows give the content of the prayers immediately before and after the Consecration. They aim at keeping constantly before the eyes of the faithful the mystery of the oblation moving them to ever richer pondering as they celebrate the service of God in divine mystery.

The symbolism is highly elaborate. More than sixty figures are grouped in unified composition, Trinity, angels, saints, instruments of the passion — Christian symbolic pictures, earthly structures . . . to the coat of arms of the patron (*Stifter*). The formal composition clearly follows the objective content of the prayer of the holy canon and is focused on the heavenly liturgy, the mystery of Consecration: chalice and host. In all this one calls to mind the turning of the spoken word into music. And chant is accompanied by sacral, instrumental music. This stained glass raised to symphony in color enhances the sacred action on the altar and raises the prayer into the outer realm of silence, which is filled with the resonance of the words, the eternal Word, imparting in the jubilation of color a reflection of the eternal image, light from light, suffering and deeds of light.

The song of praise ascends upward in burnished light of colors. The light of the heights responds as the heavens open to the great sacrifice. The three windows glow in blue, red, golden-yellow; blue of the incomprehensible dark light of the world of faith, the red of blood and love, the golden-yellow of the light of life. The green of the earth is transformed, between the blue and red, by clouds of incense, sacrificial color of violet, clouds of smoke in many layers and banks.

The left window is the green of earth's hope, dear to the memory of the living rising in the blue of faith. *Most of the halos of the saints* glow in the red of blood for not all are martyrs. Red too, the bosom of the Mother of God in the flame of the Holy Spirit. In the right window to the memory of the dead, dark shade underlies the heavy blue and violet, above glows the red of blood . . . John the Baptist stands on the vessel with his blood, which holds the head of this martyr of Christ.

The middle window, somewhat lighter, recalls the passion and the ancient patriarchs of the Old Testament, blue-violet light predominating. From God the Father golden-yellow suffuses the heavenly altar. We mark the angels of the ascension, and the angel restraining Abraham from sacrificing his son Isaac. Flaming red of angels' wings merge in the fiery winglets of the Holy Spirit. Only the angel of the sacrifice is aloft on blue-violet wings.

The Christ wears the cloak of blood-red. The crystal sea laps round the golden altar, and is overarched by the rainbow of emerald green. In the right window the golden sun with the *JHS* looms over all. In the left window the morning star emerges in the aurora with the insignia of Mary.

From the three windows a stream of light floods the high altar on which the tremendous oblation of thanksgiving is celebrated. Here all men offer to the Father of Lights the Eternal Light of True Light (*op. cit.*, p. 202-205 adapted).

CHAPTER FIFTEEN

THE ULTIMATE FRUIT OF
THE SANGUIS CHRISTI

MARIA REGINA MARTYRUM
IN EVERLASTING REMEMBRANCE

The triumph of defeat, the rising to glory from shameful torture and death, central to our study of the *Sanguis Christi*, is exemplified in every martyr for the cause of Christ, but never so splendidly as in the victims of the Nazi persecution in our own times. And never so splendidly has the genius of modern art-forms linked them with Mary — the sorrowing Queen of Martyrs and the crucified Christ — for our perpetual memory and instruction in the great shrine *Maria Regina Martyrum*. On the site of the most diabolical persecution in human history, when Nazi fury made the profession of the Christian faith a cause of most cruel death, the shrine teaches its meaning for generations yet unborn. Many appeals to the German people urged the construction of the memorial, among them that of Pius XII:

> At a place where in dark times death sentences were continuously carried out, you (should) plan a sanctuary in honor of the Regina Martyrum in memory of those who shed their blood for the rights of God and conscience. Heroic confessors of the past, they teach us that moral values, the divine rights and the true faith by far excel all that is temporal: they demand your unconditioned consent even to the sacrifice of your lives. Indeed, those of you who are in distress and danger can find in their example the consolation and strength to carry on.

A beautiful pamphlet entitled

MARIA REGINA MARTYRUM
BERLIN-CHARLOTTENBURG
Memorial Church of the German Catholics
IN HONOR OF THE MARTYRS
For Freedom of Religion and Conscience
From 1933 to 1945

tells the story of the construction by noted artists and of the consecration by noble prelates of the center of remembrance and atonement. Here we have the congregation of those who have been *called out,* the *ecclesia.* Deep is the meaning: the *parish* in the living Church makes the remembrance of those who have been *called out,* chosen by special divine grace and election, continues their noble example, and appeals for their intercession, looking forward to sharing their glory. A sacred place within a modern housing area: a large enclosed site in which church, rectory, tower, school, place for youth activity tell a busy, active world the real, deeper meaning of life in Christ, as it pictures the martyrs of Christ with their sorrowing Mother, the Queen.

In these few pages we can refer only to the most pertinent monuments.

> We enter the church building, proceed past the stairway and approach the smaller lower church — the main sanctuary of the memorial place. A few steps lead down to this crypt, purposely left in twilight, since it serves as a sepulchral church. The walls are blackish grey — only the wall behind the altar glimmers with golden warmth. To the right of the altar three graves have been embedded in the floor. The right one contains the ashes of Dr. Erich Klausener, which were transferred from the St. Matthias cemetery. The left grave still waits for the remains of prelate Bernhard Lichtenberg who was buried in the St. Hedwig's cemetery, now in East Berlin. So far the East Berlin authorities refused the transferring of his body to West Berlin. Between these two martyrs — one a priest, the other a layman — a third grave is dedicated
>
> > To all martyrs to whom a grave was denied.
> > To all martyrs whose graves are unknown.

Here the concept of martyrdom which essentially formed the plan and the design of this church found its truest realization. The same idea also materializes in the grandiose figure of Mary, the Pieta.

> Behind the graves, against the gold background, the bronze pieta by Fritz Koenig has been placed. The tender piety of the middle ages yields to a different expression of mourning. The dominant and frightening marks of this bronze are bareness of beauty, unity of mother and son in the form of the cross. The worn-out body of our Lord, his limbs mere skin and bone, the wretchedness of the shrunken bald head bending down from the shoulders, as if it were cracked, the skinny legs that hang down as heavy as lead, all present a figure that is scarcely human: but it reminds us of something. Christ our brother — dishonored, despised, murdered in the concentration camp. The sculptor, Koenig, forces us to face Golgotha's naked horror — never joined by *beauty* — not only to increase our fright, but to let us reach a deeper stratum where quiet and peace prevail. And that great quiet is present here. It is given by the linking of both figures to the indissoluble unit of the

cross, by the tenderness, intimacy and even beauty which will reveal themselves only to the contemplating eye. Mary offers her entire body to her dead son; she embraces him so full of compassion that she becomes a shell in which her son sinks and also a throne on which she holds him and presents him to the world, giving him away a second time. She only needs her feet to support herself and him, her arms are interwoven with the whole movement of offering and accepting, of embracing and holding. Only her head stands out. The spare outline of her face expresses hope in the midst of sorrow, peace in the midst of pain, immense majesty and dignity in the presence of such distortion and deprivation. This church is dedicated to Mary, *Queen of Martyrs*. Koenig's sculpture makes us see in Mary the Mother of the living, the royal Mother of all the tormented. She who sheltered her dead son in her lap and was united with him in the sign of the cross, she will also shelter the martyrs and those who mourn.

Mary is also presented as the Woman of the Apocalypse. She is the Mother who brings forth the children who form the New People of God, whose birth the Dragon seeks to prevent. The martyrs are his prey. There is a bond between the *Woman of the Apocalypse* and the *Queen of Martyrs*. The Virgin-Mother Mary — type of the Church who is oppressed and persecuted by the Dragon — defends the precious life of the martyrs against the enemy that wants to devour her new-born children. There is also represented the Lady who resembles the resurrected body, thus becoming an explanation of what we profess in the Creed: "I believe in the resurrection of the body." The Dragon has scattered the corpses and the ashes of human beings all over the tortured earth. But the assumption of Mary gives rise to our conviction that they shall rise again.

We can merely mention the picture of the Lamb of the Apocalypse, who at Judgment takes over the struggle which was carried on by Mary representing the Church. The Lamb leads to victory and makes Judgment Day dawn in splendor and power. The way of the cross is set in great groups, the seventh being the resurrection. After the cross, the Easter morning is dawning. An almost classic beauty is shed over this last group, a shine of the invisible. The way of the cross points to the altar of the sacrifice:

> The consolation resulting from the faith in the Last Things is not a distant one; it is near to every generation, near also to this memorial place in honor of the martyrs of our time.

Fittingly we conclude our study of the spirituality of the Precious Blood with this reference to the Memorial of the Martyrs of Christ, who, grouped about Mary their Queen, are the most glorious fruit of the *Sanguis Christi*.

NOTES AND REFERENCES

1. Karl Rahner reduces the great mysteries to these three: Trinity, Incarnation, Grace-Vision. Tullio Citrini in his *Gesu Cristo, Rivelazione di Dio* (Milano, 1969) comments beautifully on this approach to the mysteries and God's communication of himself to creatures as God (cf. p. 147). We attempt in our study to show the profound bond of the mysteries in our Precious Blood theology. (Rahner states the truth very simply in *Do You Believe in God?* p. 103, Paulist Press, 1969, translation by Richard Strachan).

2. Thomas Ohm, O.S.B., *Die Liebe zu Gott in den nichtchristlichen Religionen*, (Wewel Verlag, Muenchen, 1950).

3. Our reference is the MS, vol. 1, p. XXIII (Benziger, Einsiedeln, 1965). Following is the statement prepared for the Council: *Omnes vero disciplinae theologicae, in Ratione Studiorum determinatae, ita doceantur ut harmonice in hunc finem conspirent, quippe quae singulae, ex intrinsecis proprii objecti rationibus, mysterium Christi in historia salutis a divinis scripturis annuntiatum et in ecclesia semper in actu clara in luce ponant.*

4. *DOV* America Press, no. 2, 3.

5. In every age the contemporary scene must be faced and studied by our theologians, our spiritual writers, and our directors and guides in the movements of youth. In a sense the entire People of God must be reinstructed. This is especially true for the present age, which to our mind presents the greatest challenge in all man's history, relating to his work, his culture, research, his total manner of being. The past two decades have witnessed a greater transformation in man and his universe than all the previous centuries of recorded history. For this very reason every historic institution must have tremendous problems of *adjustment*. The insight is from *Muehlen*, o.c., p. 36; the very technical nature of our age makes it possible for us to experience as never before the *we-structure* of the divine *being-ness*. "Insofar as Christ is present through his Spirit in all men who love through the power of this Spirit," we make room for the *"we-Christology."* This love is present in the we-operative Spirit in the history of the mature personalized socialization of the entire race amidst all distinctions of persons, peoples, races, even "separated churches" (adapted). In the context of a totally new world — historic past, evolving future — the Precious Blood spirituality must give the new Christian redemptive response to today's challenge, response which is defense in a positive all embracing Christocentrism..

6. Note especially Lv 17:12ff: "No one among you, not even a resident alien, may partake of blood. Any one hunting, whether of the Israelites or of the aliens residing among them, who catches an animal or a bird that may be eaten, shall pour out its blood and cover it with earth. Since the life of every living body is its blood, I have told the Israelites: You shall not partake of the blood of any meat. Since the life of every living body is its blood, any one who partakes of it shall be cut off." Cf. also the author's *The Everlasting Covenant*, p. 144ff. It is far beyond the writer's capacity and research and as well beyond the scope of this study to inquire at any length into the theological significance of blood in the context of other ancient peoples. Or, in the very nature of man's language and thought. However, he finds great significance in the following note from Robert Schreiter of our Society of the Precious Blood, and a comment made

by Karl Rahner in his explanation of the Devotion to the Sacred Heart. In a note of June 9, 1976, Father Schreiter writes:

> Enclosed is a segment of a paper on the theological significance of blood in the Melanesian context . . . This paper forms part of a larger paper entitled "Toward a Local Theology for Melanesia," produced by the Melanesian Theology Workgroup in my seminar, Constructing Local Theologies. The paper has a common introduction and then sections on blood, religious experience, grace and the Church. Philip Gibbs, author of this section I am sending you, is a native of New Zealand. He has an M.A. in anthropology and is pursuing an M.A. in theology . . . at CTU. He has worked among the Enga peoples in the Highlands of New Guinea. To my knowledge, this is the first attempt to think further the theology of the blood of Christ outside the older Christian oecumene. I think (his) . . . presentation reaffirms much of our theology of the Precious Blood while at the same time opening up new possibilities in a different cultural setting.

In the context of the above note — and of our entire study — we wish to restate that we do not look upon the Blood of Christ as merely a part of his sacred adorable humanity. It is Rahner who suggests that heart should be considered URWORT. But it is impossible for us to agree with the noted theologian (cf. his penetrating study in *Theological Investigations,* Vol. III, *Theology of the Spiritual Life,* Helicon Press, Baltimore, 1967, p. 321-352) in the statement on p. 336 which obviously limits the concept of *blood* to a " 'part' of the person of Christ (the face, the *blood,* the hand, and so on)." The entire direction of our study rules out any narrow concept of blood, though we have not expressly spoken of it as *Urwort.* We do, however, agree with Rahner's explanation of the Devotion to the Sacred Heart with all its background and its varied stress. The pages merit the careful reflection of our students of Precious Blood spirituality.

7. The sacrifice of Christ insofar as it is bloody immolation approaches by its nature the Jewish sacrifices. However, it transcends them mightily, indeed infinitely because of the motive involving perfect knowledge and will in the immolation. But this same bloody immolation (with the most profound sentiments of mind and heart which accompany it) derives its value from the dignity of him, whose Body and Blood are offered on the cross to God in an infinitely perfect sacrifice (Fernandes, *Sanguis Christi,* p. 164). Later in our study we shall clearly broaden this concept of sacrifice based entirely on Christian sources, of which the Letter to Hebrews is the most exemplary. This broader concept does not lessen the value of the present context of our work on this point, though the writer has come to accept it in the course of the study itself.

This present note (7) is to stress: *both* the bloody immolation and the interior sentiment of mind and heart in Jesus are embraced in the term we use consistently: *Blood* of Christ . . .

. . . In fact in the Hebrew concept, the blood because of the conjoined specification *nefesh* — which is also the principle of the spiritual activity — designates the concrete individual or concrete personality: and hence in the instance of a rational victim, also the personality of that victim, his immolation and the spiritual acts which accompany the sacrifice or those which are strictly bound up with it.

Thus considered, the New Testament expression, *Blood of Christ*, correctly includes the *integral personality of Christ*, the *God-man in the act consciously and voluntarily sacrificial, physical as well as spiritual.* And hence also the spiritual acts of love, of obedience . . . are included as bound up with the sacrifice of the Cross. (Again we refer to our broader concept of sacrifice which would include the entire life of Jesus as we shall explain later.)

The author then cites the following texts:

> But now in Christ Jesus you who once were far off have been brought near *through the blood of Christ.* It is he who is our peace, and who made the two of us one by breaking down the barrier of hostility that kept us apart. *In his own flesh* he abolished the law with its commands and precepts, to create *in himself* one new man from us who had been two and to make peace, reconciling both of us to God *in one body* through his cross, which put that enmity to death (Eph 2:13-16).

The author makes the *point* that the passage refers to the redemptive death of Christ, and the term *Blood of Christ* is equivalent to *body, flesh,* of Christ and also to *he* and *in himself.*

The other text is from Hebrews; it retains the full sense of the *Blood of Christ*:

> For if the blood of goats and bulls and the sprinkling of a heifer's ashes can sanctify those who are defiled so that their flesh is cleansed, how much more will the blood of Christ, who through the eternal spirit offered himself up unblemished to God, cleanse our consciences from dead works to worship the living God! (Heb 9:13-14).

8. We can do little more in this brief note than to touch upon the extensive summary of the views of authors made by Father Alphonse Spilly in a careful manuscript study: The Synoptic account seems to present the Last Supper as the *Paschal Meal* whereas John (18:28) implies that the Jews had not yet eaten the Passover Supper when Jesus was arraigned before Pilate. Joachim Jeremias argues that the Last Supper was identical with the Passover meal. In addition to other possibilities (Last Supper was a kiddus meal . . . a Haburah meal . . . an Essene meal, etc.) he submits fourteen arguments to show that the Last Supper was a Passover meal, and answers ten objections to his own position. Father Spilly then presents the opinions of various authors from periodical literature of the past ten years listing about six authors. Then he offers this brief balanced summation:

"There is at least one major author (Jeremias) who argues that the Last Supper was indeed a Passover meal. My own feelings are somewhat mixed. I don't think all the problems are solved by any means. It is possible that the Last Supper was originally a Passover meal and that its traditions were developed and altered to fit early Christian liturgical practice. It is also possible that the Last Supper itself was not precisely a Passover meal. but that early Christian descriptions of its significance interpreted it in the light of Passover theology. In both cases, there is a strong connection with the Paschal meal, at least with its theology" (Ms. of Rev. Alphonse Spilly, *The Last Supper as Paschal Meal*).

To the above we add the statement of the *DB*: "all the sources unite in affirming that the Supper itself was the Passover dinner of Jesus and his disciples" although the writer admits the difficulties involved (p. 250). The *EDB* seems somewhat less positive, col. 698. Both articles are entitled: *Eucharist.*

9. The categories are obviously not rigidly fixed (Cf. *The Everlasting Covenant,* chapter nine for a more complete terminology.) We stress above all Redemption after the manner of efficacy, which includes all the other categories, extending from Christ's earthly life, passion, death, to resurrection, life in the Church and in glory through all eternity (ibid., chapter twenty four, p. 246ff). Note also *Christus Victor Mortis,* in Gregorianum, vol. 39, 1958. And as well F. J. Schierse, *Verheissung und Heilsvollendung* (Muenchen, 1955) which German critics acclaimed as a great pioneering work (*bahnbrechend.*)

10. This teaching is stoutly defended by Felix Malmberg, *Ueber den Gottmenschen* (Herder, Freiburg, 1960). One wonders how theology persisted so long in disputing the motive of incarnation, along the usual lines of our text book manuals, *if* man had not sinned, etc. This tract was made a mere incidental question, though it should be central in all theology. The Christocentrism we have proposed in this study brings Christ directly into contact with *our world.* It raises many problems regarding creation, the fall or/and Original Sin, the natural and supernatural order. In no wise, however, does it make God the Author of Sin. Cf. Chapter One in *The Everlasting Covenant*: the Motive of Incarnation, p. 11ff. According to a review, which we suggest the reader study carefully, by Alois Guggenberger in *TR* #3, 1976, Bishop Zoghby introduced into the discussions at Vatican II the concept: there is no breach (*Bruch*) between "*the Creative Word and the Redemptive Word*" (col. 232). He deals with a recent work on Theilhard de Chardin and Vatican II by Wolfgang Klein.

11. In a magnificent essay on Bonaventure, Hans Urs von Balthasar studies the concept of the *humility of God.* By creation he descends *into nothing,* fashioning creatures other than himself. Through *Incarnation* he unites *human clay* to *Infinite Logos.* He conceals his glory beneath betrayal, desertion, scourge and cross. His deformity conceals his glory and becomes the price of our beauty. To vilify ourselves for Christ is the acme of following him. The hypostatic union is utter abandonment to God. His union with man and submission to bloody death is supreme veneration for the Father and brings all men to sanctification. His Blood diffuses his spirit among them, the Spirit who unites him and men to the Father in love. The divine life communicated to him sanctifies, vivifies the *Life Blood* which justifies men in the Mystery of the Church. The tremendous cycle is completed in the Blood offered to God: The ignominy of the Cross, followed by the glory of resurrection and return to the Father. Thus men who have suffered and died with him bear his unveiled glory and all the Church finally shares with him the eternal life. (Suggested by *Herrlichkeit,* vol. II, p. 353 and elsewhere.)

Similar is the reflection suggested by Joseph Ratzinger, *Einfuehrung in das Christentum* (Koesel Verlag, Munich, 1968, p. 111ff) on the words taken from the epitaph of Ignatius of Loyola discussed in length in an article by Hugo Rahner in *Stimmen der Zeit,* Feb. 1947. Ratzinger applies the words: *Non coerceri maximo, contineri tamen a minimo divinum est,* to the Christian concept of the true greatness of God. The *Infinite Transcendent* reaches infinitely beyond this vast creation of which he is not a part, but which he created and governs, but he also descends into the tiniest atom: our modern science has in reality quite unconsciously written a great theological context for the *power and presence of God.* But the Incarnation goes far beyond this created concept. He whom the heavens cannot contain has in his own union with creation, linked the very Godhead, the divine nature in a union of Person with singular human nature: tiny human eyes look out upon a world which is truly governed by tiny human hands. A tiny heartbeat is the pulse of the throbbing Universe. The tiny babe is Son of Eternal Father and of human Mother, he learns to walk, who guides the stars, he grows, learns, reads, preaches, is nailed helpless to a Cross. In him is contained the omnipotent God. Thus we must view our Christocentrism — the basis of Precious Blood Spirituality.

12. Wolfgang Borchert (1921-1947), fought for the Germans in World War II. He went to the East Front in 1941, where he was seriously wounded. Then he became ill with jaundice and diptheria, was imprisoned in this condition for *unpatriotic remarks,* condemned to death but sent back to the East Front instead. Ultimately released because of ill health, he got himself thrown into prison again. In 1945 he returned to Hamburg in very poor health, with a chronic fever, but wrote and performed in cabarets over the next two years until he broke down completely. He went to Switzerland for *a cure* and died there at the age of 26. Besides the play *Draussen vor der Tuer,* which has been translated into English under the title *The Man Outside,* and deals with the problems of the *Heimkehrer,* the *Returnees* from the war, he wrote many short works in prose. His style is *Expressionistic.* Almost all his works deal in one way or another with the terrible effects of the war on the lives of the people. (From the notes of Cynthia Felch.)

Under this note we call to mind the thought of Rahner regarding the *silence of God,* the *inaccessibility of God,* in relation to the vastness of our universe by comparison with the petty comfortable world of the Middle Ages. The very vastness helps to explain "Rahner's atheism" which is not really atheism embodied in his concept of the *anonymous believer.* (Cf. *Do You Believe in God,* p. 101 ff, Paulist Press, and elsewhere.)

13. Franz Nikolasch, *Das Lamm als Christussymbol in den Schriften der Vaeter,* Herder, Wien, 1963, p. 21. Cf. also Stephen Virgulin in *Scripture,* July 1961, Recent Discussion of the Title: 'Lamb of God' p. 76.

14. Liturgy of the Easter Vigil.

15. The Woman and the Hour, *Precious Blood Study Week, III,* 1968, Messenger Press, p. 195 ff.

16. All this must be studied in the light of our theology of grace which goes far beyond the metaphysical terms of the *res creata* within us and the traditional categories. Very helpful is the explanation of Francis Colborn in *Theological Studies,* Theology of Grace: Present Trends and Future Directions, Dec. 1970, pp. 692 ff. Surely in our interior acts of Christian love we experience more than our own achievement. Do we not also experience the gift of this achievement as divinely bestowed? Not indeed as reflexly conscious insight but as direct co-experience of God-love moving us and within us. (*TR* 1964, no. 3, col. 150, Johann Auer, *Das Werk Karl Rahners*). Nevertheless, grace itself — Auer makes clear — transcends every explanation of grace. We add what we consider the Thomistic teaching on increase in sanctifying grace as conferred only with increase in our spiritual efficacy and effort of which one must in great measure be reflexly aware.